Constitutional Law in the Netherlands

Constitutional Law in the Netherlands

Fourth Edition

Paul Bovend'Eert
Constantijn Kortmann

This book was originally published as a monograph in the International
Encyclopaedia of Laws/Constitutional Law.

Founding Editor: Roger Blanpain
General Editor: Frank Hendrickx
Volume Editors: André Alen & David Haljan

Wolters Kluwer

Published by:
Kluwer Law International B.V.
PO Box 316
2400 AH Alphen aan den Rijn
The Netherlands
E-mail: lrs-sales@wolterskluwer.com
Website: www.wolterskluwer.com/en/solutions/kluwerlawinternational

Sold and distributed by:
Wolters Kluwer Legal & Regulatory U.S.
920 Links Avenue
Landisville, PA 17538
United States of America
Email: customer.service@wolterskluwer.com

DISCLAIMER: The material in this volume is in the nature of general comment only. It is not offered as advice on any particular matter and should not be taken as such. The editor and the contributing authors expressly disclaim all liability to any person with regard to anything done or omitted to be done, and with respect to the consequences of anything done or omitted to be done wholly or partly in reliance upon the whole or any part of the contents of this volume. No reader should act or refrain from acting on the basis of any matter contained in this volume without first obtaining professional advice regarding the particular facts and circumstances at issue. Any and all opinions expressed herein are those of the particular author and are not necessarily those of the editor or publisher of this volume.

ISBN 978-94-035-0367-7

e-Book: ISBN 978-94-035-0377-6
web-PDF: ISBN 978-94-035-0387-5

The Authors

Paul Bovend'Eert (born 26 June 1957) is a professor of Constitutional Law at the Radboud University of Nijmegen, Netherlands. In 1988, the University of Nijmegen awarded him a doctorate degree in Law for a thesis on coalition agreements in the Dutch parliamentary democracy. He teaches Constitutional Law and Comparative Constitutional Law. He has been dean of the Faculty of Law at the Radboud University (2010-2014). He is joint editor and co-author of a handbook on *Constitutional Law of the EU Member States* (2014). He is the author of *Introduction to Dutch Constitutional Law* (2019), co-author of *Manual on the Dutch Parliament* (2023), co-author of a handbook on Dutch Constitutional Law (2021) and author of *Treatise on the Judiciary and the Administration of Justice* (2022).

Constantijn Kortmann (born 14 March 1944, deceased 24 January 2016) was a professor of Constitutional Law and General Theory of State at the Radboud University of Nijmegen, Netherlands (1981–2009). He received his doctorate degree in 1971. He was a professor of Dutch and Comparative Constitutional Law at the University of Amsterdam (1976–1981). His publications include a Manual on *Constitutional Reforms of 1983 and 1987* and *Treatise on Constitutional Law* (2008). He was joint editor of a handbook on *Constitutional Law of the fifteen EU Member States* (2004). He was dean of the Faculty of Law at the Radboud University and at the University of Amsterdam. He was doctor *honoris causa* at the University of Poitiers, France.

The Authors

Table of Contents

Table of Contents

Table of Contents

Text of the Constitution for the Kingdom of the Netherlands;
Text of the Charter for the Kingdom.

Table of Contents

10

List of Abbreviations

ARP	Anti-revolutionaire Partij
CDA	Christen-Democratisch Appel
D66	Democraten 66
ECHR	European Convention on Human Rights
ECtHR	European Court of Human Rights
EEC	European Economic Community
EU	European Union
GRECO	Group of States Against Corruption
ICCPR	International Covenant on Civil and Political Rights
MP	Member of Parliament
OWN	Oorlogswet voor Nederland
PvdA	Partij van de Arbeid
PVV	Partij voor de Vrijheid
SER	Sociaal-Economische Raad
SP	Socialistische partij
VVD	Volkspartij voor Vrijheid en Democratie
Wet BBBG	Wet Buitengewone Bevoegdheden Burgerlijk Gezag

List of Abbreviations

Preface

This book offers an introduction to Dutch constitutional law. It describes the present form of government in the Netherlands and in the federation of the Kingdom of the Netherlands. The present-day Constitution of the Netherlands dates from the general constitutional revision of 1983. The first Constitution was established in 1814. The constitutional reform of 1848 led to a gradual development of parliamentary democracy and the rule of law in the Netherlands. This survey of Dutch constitutional law is also focused on these constitutional developments since 1814. The different parts of the text of the 1st edition have been written in close collaboration by the two authors.

The 2nd edition (2012), 3rd edition (2017) and this 4th edition (2023) were prepared by Paul Bovend'Eert. Nijmegen as of 1 January 2023.

Preface

General Introduction

Chapter 1. Constitutional History

1. The Kingdom of the Netherlands (*Koninkrijk der Nederlanden*) dates from 1814. In that year, Prince William I, a descendant of William of Orange along the female line, accepted the sovereignty offered to him, after the period of French rule ended in 1813. It is certainly also useful to recall some salient features of earlier periods.

The greater part of the current territory comprised a number of provinces, which were small, more or less independent republics. These seventeen provinces, also including the territory of present-day Belgium and Luxembourg, had some mutual links. During the fifteenth and sixteenth centuries, they gradually came under the rule of the Dukes of Burgundy, later the Habsburgs. Representatives of the provinces gathered in the States General. In 1477, there was a revolt against Burgundian rule, and the provincial states gained some concessions, but after a while, these were lost again to the Habsburg rulers. When Charles V succeeded to the Spanish throne (1517), the Habsburg Netherlands was placed under a series of regents. For a while, the Netherlands was part of a Kingdom. However, in 1572, the provincial states again revolted, this time more successfully, against King Philip II of Spain, their sovereign lord. The seven northern provinces (of which the province of Holland was by far the most important) split off and joined together in the Republic of the United Netherlands (*Republiek der Verenigde Nederlanden*) as the Dutch Republic was officially called. The Union of Utrecht (1579) was the founding treaty of this confederation, which lasted right up until 1795. However, the Union did not have a strong central authority. The Union did not possess a Head of State, and the assembly which met at the level of the Union, still called the States General, was considered to be a meeting of state envoys (of the provinces) rather than a national parliament.

With the Napoleonic era, there was a brief interlude (the Batavian Republic), and then in 1798, under French rule, the whole previous structure was swept away, and the government was centralized. The advantages of this from an administrative viewpoint turned out to be so great that in 1814 when the first written Constitution (*Grondwet*) for the Netherlands was drawn up, it was decided to establish a unitary State. Although the 1814 Constitution recognized provinces and local authorities, neither possessed sovereignty. Sovereignty was vested jointly in the central institutions of the State.

It is remarkable that the 1814 Constitution introduced a monarchy, which had not been recognized in the country since the formal abjuration of the Spanish King

Philip II in 1581. Where other countries, such as France, were experiencing a res-toration, monarchy was new for the Netherlands. The Netherlands had a long repub-lican history, and this was to continue, as we shall soon see. But let us first look at the establishment of the Kingdom.

Besides the monarchy, the 1814 Constitution established a parliament – the States General – consisting of one Chamber, which exercised legislative power together with the monarch. However, the King also possessed autonomous rule-making pow-ers, which he frequently made use of. There was as yet no government in the mod-ern sense, with ministers responsible to parliament. There were ministers, it is true, but they were only advisers to the King. The Constitution did, however, institute an independent Judiciary.

2. 1815 (Treaty of Vienna) brought the unification of the present-day Nether-lands with present-day Belgium. International politics required that there be a suf-ficiently large and powerful State on the northern border of France. On the instigation of the Belgians, who wished to see the nobility represented in parlia-ment, the new Constitution introduced a bicameral system, in which the Second Chamber consisted of elected members and the First Chamber of members appointed by the King for life.

3. The unification of the two countries did not last long, though. King William I's regime, which displayed certain authoritarian traits, met with particular resis-tance among the liberals and Catholics in the South. The latter objected to the King interfering in religious matters; while the liberals, who were mainly French-speaking, resented the King's Dutch language policy. The Belgians rose up in 1830 and declared their independence; in 1831 a Belgian Constitution came into force. However, the separation of Belgium and the Netherlands was only sealed in 1839 by the Treaty of London. The revision of the Constitution in 1840 then provided the initial impetus for the growth of a modern system of government. Ministers had to countersign the King's decisions and were made liable under criminal law for acts contravening the Constitution or the law. Since 1840, the government has com-prised the King and the ministers.

The most important constitutional reform the Netherlands experienced was that of 1848. It introduced political ministerial responsibility and the government's power to dissolve parliament. It prescribed that the members of the Second Cham-ber should be directly elected (albeit by a limited electorate), and it gave the Sec-ond Chamber important powers, such as the right of amendment and the right of interpellation. At the same time, the foundation was laid for a modern and uniform government of the provinces and municipalities.

Despite these constitutional changes, the King's role had certainly not come to an end. The Second Chamber was weak and internally divided, partly because there were as yet no political parties or parliamentary groups. The King still retained his autonomous rule-making power, even though he now shared it with a minister. This situation did not last long, though. The years 1866 and 1868 witnessed conflicts between the government and the Second Chamber which were finally decided in favour of the latter. Since then, it is firmly established that a minister or a cabinet, that loses the confidence of the Second Chamber or the First Chamber, must resign, unless the Chamber is dissolved. The parliamentary system was definitively established.

A Supreme Court ruling of 1879 (Supreme Court 13 June 1879 *Meerenberg*), followed by the 1887 revision of the Constitution, virtually abolished the autonomous rule-making powers of the government. Since then, all regulations made by the government to which penalties are attached must be pursuant to an Act of Parliament. Also, from 1887 onwards, there was a gradual expansion of the franchise to include broader sections of the population.

Notwithstanding later constitutional reforms, the reform of 1917 can be regarded as the culmination of the construction of the constitutional system of the Netherlands. It introduced universal suffrage for men and women as well as the system of proportional representation. Furthermore, it put an end to the long-standing political conflict on the financing of denominational education. The political parties on the left agreed to state subsidies for denominational education in exchange for recognition of universal suffrage by the religious parties.

Many of the topics outlined above will receive more detailed consideration later.

4. To summarize, in the constitutional development of the Netherlands, a number of principal threads can be identified: broadening of the franchise, increasing power of the States General, enhancement of democracy, reduction of the autonomous powers of the government, restructuring the organization and powers of the decentralized authorities to bring about some uniformity, and an emphasis on fundamental rights and legal protection against the actions of government authorities. Despite these developments, and despite another complete revision of the Constitution in 1983, little has really changed in the substance of the Constitution since 1848. The most important changes to constitutional law have resulted from European Union (EU) law, treaties, and supranational and international case law. In addition, parliamentary and political relations have evolved independently of any formal constitutional amendments.

5. A number of characteristic features of Dutch constitutional law can be identified. In the first place, Dutch constitutional law is relatively free of ideological tinges compared with a number of other West European countries. Neither does it contain an unequivocal concept of the foundation of government power. In Belgium, the situation is very different; there, the Constitution states: 'All powers emanate from the nation'. The French Constitution also takes as its starting point the *souveraineté nationale*, together with a recognition of the *droits de l'homme* and *démocratie*. The *Grundgesetz* of the Federal Republic of Germany is based on the principle of popular sovereignty and declares that the Federal Republic is a democratic and social federal State. Furthermore, the *Würde des Menschen* is inviolable and must be defended and taken into consideration by the government. British constitutional law has as its central concept the sovereignty of parliament.

In Dutch Constitutional Law the ultimate source of authority is not indicated. A preamble, to be found in many other Constitutions, referring to a deity, the nation or the people, is absent in the Dutch Constitution. However, it cannot be said anymore that the Dutch Constitution is without any leading principles. In 2016, the

Dutch government introduced a bill in parliament to revise the Constitution. This bill contained a new general provision, according to which the Constitution would guarantee fundamental rights and democracy based on the rule of law (*democratische rechtsstaat*). This partial revision of the Constitution succeeded in 2022. So the Dutch Constitution has joined other Western European constitutions by including, in a new general provision, guiding principles of constitutional law.

Besides this new general provision, a number of leading principles are implicitly embodied in Dutch constitutional law: the monarchy, representative democracy (the States General and franchise), the 'social State' (fundamental social rights) and recognition of human rights.

6. In the second place the Constitution traditionally has a strong emphasis on the monarchy and the King. Although the history of the Netherlands is republican rather than monarchical, in 1814 the choice was made for a monarchy with a King as Head of State. Present-day constitutional law is not easy to understand, especially its terminology, without taking into account the 1814 Constitution, which accorded the King a central position, and which was interpreted in monarchical terms until well into the nineteenth century. However, since 1848 collegiate decision-making by the ministers has become a characteristic feature of Dutch constitutional law and has gained in strength. The role of Head of State in Dutch constitutional law is not like that of the French or the American President. For a long time, the Netherlands has not had power vested in one person, in the sense of a powerful sovereign or president. Nevertheless, the Constitution still often speaks of 'the King' and 'a Royal Decree' where it means the government (King and ministers), and in Acts of Parliament, the royal 'We' is repeatedly used, the *pluralis majestatis* for the King.

7. In the third place, during the course of history, it has become clear that Dutch constitutional law is an open system. Important changes have occurred without formal revision of the constitutional law. In particular, the provisions relating to the powers of the government and the States General and their relationship with each other, which date almost completely from 1840 to 1848, have not hindered the development from a monarchy with the monarch in charge to a parliamentary system, in which members of the cabinet resign if they lose the confidence of one of the Chambers of Parliament (the so-called confidence rule). Likewise, the curtailment of the King's autonomous rule-making powers was first brought about by the Supreme Court, in the *Meerenberg* ruling, mentioned above. The Constitution leaves a great deal open in other areas too, referring to the legislature to make further regulations. This is the case not only in relation to fundamental rights but also on the question of the organization and powers of the decentralized government bodies.

Under the existing constitutional law, there is plenty of scope for the government, the States General or the courts to adjust to changing social and political circumstances without the Constitution itself having to come under discussion or be amended. Changing the Constitution is not a simple matter in the Netherlands, as the revision procedure is burdensome. If it is desired that the existing openness and flexibility in constitutional law be maintained, then there needs to be a cautious acceptance of unwritten constitutional law.

8. The fourth characteristic trait of Dutch constitutional law which should be mentioned is the absence of a single central authority responsible for the final interpretation and upholding of constitutional law. In the Netherlands, neither the courts nor any other institution is authorized to review Acts of Parliament against the Constitution (Article 120 of the Constitution). It is the legislature itself which decides whether an Act of Parliament is constitutional in its content and whether an Act of Parliament has been established according to constitutional procedures. This means that the 'political' institutions, government and States General are important interpreters of Dutch constitutional law. One must not forget, however, that Acts of Parliament also have to comply with the provisions of international law and EU law. The upholding of these norms – EU law and all directly applicable provisions contained in treaties and decisions of international organizations – rests in part with national and supra- or international courts. The effect of this judicial review is that the interpretation of Acts of Parliament and of the Constitution by government and States General has to concur with, or is bounded by, the interpretation of supra and international law by the courts.

9. The relationship between the government and the States General is not strictly regulated. The exact nature of ministerial responsibility, the circumstances under which the confidence rule and the power to dissolve parliament may or may not be applied, and the question of when a bill may or may not receive royal assent, are all questions which are open to more than one interpretation. In Dutch constitutional law, this interpretation is a matter for the government and parliament. Courts do not get involved in the (political) question of whether a minister was right to withhold information from parliament, whether a decision to dissolve parliament was right or not, or whether the decision not to give assent to a bill was the correct one. These kinds of decisions are left to the political offices mentioned above, who function as guardians of the Constitution. The role of the judiciary in this respect can be explained both by the principle of the separation of powers and by the fact that these are legal relationships which exist solely between the government and the States General.

10. To summarize, it can be stated that under Dutch constitutional law, the role of upholding the Constitution has been left in the hands of various institutions, depending upon the type of rule involved. However, there is a certain trend towards greater judicial involvement concerning constitutional law, especially as a result of the increase in the number of inter- and supranational standards, in the interpretation of which courts do play an important part these days.

Chapter 2. Form of Government

11. The form of central government is a parliamentary democracy with a constitutional monarchy. Since 1814, there has been a hereditary monarchy exercised in turn by Kings William I, William II and William III, followed by Princess Regent Emma, Queens Wilhelmina, Juliana and Beatrix, and King Willem Alexander. The King enjoys immunity; ministers are politically responsible to parliament for all actions of the government, including all actions of the King. According to the Constitution, the King forms part of the government (Article 42 of the Constitution), but in fact, it is the ministers who actually make policy. During the Second World War, when the government was evacuated to London, this was not the case. Queen Wilhelmina really participated in the government for that extraordinary period.

As has already been pointed out, under the parliamentary system ministers are responsible and accountable to Parliament. A minister who loses the confidence of the Second or the First Chamber of the States General must resign, except in the case where the relevant Chamber of Parliament is dissolved.

12. The constitutional character of the Dutch State is expressed in a number of ways. Besides a parliamentary democracy and a constitutional monarchy, the Dutch state is also characterized by the rule of law and by the principle of separation of powers.

13. The rule of law (*rechtsstaat*), one of the principles included in the new general provision of the Constitution, implies in the first place that, in principle, the government is only empowered to act if its action is founded on a previously established general rule. In practice, this means that all government action must be based upon a provision of an Act of Parliament.

A second important feature of the rule of law is the independent administration of justice. In theory, every action taken by the government towards a subject is liable to review by either the ordinary (civil) courts or the administrative courts. As we have seen already, there is one important exception to this: courts are not empowered to review Acts of Parliament against the Constitution.

A third element in the rule of law is the concept of fundamental rights, which aim to prevent the development of a totalitarian State. A number of fundamental rights are laid down in Chapter 1 of the Constitution. The Netherlands is also a signatory to the European Convention on Human Rights (ECHR), the International Covenant on Civil and Political Rights (ICCPR) and a number of other international conventions which aim to protect citizens in their fundamental rights against public authorities. National law must conform to these conventions and is, in principle, subject to judicial review on this point.

The constitutional character of the Dutch State is also expressed through Separation of Powers (*trias politica*) and an extensive system of checks and balances. The Constitution more or less follows the traditional classification of the principle of separation of powers. In concrete terms, this means a division of government into legislative power, executive power and judicial power. Chapter 5 of the Constitution deals with the legislative and executive functions, and Chapter 6 with the administration of justice. These three leading governmental functions are assigned in the Constitution to the three most important government institutions, namely the States General (Chapter 3), the government (King and ministers) (Chapter 2) and the judiciary (Chapter 6). The underlying premise is that these three state institutions are equal in authority and independent from each other. The judicial branch, which has exclusive authority to administer justice, is most distant in relation to the two other state authorities. The government and parliament, on the other hand, are less separated in a parliamentary democracy, in part because they share the legislative power. The organizational and functional separation of powers is thus not absolute. Various checks and balances constitute part of the principle of the separation of powers.

Checks and balances come from various sources: the bicameral system, judicial review, administrative supervision, the right of amendment of the Second Chamber, the confidence rule and the government's power to dissolve a Chamber of Parliament, to name the most important.

Chapter 3. Territory and Population

14. The Netherlands was a major colonial power for a long time. It had possessions in the East Indies (present-day Indonesia), present-day Surinam and a number of Caribbean Islands. This situation changed drastically following the Second World War. Indonesia became independent in 1949, and Surinam in 1975. The Caribbean Islands Aruba, Curaçao, Bonaire, St. Maarten, St. Eustatius and Saba (joint population slightly over 300,000) are still part of the Kingdom. Curaçao, Aruba and St. Maarten form as autonomous countries a federation with the Netherlands, the territory in Europe. The other three (smaller) Caribbean Islands are part of the Netherlands. The Charter for the Kingdom forms the Constitution for this federation. This Charter is of higher rank than the Dutch Constitution.

15. Since 1814, the territory in Europe has been what is known as a decentralized unitary country. The legislative and administrative functions are exercised not only at central but also at regional and local levels: that is, by the twelve provinces and around 340 municipalities. A number of matters are however handled entirely at national level: these include defence, foreign affairs and the administration of justice.

The Netherlands is very densely populated, with approximately 17.5 million inhabitants, including a number of foreigners originating mainly from Mediterranean countries, Surinam and the Caribbean. The highest population concentrations are found in the west (the *Randstad*) and in the south of the country. Until recently, the dominant religions were Roman Catholicism and Protestantism; however, the last fifty years have witnessed a major secularization process. Now, the two other main religions, Islam and Judaism are also represented.

There is a long history of antithesis between Catholics and Protestants in the population. Catholics who lived south of the rivers Rhine and Maas used to be discriminated against in fact, if not legally. However, that came to an end after the Second World War.

The territory in Europe comprises 41,160 square kilometres. The land is mainly flat and one-third lies below sea level, which means that coastal defences, the regulation of the water level and water management, in general, are of vital importance. The country is cut through by major rivers. It is bounded on the east by the Federal Republic of Germany, by the Kingdom of Belgium to the south and by the North Sea on its western and northern sides. There are few natural resources except for large quantities of natural gas in the north of the country.

Part I. Sources of Constitutional Law

16. Dutch constitutional law is contained not just in the Constitution (*Grondwet*). It is also shaped by a considerable number of Acts of parliament and other regulations. In addition to that, there are other sources of law, often not set out in writing. The question is which Acts of Parliament and regulations and other rules of law together represent constitutional law, in other words, 'the constitution'. What are the legal sources of constitutional law? Generally speaking, the constitution can be seen as the overall embodiment of the set of rules of law that serve as the foundations for the structure of governmental organization and that pertain to the relationship between government institutions and citizens. Following this general constitutional concept, legal doctrine tends to distinguish between the constitution in the formal sense and the constitution in the substantive sense. What the formal constitution entails is determined by formal characteristics. The first is that constitutional rules are included in an Act of Parliament. For this particular Act of Parliament, a second characteristic applies, namely a specific method of enactment and amendment that differs from 'ordinary' Acts of Parliament. The specific amendment procedure is set out in the Constitution itself. A third distinguishing characteristic of a formal constitution is the special name. A final special characteristic is its unique position versus 'ordinary' Acts of Parliament and other regulations. The formal constitution has a higher force of law than ordinary Acts of parliament and other regulations. These may not deviate from the constitution in the formal sense. In many countries courts are qualified in this context to declare Acts of Parliament to be non-binding, if they deviate from, i.e., are contradictory to, the formal constitution. In the Netherlands, the courts are, as stated above, not authorized to review Acts of parliament against the Constitution (Article 120 of the Constitution). It is the legislature's responsibility to determine whether a law is in line with the Constitution before it is enacted.

In the Netherlands, the constitution in the formal sense is identified since 1814 as the 'Constitution of the Kingdom of the Netherlands', in Dutch '*Grondwet voor het Koninkrijk der Nederlanden*' (hereinafter referred to as the Constitution, i.e., with a capital letter). The special amendment procedure involving two readings is described in Article 137 of the Constitution. After the first reading, the Second Chamber must be dissolved for the second reading, which requires the amendment procedure to be adopted by both Chambers with a two-thirds majority.

In 1954, at the time of the formation of the federal alliance of the Kingdom of the Netherlands, nowadays consisting of four Member States (the Netherlands, Aruba, Curaçao and Sint Maarten), a special arrangement was made for the organization of this alliance through the Charter for the Kingdom of the Netherlands

(Statuut voor het Koninkrijk der Nederlanden). This likewise contains a special amendment procedure. In the hierarchy of norms, the Charter for the Kingdom takes precedence above the Constitution. The Charter for the Kingdom is presently, next to the Constitution, a part of the formal constitution in the Netherlands.

The constitution in a substantive sense pertains to a much broader system of rules of law. As a starting point, the substantive constitution may be described as the totality of written and unwritten rules of law that, based on their content, may be interpreted as norms that set out the principles for the structure of the organization of a nation and the relationship with its citizens. In this doctrine a distinction is also made in that constitutional law has three functions, namely: (1) constituting government institutions, in other words, their establishment; (2) attributing powers, in other words assigning authorities to government institutions; and (3) regulation, in other words regulating the relationships between the government institutions and the citizens. By extension, the constitution in a substantive sense is the totality of regulations that have a constituting, attributing and/or regulating function. In other words, it must concern rules of law that establish government institutions in the state, attribute powers to them, and regulate their mutual relationships as well as the relationships with citizens.

In this line of thought, the substantive constitution encompasses first the constitution in the formal sense, namely the Constitution and the Charter for the Kingdom. Aside from this, the substantive constitution encompasses various other types of regulations that fulfil the above functions of constitutional law. It should be clear that this approach leads to a broad concept of the constitution. Regulations of the constitution are not necessarily 'fundamental': they must be constitutive, attributive and/or regulatory. The Elections Act, for example, falls in this approach under the laws that are constitutive. It establishes government institutions such as the Electoral Council, assigns powers to these institutions, and regulates the elections for, amongst others, the First and Second Chamber of Parliament. Aside from this, also unwritten rules of law that come about through rulings of the courts, or unwritten rules of law (conventions) that arose in the relationship between government and parliament, can become part of the substantive constitution.

It may be argued that also certain legal principles that are anchored in written or unwritten law should be considered to belong to the constitution in a substantive sense. This applies, for example, to the above-mentioned legal principle of the separation of powers and the principle of the rule of law. In itself there is no objection against inclusion of such legal principles under the concept of constitution, so long as these principles of law, or elements thereof, are sufficiently anchored in written or unwritten constitutional law. The risk of including all sorts of vague, multi-interpretable legal principles under the concept of the constitution must be avoided for reasons of legal certainty. Unmistakable anchoring in positive law is therefore a key requirement.

The remainder of this chapter covers the various types of written and unwritten rules of law that together form the constitution in a substantive sense in the Netherlands. This includes discussion of the interrelationship between these rules.

Chapter 1. Supra and International Law

§1. Primary and Secondary EU Law

17. European law, as the source of law of Dutch constitutional law, deserves separate mention. At this time, in 2023, a total of twenty-seven Member States are joined together in the EU by virtue of various treaties. This alliance of nations has strong federalist features. Through the European treaties, starting with the treaty of 1957 that established the European Economic Community (EEC) and up to the Treaty of Lisbon of 2007, a full-fledged governmental organization has been created, charged with legislation, administration and administration of justice, as well as a Community-wide legal system. In the context of the establishment of an economic and monetary union, the Member States have transferred extensive sovereignty to European institutions. Aside from that, it cannot go unnoticed that the number of other government tasks of the EU has over the years expanded substantially. In the context of the EU, a separate governmental organization has been established that in various respects is quite similar to that of the central government in a federal state. The EU has a representative body (the European Parliament), an executive function (the European Commission) and a separate court (the European Court of Justice). None of these bodies consists of representatives or emissaries of the Member States. Aside from this, the Council of Ministers and the European Council act as institutions of the EU, even though these bodies mostly consist of representatives of the Member States. The regulations that are established in this European legal system also constitute part of the Dutch legal system. Furthermore, European regulations take precedence over national regulations (*see* Court of Justice, 15 July 1964, Costa/Enel). Strictly speaking, this means that the treaty provisions regarding this European government organization are an integral part of Dutch constitutional law. After all, under these treaties, special governmental functions have been set up that exercise authority in the fields of legislation, executive administration and jurisdiction in the Dutch legal system.

In actual practice, European law has great impact on the legal position of the citizens of the EU countries. The provisions of primary EU law – the Treaty on the EU, the Treaty on the Functioning of the EU, the Charter of Fundamental Rights of the EU, and the general principles of EU law – as well as the provisions contained in secondary EU law (regulations, directives and decrees) can be directly operative. Insofar as they are directly operative they extend, as already stated, to the national legal systems and take precedence over national law. Directly operative provisions of EU law grant citizens not only rights but can also impose obligations on them.

§2. Treaties

18. International laws can be part of a constitution insofar as such laws establish government institutions, grant powers and regulate the relationships between governments and their citizens. As far as the effect of treaties and decisions by international organizations is concerned, Dutch constitutional law favours monism. For the applicability of treaties and decisions by international organizations within the national legal system, no national Act of Parliament or regulation is needed to convert an international rule into national law. As such, the international rule applies automatically within the national legal system. Consequently, certain treaties and decisions of international organizations may be regarded as constitutional law.

In terms of international law, the most important treaties in practice for Dutch constitutional law are the European Convention for the Protection of Human Rights (ECHR), the protocols related thereto and the ICCPR. The ECHR is in various respects particularly important for the Dutch Constitution. This convention, which came about within the context of the Council of Europe, first contains a large number of classic fundamental rights, which the Dutch courts regard as binding on all citizens within the meaning of Articles 93 and 94 of the Constitution. Citizens may thus appeal where applicable before the courts both to their fundamental rights under the Constitution and their fundamental rights under the EHCR.

The fundamental rights under the EHCR are secondly of special importance for the Dutch constitutional legal system in light of the prohibition of judicial review contained in Article 120 of the Constitution. While the courts may not conduct such a review, as we saw earlier, with regard to Acts of Parliament, no such prohibition applies with regard to treaties.

Article 94 of the Constitution allows Dutch courts to decide not to apply Acts of Parliament or other regulations if such application is incompatible with generally binding treaty provisions. Article 94 of the Constitution thus gives the courts the possibility of constitutional review of laws against fundamental rights under the ECHR.

Thirdly, the ECHR is particularly important for the Dutch Constitution since it contains fundamental rights that are not mentioned in the Constitution. This includes the right to life (Article 2 ECHR), the freedom of movement (Article 2, 4th. Protocol ECHR) and until recently the right of access to an independent and impartial judge (Article 6 ECHR). This right to a fair trial was finally included in the Dutch Constitution in 2022. In addition, the ECHR has its own rules for the limitation of fundamental rights.

A fourth relevant aspect is that a special court, the European Court of Human Rights (ECtHR), has been established to oversee compliance with the convention by the Member States. The ECHR also includes an individual right of complaint for private persons or groups. Case law by the ECtHR is binding for the interpretation of convention provisions. Rulings by the ECtHR have had significant impact in the past decades on the development of the Dutch constitutional legal system.

While the ECHR is a European convention, which the Member States of the EU and a number of other European states such as Turkey are subject to, the ICCPR is a worldwide convention that came about in the context of the United Nations. The ICCPR likewise contains a large number of classic fundamental rights, which largely correspond with those listed in the ECHR. These fundamental rights are also regarded by the Dutch courts as universally binding convention provisions within the meaning of Article 94 of the Constitution. However, the ICCPR does not have a special court of law that issues binding rulings like the ECtHR does.

Chapter 2. The Charter and the Constitution

§1. THE CHARTER FOR THE KINGDOM OF THE NETHERLANDS

19. As was indicated in the introduction, the Charter (Statuut voor het Koninkrijk der Nederlanden), which came into being in 1954, governs the mutual relationships between the Netherlands, and the Caribbean Islands Curaçao, St. Maarten and Aruba. The other three (small) Caribbean Islands are part of the Constitutional order of the Netherlands. The Charter may be seen as the Constitution for the federation formed by these four countries.

The Charter consists of a preamble, five sections and sixty-six articles. The preamble first contains a brief description of the history of the Kingdom since 1954. It then formulates the main principles that serve as the basis of the constitutional order of the Charter. The preamble makes clear that the four countries that make up the Kingdom have freely accepted this new constitutional order, in which they look after their internal interests autonomously. In that sense, the preamble is a guarantee for the autonomy of the individual countries. In addition, the preamble sets out the principle that the four countries look after the common interests of the Kingdom on a basis of equivalence. Next, it states that the countries will provide mutual assistance. The preamble is part of the Charter and is binding.

The first section of the Charter contains a number of general provisions. This section deals with the composition of the Kingdom (Article 1), determines to whom the Crown of the Kingdom devolves and who conducts the government affairs of the Kingdom (Articles 1a and 2), contains a summary of the federal or Kingdom affairs (Article 3) and describes who is charged with the executive and legislative powers (Article 4). This section also contains, in Article 5, a regulation governing the relationship between the Charter and the Constitution. Article 5, paragraph 1 of the Charter refers back to the Constitution for the regulation of a number of federal matters. As such, parts of the Constitution may be considered to apply to the entire Kingdom and not just to the territory in Europe. Article 5, paragraph 2 states that the Charter prevails over the Constitution.

Section 2 of the Charter describes the principle that the countries look after the common interest on the basis of equivalence. This section contains specific rules regarding certain government institutions of the Kingdom, such as the Council of Ministers of the Kingdom (Articles 7–12) and the Council of State of the Kingdom (Article 13). Aside from that, it contains provisions regarding the formation of a Kingdom Act (Articles 14–19). In addition, section 2 presents detailed provisions regarding the performance of certain federal matters, in particular pertaining to defence and foreign affairs. It also contains a provision on the jurisdiction in the final instance by the Supreme Court (Article 23).

Section 3 of the Charter contains various provisions regarding mutual assistance, consultation and cooperation, thus working out the principle in the preamble that the countries shall mutually assist each other (loyalty and solidarity). A prime consideration is that the cooperation between the countries is voluntary. This section includes a limited number of subjects where cooperation applies and states that the countries can agree on mutual regulations.

Section 4 of the Charter relates to the constitutional organization of the countries and presents several general provisions regarding this. The basic premise is that the countries exercise their powers independently (Article 41). The section also contains several provisions regarding the administrative monitoring of the Caribbean countries by the government of the Kingdom (Article 50).

Section 5 of the Charter contains transitional and closing provisions. The procedure for amendment of the Charter is laid out in this section. Amendment of the Charter must follow a special procedure. The point of departure is that the amendment takes place under a Kingdom Act. Revision of the Charter is a federal matter. Application of the Kingdom Act procedure implies that, in the Netherlands, the two Chambers of the States General decide by simple majority on acceptance of a bill to amend the Charter. The bill must also be accepted by Act of Parliament in each of the three Caribbean countries (Article 55). A bill to amend the Charter must in principle be adopted in two readings, i.e., in two successive voting sessions, by a simple majority. If one of these parliaments adopts the bill by a two-third majority, then a second reading in that parliament is not required. The procedure is remarkable in that the parliaments can decide on an amendment by a simple majority. In the case of revision of the Constitution, and of the constitutions of the Caribbean countries, a stricter procedure applies. A bill must then be adopted in parliament by a two-third majority.

§2. THE CONSTITUTION

20. Despite the increased, and still increasing, significance of EU law and international law for Dutch constitutional affairs, the Constitution (*Grondwet*) remains the most important document of Dutch constitutional law for the Netherlands.

As mentioned earlier, the Constitution dates from 1814, when a constitutional monarchy and a unitary state were established in the Netherlands. A drastic revision of the Constitution took place in 1815 as a consequence of the unification with Belgium. With the constitutional revision of 1840, the Constitution was amended in light of the secession of Belgium. This revision also involved the first major political reform regarding the relationship between the King and the cabinet ministers. The revision of the Constitution in 1848 was the most drastic in Dutch political history. This revision involved laying the foundations for the development of the parliamentary democracy and of the modern decentralized unitary state. Since that year, the Constitution has not drastically changed in substance. Still, there have been many minor changes to the Constitution over the years, such as in 1884, 1887, 1917, 1922, 1938, 1946, 1948, 1953, 1956, 1963, 1972, 1987, 1995, 1999, 2000, 2005, 2006 2008, 2017, 2018 and 2022. The cumbersome procedure to revise the Constitution (*see* below) was not a reason for this. In 1983, a general revision of the Constitution took place, which mainly involved modernization of the design and the text, without drastic political reforms taking place. For example, the persistent mention of the King in the old text of the Constitution of 1814 largely disappeared in the new text of 1983.

21. The way the current 'modern' Constitution is set up is comparable to that of other present-day constitutions of European nations. The Constitution consists of eight chapters and 142 articles. It does not have a preamble, but it does have a general provision as an opening statement with general principles (fundamental rights, democracy and rule of law (*democratische rechtsstaat*)) to be guaranteed by the Constitution.

Chapter 1 of the Constitution is dedicated to fundamental rights, in line with other modern constitutions. The chapter covers both the traditional civil liberties, such as freedom of speech, freedom of religion, the right of assembly and the right to privacy, but also specifically social rights, such as the government's concern to promote employment and the wealth and health of the population. It should be noted that Chapter 1 of the Constitution does not make any distinction between civil liberties and social rights.

Chapter 2 deals with the composition of the government, starting with the King. The Constitution regulates the system of hereditary succession and the special constitutional position of the King, including immunity. The chapter also addresses the main features of the organizational structure of the government, in particular Council of Ministers, the prime minister, the ministers and the state secretaries.

Chapter 3 covers the parliament, known as the States General. This chapter includes rules for the division of the States General into two independent Chambers, their modus operandi, the elections and the constitutional position of the members of parliament, including their free mandate and immunity.

Chapter 4 next contains various general provisions pertaining to the composition and powers of the Council of State, the Court of Audit, the national ombudsman and advisory bodies.

Chapter 5 contains general provisions regarding legislation and administration. The chapter opens with regulations on the drafting of Acts of Parliament. Following this, several special subjects are discussed, including foreign affairs, defence, the budget and taxation.

Chapter 6 covers the judicial organization and the administration of justice. It contains general provisions regarding the composition of the judiciary, the authority of the courts, the legal position of judges, the composition and power of the Supreme Court and the legal procedures in the courts.

Chapter 7 of the Constitution deals with decentralized authorities, including provinces, municipalities, water authorities and other public bodies, and their composition and powers.

Closing Chapter 8 covers the procedure for revision of the Constitution and provides for a transitional scheme.

22. As is customary in modern constitutions, the Dutch Constitution is mostly limited to general regulations regarding the various subjects covered. Only in a few cases does it contain a detailed and legally conclusive regulation, such as the rules for the hereditary succession of the King. Often the Constitution delegates powers regarding the specifics of the composition of government offices and their powers to the legislative branch, with or without the possibility of further delegation. In many cases the provisions are formulated in an open, even vague manner, leaving room for developments in the political sphere. In that sense, we can speak of a flexible constitution that is open to changes that occur over time, and the legislature has ample room to establish regulations that consider practical circumstances. The Constitution furthermore hardly contains a conclusive regulation of authorities at the various government levels and fields. Important government tasks, such as the police and the prosecution service, are not mentioned at all.

In several areas, we can speak of notable gaps. For example, the Constitution still does not say anything about the key rule of parliamentary democracy, that ministers are expected to offer their resignation when they lose the support of a majority of one of the chambers of parliament (the confidence rule). This rule is based since its origin in 1866–1868 on unwritten law. Also in other regards, the Constitution does not provide specific regulations, such as regarding the appointment and dismissal of ministers.

23. The procedure for revising the Constitution is not simple. Basically, it takes place in two stages. In what is called the first reading (*eerste lezing*), one or more bills are submitted which follow the normal procedure for debating and voting on bills, except in one detail: the so-called right of division of the Second Chamber, whereby the bill may be divided into two or more separate bills (*splitsingsrecht*). This first stage is completed when the bill is passed and ratified (or a number of bills, if the right of division has been exercised), and the so-called First reading Acts are published. After this, the Second Chamber has to be dissolved and elections held. In practice, it is usually arranged in such a way that these elections coincide with the normal general elections for the Second Chamber. This has the effect that the question of constitutional reform becomes submerged in the general election contest. The second stage, called second reading (*tweede lezing*), follows as soon as the newly elected Second Chamber meets. This Chamber has to make a decision on the second reading of the bill, or else the proposal for a constitutional reform lapses. The bills debated in this second reading must have the same text as those passed in the first reading. Revision of the Constitution requires a two-thirds majority vote in both Chambers at this second reading. Amendments, that is, changes to the proposals under consideration, are not allowed.

24. After the bill has been passed at second reading, it must be ratified by the government. Once this has happened, the revision comes into force. Despite this cumbersome procedure, the Constitution has been repeatedly revised since 1814, as we have indicated. This can be explained by the fact that the changes often concerned issues which were of little political significance or resulted from changes in international relationships, such as decolonization. It is not going too far to suggest that only the 1848 and 1917 revisions were of any substantial significance.

25. In the context of constitutional revision, the arrangements for transitional constitutional law deserve some mention. Constitutional changes do not usually take immediate effect in the system of law. This follows from Article 140 of the Constitution, which states that legislation preceding an amendment of the Constitution, which as a result of the amendment is brought into conflict with the new constitutional law, remains in force until it has been revised to conform to the new law.

Chapter 3. Statutes and Other Regulations

26. In its substantive sense a constitution includes, as mentioned earlier, much more than the formal Constitution. Numerous laws and other written regulations can in practice be regarded as part of the constitution. Constitutional doctrine uses the term organic laws and organic regulations to identify these other elements. Sometimes these laws or regulations have come about by virtue of an instruction contained in the Constitution. The Constitution establishes, for example, that the members of the Chambers of the States General must be elected on the basis of proportional representation within the limits set by law (*see* Article 53 of the Constitution). The Elections Act, as an organic law, regulates, by virtue of this constitutional instruction, the elections on the basis of proportional representation.

Linkage of organic laws to explicit constitutional provisions is not automatic, however. It regularly happens that laws or regulations are adopted without a specific instruction thereto in the Constitution, but that they nonetheless contain important provisions of a constitutional nature. The Rules of Procedure for the Council of Ministers are an example of this. The Constitution does not prescribe, in the article about the Council of Ministers (Article 45), that detailed regulations must be established. Nonetheless, the Rules of Procedure for the Council of Ministers regulate in detail since 1850 the powers of the Council, the Prime Minister and other officials of the Council. Without doubt, this regulation can be regarded as an important organic regulation within the Dutch constitution. It is best therefore to regard as organic those regulations that establish government functions and that assign or regulate powers. The constitutional basis is not decisive.

For an indication of organic laws and regulations that thus fall under the substantive concept of constitution, the following – far from complete – summary can be given.

In the area of government, aside from the Rules of Procedure for the Council of Ministers mentioned earlier, it is worth noting the Ministerial Responsibility Act, the Membership of the Royal House Act and the Government Accounts Act.

Regarding the States General the above-mentioned Elections Act should be noted, but also the Rules of Procedure of both Chambers of Parliament and the Parliamentary Inquiry Act of 2008. With regard to legislative and executive powers, there are the Publication Act, the Council of State Act, the Treaties (Approval and Publication) Kingdom Act, the Civil Servants Act, the General Administrative Law Act, the War Act and the Civil Authority Special Powers Act.

Relevant to the judiciary system are the Judiciary (Organization) Act, the General Provisions Act, the Judicial Officers (Legal Status) Act, the General Administrative Law Act, the Council of State Act, the Social Security Appeals Act and the Administrative Jurisdiction (Trade and Industry) Act. For the organization of local and regional authorities the Provinces Act, the Municipalities Act and the Water Boards Act are relevant.

Lastly, as to the fundamental rights, it applies that organic laws give substance to the regulatory function of constitutional law. This is expressed in the Equal Treatment Act, the Public Assemblies Act and the Personal Data Protection Act.

This summary of organic laws and regulations makes clear that much of constitutional law is to be found in laws and regulations outside the Constitution.

Chapter 4. Case Law

27. When deciding disputes and adjudicating criminal offences, in particular when the government is involved in a dispute, the courts must where applicable rule in accordance with the Constitution and the organic laws and regulations, explain these constitutional norms and apply them. Even though the Constitution forbids the courts from evaluating Acts of Parliament for any inconsistency with the Constitution (Article 120), the courts must decide with regard to all other regulations, decrees and actions of government institutions whether such regulation, decree or government action is compatible with the Constitution.

The courts are thus fully authorized to conduct reviews for compatibility with the Constitution. In applying constitutional provisions, the courts develop unwritten rules of law that, according to the case law that they establish, assign a specific interpretation or meaning to these provisions. These unwritten rules of law are also an important source of Dutch constitutional law. It is important in this context that, especially with respect to the fundamental rights of Chapter 1 of the Constitution, the courts have explicitly contributed to the development of unwritten constitutional law. For example, the Supreme Court has through its rulings shaped, in a far-reaching way, the meaning of the freedom of the printed press and the freedom of speech of Article 7 of the Constitution by deducing a core right (right of communication to the public) and a 'connex' right (right of distribution) from this fundamental right and developing a special limitation regime in that context (*see* below).

In the judicial system, unwritten rules of law usually pertain to disputes between government bodies and private citizens. As to disputes between one political institution and another, within the scope of parliament or in the relationship between government and parliament, unwritten rules of law in the judicial system have hardly developed. Judge-made law (case law) is not or hardly available. A first explanation for this can be found in the principle of the separation of powers. Under this principle, not only the parliament but also the government takes up an independent and self-supporting position. Court intervention in the structure of parliament, or in the functioning of government and parliament, would compromise their autonomy.

From the viewpoint of checks and balances, it would, however, be quite justifiable to grant a judicial body the authority to review internal decisions or disputes between political institutions against the Constitution and organic regulations, thereby developing unwritten rules of law regarding the political functioning of these institutions. In other European countries, such as Germany, the constitution has specifically chosen to allocate such administration of justice to a special constitutional court.

In the Netherlands, no such choice has been made by the Constitution, so there is no special constitutional court. The 'ordinary' courts in the Netherlands do, however, have substantial authority by virtue of Article 112 of the Constitution (*see* below). In practice, however, the courts are very reticent to deal with such disputes. The courts are after all not political institutions that take part in the political decision-making process. As such, they are expected not to get involved in such issues. The courts confine themselves to disputes on the basis of law. They issue legal rulings, not political opinions. It is therefore logical that they cannot be asked to decide in strictly political disputes.

The Supreme Court generally does not get involved in disputes in the political arena. However, it is not entirely excluded that a court would involve itself in disputes that arise within the scope of parliament and government. The Supreme Court ruled in 1988 (Supreme Court, 18 November 1988, *Arubaanse verkiezingsafspraak*) that members of parliament have a free mandate. They cannot be forced by their political party to resign before the end of their term on the basis of an election agreement. The Supreme Court deduced this principle of free mandate from various constitutional regulations.

Such involvement in politics is, however, exceptional. As such, the Supreme Court ruled in 2003 (Supreme Court, 21 March 2003, *Waterpakt*) that the courts cannot force the State to prepare legislation, even though it is clear that the State is required to do so under European law. The Supreme Court made clear in this ruling that a court is not expected to get involved in strictly political decision-making processes. The question whether legislation must be enacted and what this must entail requires, according to the Supreme Court, a political assessment by the government and the States General, which the courts cannot get involved in. In this ruling, the Supreme Court rightly emphasizes the importance of separation of powers. The courts in the Netherlands are not expected to get involved in strictly political deliberations. However, in the *Urgenda Climate* Case (Supreme Court 2019), the Dutch Supreme Court reversed its ruling in the *Waterpakt* Case (2003) in part. In *Urgenda,* the Supreme Court regards an order to legislate permissible ' … in order to achieve a specific goal, so long as such an order to legislate is not tantamount to an order to establish legislation with a certain specific substance.' When the court limits itself to a general order to take measures, then, according to the Supreme Court, there is no drawback that third parties would be indirectly bound by the judgement. After all, the Supreme Court reasons, the court does not by means of its order determine the content of the regulation; that remains within the sphere of authority of the legislature involved. With this reasoning, the Supreme Court thus justifies its decision that a general order to create legislation regarding the reduction of CO^2 by 25% by the year 2020 is justified. In *Urgenda*, the Dutch Supreme Court for the first time forced the government to take legislative measures to combat climate change. The verdict by the Supreme Court is particularly relevant from the viewpoint of separation of powers and the rule of law. In the *Urgenda* ruling, the Supreme Court especially considers its own role in the rule of law, while ignoring the interests that are at stake regarding other state authorities, government and parliament. The judicial order to create legislation is difficult to unite with constitutional arrangements regarding the independence of parliament and its members (free mandate) in the context of separation of powers. The ruling furthermore clashes with the legality principle in the rule of law. The Supreme Court departs from the principle that a court dispenses justice in accordance with the wording and intention of the law. The Supreme Court bases its ruling in *Urgenda* primarily on political and scientific insights. In that way, the Supreme Court assigns itself a role in the political domain. There is reason to consider whether it is acceptable in a system of separation of powers for the Supreme Court to get involved in this way in the political decision-making process regarding climate policy and to order the government and the parliament to initiate legislation.

Chapter 5. Other Sources of Constitutional Law

§1. CONVENTIONS

28. There are certain unwritten laws or conventions which concern parliamentary and political relationships. These are not upheld by courts, but they are heeded by the offices involved, namely the ministers (the government) and the Chambers of the States General.

There is no consensus in the Netherlands on the question of which political practices are merely accepted practices and which must be considered as conventions. However, there are two conventions on the relationship between the government and parliament on which there is general agreement: The first is the confidence rule, which requires that a minister who has lost the confidence of one of the Chambers of Parliament must resign, except for the dissolution of the Chamber concerned. The second is that the government may only dissolve a Chamber of Parliament once for the same fact. Both of these unwritten laws became established in the period 1866–1868 and have never been seriously questioned since.

§2. DOCTRINE

29. Legal doctrine – writings by legal scholars – is not generally considered to be a source of constitutional law, nevertheless, it has clearly had an influence upon it on many occasions. For instance, large parts of the text of the 1983 Constitution were taken from the reports of an Advisory Committee, in which leading academic lawyers participated. Politicians also regularly request the advice of distinguished constitutionalists. It is probable that their opinions have become more important in recent years, now that there are only a few lawyers in parliament, most of whom have not been trained in constitutional law. The time when parliament included many renowned lawyers is long gone.

§3. ADVISORY BODIES

30. Although as a general rule, the advisory bodies cannot be considered to be a source of constitutional law, they do contribute to its development. In particular, since the decision to start publishing the recommendations of the Council of State (*Raad van State*), considerable attention has been paid to its views on constitutional and other important legal questions, even though its recommendations are not always followed. Other advisory bodies such as the Social Economic Council (*Sociaal Economische Raad*) have played a similar role from time to time.

Chapter 6. Codification, Interpretation and Hierarchy of Legal Rules

31. As the above summary of sources of constitutional law shows, Dutch constitutional law has been codified in different ways. In the first place, there are the Charter and the Constitution, the two basic laws of the Kingdom of the Netherlands. In addition, there is a wide range of Acts of Parliament and other organic regulations, which enact government institutions, grant government powers or regulate government relations. Case law is also considered an important source of constitutional law.

There is no single institution with powers to give a final interpretation of constitutional provisions. This results from a number of characteristic features of constitutional law: In the first place, the interpretation of the Constitution by the legislature is binding upon the administration and judiciary, given that Acts of Parliament cannot be tested against the Constitution (Article 120 of the Constitution). Second, there are a number of constitutional rules which, according to case law, cannot be enforced by the Judiciary such as rules on the relationship between the government and parliament. Third, the Netherlands does not have one single court at the highest instance, but several highest courts. Their interpretations of constitutional law can of course differ.

32. The hierarchy of legal rules can best be represented schematically as below:

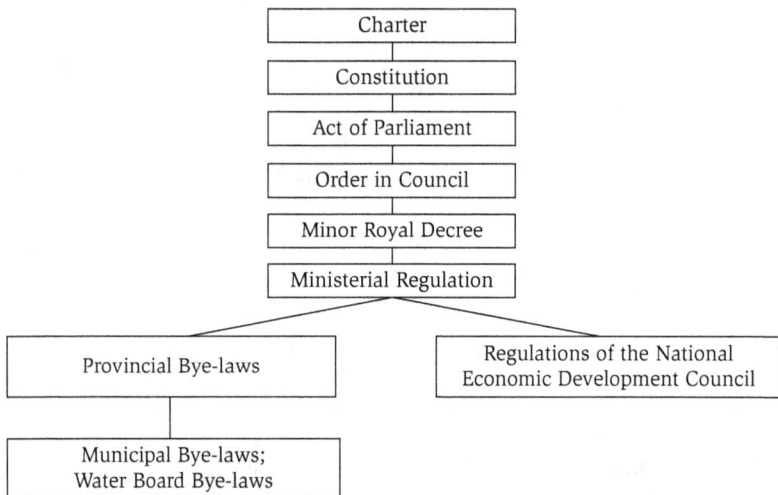

It should also be noted, in relation to this diagram, that EU law, as mentioned, prevails over the Constitution and other national regulations. As for treaties and decisions of international organizations, it cannot, strictly speaking, be said that they prevail over national statutory regulations. Article 94 of the Constitution does not lay down a hierarchy of norms but is only a provision relating to the application of national regulations which conflict with one particular type of international norm, that is, provisions that are directly applicable. We shall return to this topic later.

Part II. The State and Its Subdivisions

Chapter 1. The Form of State: The Federation of the Kingdom of the Netherlands

§1. HISTORICAL DEVELOPMENT

33. Since 1814, the Kingdom of the Netherlands has encompassed not only the territory in Europe but also colonies in other parts of the world. The Netherlands – the Country in Europe – as the 'motherland', formed the heart of the Kingdom. The other countries, the Dutch East Indies, Surinam and the Netherlands Antilles were more or less considered appendages.

34. For a long time, governmental authority in the overseas territories lay entirely in the hands of Dutch constitutional institutions. The 1815 Constitution stated that the King had supreme authority over the colonies. King William I, took this to mean that he was authorized to rule the colonies completely autonomously. He exercised the legislative and executive power over them personally. However, the constitutional revisions of 1840 and 1848 and the introduction of the parliamentary system brought about a gradual shift in government power away from the King and towards the Dutch legislature. Thus, from the middle of the nineteenth century, the Dutch parliament gained more influence over colonial policy.

35. In the Netherlands, it gradually came to be realized that the principal task of the motherland was to assist in the political, social and economic development of the colonies instead of treating them as conquered territories. This ethical policy, which won broad support in the government and in parliament, led to government institutions being set up in the colonies responsible for regulating internal matters. At the same time, a degree of democratization took place, albeit somewhat hesitantly, through the establishment of representative bodies. Thus a process of decolonization was started which was eventually supposed to lead to the overseas territories gaining autonomy and equivalent status with the motherland.

Some important steps were taken in the first decades of the twentieth century, but the ultimate goal was still a long way off. Dutch government power continued to dominate the colonies. Moreover, the European population ran the most important government institutions overseas. However, the elected representative bodies increasingly provided an important forum for the indigenous population groups to realize their struggle for greater independence.

The decolonization process accelerated after the Second World War. Immediately after the war, the Kingdom underwent a radical change. In the Dutch East Indies, attempts to restore the pre-war power relationships met with fierce resistance. Following an armed struggle, and under pressure from the United Nations and the United States, the motherland was forced to grant Indonesia its independence through a transfer of sovereignty in 1949.

36.   In the meantime, in the Netherlands Antilles and Surinam it proved possible to reach a negotiated solution, whereby a new federal structure was determined for the Kingdom, which guaranteed the autonomy and equivalent status of these overseas territories vis-à-vis the Netherlands. This new legal system came into operation in 1954. The Charter for the Kingdom of the Netherlands, which was democratically adopted in the three states, or 'countries'(*landen*) that made up the Kingdom, laid down the fundamental principles of the new legal system. The Charter functioned unchanged for about twenty years. Then, at the end of the 1960s, dissatisfaction with the political relationships within the Kingdom manifested itself among large sections of the population, especially in Surinam, but also in the Antilles. The struggle for complete independence gained more and more support. Against this background, the Dutch government felt compelled to draw up a policy to revise the Charter to give priority to the realization of autonomy.

In 1975, Surinam left the federation of the Kingdom and became an independent State. In 1985, the Charter was changed again, when the island of Aruba split away from the Netherlands Antilles. Since then, Aruba formed the third state in the Kingdom alongside the Netherlands and the Netherlands Antilles, which now comprise five islands. The concept of the Netherlands Antilles as a separate state within the Kingdom of the Netherlands never enjoyed full support of all the five islands involved. The transformation of Aruba into a separate state within the Kingdom in 1985 led to calls for similar arrangements concerning the other islands. Following referendums on all five islands, the Netherlands Antilles was finally dissolved on 10 October 2010. Curaçao and Sint Maarten became two new countries within the Kingdom of the Netherlands. These two states nowadays form together with Aruba and the Netherlands, the territory in Europe, a federation of four separate countries.

The three smaller Carribean Islands, Bonaire, Saba and Sint Eustacius became a direct part of the Netherlands. They are considered special municipalities, and public authorities as outlined in Article 132a of the Dutch Constitution. These Caribbean municipalities resemble Dutch municipalities in many ways. Dutch legislation will be enacted on these Caribbean Islands unless derogations are necessary.

§2.   THE STRUCTURE OF THE KINGDOM

37.   The Charter contains the Constitution for the Kingdom. It is also the highest constitutional document of the four countries of the Kingdom. The form of State which it lays down resembles at first sight a federation or federal State. The federation of the Kingdom functions over and above the four separate states (The Netherlands, Curaçao, Aruba, Sint Maarten) (Article 1 Charter). The Charter lists the institutions of the Kingdom. These include the Crown of the Kingdom (Article 1a

of the Charter), the government of the Kingdom and the executive power (Articles 2 and 4), the legislative bodies of the Kingdom and their legislative power (Article 4), the Council of Ministers of the Kingdom (Articles 7–12), and the Council of State of the Kingdom (Article 7). In addition, the Charter sets out the various federal affairs of the Kingdom (Article 3).

The four participating countries possess the principal features of states. They all have their own constitutions, called '*Grondwet*' in the Netherlands and '*Staatsregeling*' in the Caribbean part of the Kingdom. They have their own governmental organizations (parliament, government and judiciary), full legislative, executive and judicial powers and extensive governmental functions.

The preamble to the Charter declares that the four participating states have expressed their will to establish this new constitutional order in the Kingdom of the Netherlands in full freedom. According to the preamble, they will conduct their internal affairs autonomously and represent their common interests on a basis of equivalence. The preamble also emphasizes the need for mutual assistance and cooperation between the countries (loyalty and solidarity).

38. Despite the fact that it has these federal traits, it would not be correct to classify the Kingdom as a common federal State. When the institutions were constituted in 1954, no separate federal government was created. On the contrary, the institutions of the Kingdom are primarily Dutch institutions, which may or may not be provided with a certain overseas component. That is why the Dutch Constitution, which regulates the composition of these institutions, is not merely the Constitution for the state of the Netherlands, but also regulates to a great extent the organization of the Kingdom. Therefore, since 1954 the Constitution has continued to be entitled: Constitution for the Kingdom of the Netherlands (*Grondwet voor het Koninkrijk der Nederlanden*).

The choice of this federation sui generis, in which the institutions of one state occupy a dominant position at federal level was and is considered to be acceptable, given the enormous differences between the Netherlands and the two other countries. The large difference in population size alone justifies an imbalance in favour of the Netherlands. It is not without reason that the Preamble to the Charter assumes equivalent status between the three countries, rather than equality.

39. How are the government institutions of this federation *sui generis* composed and what powers do they have?

First and foremost, the Charter sets out that the Crown of the Kingdom of the Netherlands devolves upon the King. Article 1a of the Charter mentions Juliana, the reigning queen in 1954, and her lawful successors. All rules concerning succession of the King and his constitutional status are found in the Constitution (Articles 24–41 of the Constitution). The King is head of state of the Kingdom of the Netherlands. Besides being the first representative of the Kingdom, the King is also part of the government in the four participating states. Article 42 of the Constitution declares that the government comprises the King and the Ministers. In the three Caribbean states, the King has the same position in each of the governments, in accordance with the constitutions of these states.

Because the King normally resides in the Netherlands, a governor represents the King in Aruba, Curaçao and Sint Maarten. The governor, in his capacity as government institution of the Caribbean countries, is an integral part of the local governments together with the ministers.

The governor has a dual role. Not only is he a member of the local government of his Caribbean country, but he also represents the King in his capacity as part of the Government of the Kingdom (Article 2 of the Charter). As an institution of the Kingdom, the governor must implement the policies of the Government of the Kingdom. There are certain risks to this dual role, as the interests of the Kingdom and the Caribbean state may conflict. The governor is appointed and dismissed by the Government of the Kingdom (Article 2 of the Charter).

The King and the ministers of the Kingdom together form the Government of the Kingdom (*Koninkrijksregering*). The ministers of the Kingdom are in fact the Dutch ministers. Article 2 of the Charter suggests that the King as head of the Kingdom personally reigns over the Kingdom. However, in the context of Article 42 of the Constitution, it is clear that this needs to be interpreted as the King together with the (Dutch) ministers, forming the Government of the Kingdom.

To decide a matter in the Government of the Kingdom, the Council of Ministers of the Kingdom shall consider and decide upon the matter (Articles 7–12 of the Charter). According to Article 7 of the Charter, the Council of Ministers of the Kingdom is comprised of the Dutch ministers, appointed by royal decree according to Article 43 of the Constitution, and the Ministers Plenipotentiary (*gevolmachtigde ministers*), appointed by the Governments of Aruba, Curaçao and Sint Maarten. Following instructions from their Caribbean Governments, these three Ministers Plenipotentiary participate in the discussions of the Council of Ministers of the Kingdom. However, their influence on the decision-making process is limited.

40. During deliberations in the Council of Ministers, the plenipotentiary minister may declare that his state has serious objections to a particular ruling (Article 12 Charter). In those circumstances, the Dutch Prime Minister and two other Dutch ministers will enter into deliberation with the plenipotentiary minister and a second specially designated minister from the country. The Council of Ministers finally comes to a decision based on the outcome of the deliberations. Because the Dutch ministers are always in the majority, the others will usually lose the case.

41. The legislature for the Kingdom is comprised of the Government of the Kingdom and the Dutch States General. There is no separate federal parliament. In the legislative procedure for an Act of the Kingdom, there is an opportunity for overseas public authorities, including the plenipotentiary ministers, to exercise some degree of influence, but here too the final decision rests with the Dutch institutions.

According to Article 15 of the Charter, a bill for a Kingdom Act is forwarded not only to the Dutch States General but also to the parliaments of Aruba, Curaçao and Sint Maarten. These parliaments can issue written reports on the bill (Article 16). The Ministers Plenipotentiary may attend the debates on the bill in the States General and provide information (Article 17). They can express their opinion and propose amendments to the bill. The Minister Plenipotentiary can also state his opposition to the proposal and request postponement of the vote on the bill (Article

18). All these provisions concerning the legislative procedure for an Act of Parliament of the Kingdom nonetheless lead to very limited influence for the Caribbean countries.

42. Likewise, there is no separate (federal) judiciary at the level of the Kingdom. The Charter declares that the Dutch Supreme Court (*Hoge Raad*) has legal authority in Aruba, Curaçao and Sint Maarten as the highest court of law. Finally, it should also be mentioned that the Council of State (*Raad van State*) functions as the most important advisory body for the Government of the Kingdom. The Charter also creates the possibility for participation in the Council of State by an official from the overseas countries; it states that a member of the Council of State can be appointed in agreement with the Governments of Curaçao, Sint Maarten or Aruba, respectively if they so desire. Since 2010, the Charter for the Kingdom declares in Article 12a that provisions shall be made in a Kingdom Act for settling disputes between the Kingdom and the countries. The Caribbean countries would like to see an independent court, such as the Dutch Supreme Court, settling these disputes concerning Kingdom affairs, but the Dutch Government is up to now unwilling to go along with this idea. A Kingdom Act has not been established.

43. With respect to the powers of these institutions of the Kingdom, the following observations can be made. The Charter operates on the principle that the three countries run their domestic affairs completely autonomously. In principle, only common interests are dealt with by the institutions of the Kingdom. The Charter speaks in this context of the affairs of the Kingdom (*aangelegenheden van het Koninkrijk*) and lists a number of subjects which are 'federal by nature' (Article 3 Charter). These include: the defence of the Kingdom and the preservation of its independence, international relations, Dutch nationality, and the admission and expulsion of foreigners and extradition. On the basis of joint consultation, other subjects may also be declared to be affairs of the Kingdom, though this has so far never happened. For the number of affairs of the Kingdom to be expanded in this way, the (cumbersome) procedure for amending the Charter has to be followed. This prevents the autonomy of the separate countries from being infringed on too lightly.

Although affairs of the Kingdom are dealt with in the first place by institutions of the Kingdom, the possibility for institutions of the separate countries to assume these functions and thus exercise federal powers is not entirely excluded. Here, too, one sees an important departure from the usual federal structure. First, the Charter creates the possibility for the Dutch Constitution and international law to regulate affairs of the Kingdom. In addition, the Dutch legislature or the Dutch Government may draw up rules on such affairs, providing they do not apply in either Curaçao, Sint Maarten or Aruba. It follows from this that the legislature of the Kingdom only needs to become involved if the regulation in question is to apply in the territory of (one of) these countries.

Lastly, it should be noted that, according to Article 43 of the Charter, the Kingdom is likewise responsible for the safeguarding of fundamental rights, the protection of legal interests and good governance. In first instance, the individual countries are themselves responsible for ensuring that these legal safeguards are fulfilled. The Kingdom is to intervene only when a country is itself unable to comply with Article

43. According to the explanatory notes to Article 43, this will not readily apply. Under certain circumstances, however, the Government of the Kingdom can thus intervene in the governance of an individual country.

Article 50 of the Charter does allow the Government of the Kingdom to suspend or nullify legislative and/or executive measures in the Caribbean countries if these conflict with the Charter, an international treaty, a Kingdom Act or interests whose implementation or safeguarding is a responsibility of the Kingdom.

44. It has already been mentioned above that Kingdom affairs are limited and that the four countries are generally independent in the handling of their government tasks. Article 41 of the Charter determines in this context that the separate states shall conduct their internal affairs independently. The states are 'autonomous', conduct their own financial affairs and have their own health care, social security, police, courts and educational systems.

With the reform of the Kingdom of 10 October 2010, this 'federal' principle of control over internal affairs regarding a number of important governmental tasks was concretized in a new way. In the political negotiations preceding the reform, it was agreed that henceforth a number of 'state affairs' (*landsaangelegenheden*) would be regulated jointly and that these would be set out in so-called consensus Kingdom acts (*consensusrijkswetten*).

Article 38, paragraph 2, of the Charter, represents the basis of these consensus Kingdom acts. This paragraph sets out that it may be mutually decided that a mutual regulation for the states will be established by Kingdom act or by Kingdom order in council. The concept of 'mutual consultation' is interpreted as 'consensus requirement'. How this consensus between the states involved must take shape, is not described in Article 38. In the political reform of 2010, the various countries decided to incorporate as 'consensus requirement' in the procedure for the enactment of the Kingdom acts involved that the individual governments of the countries must consent to the mutual regulation.

Important examples of consensus Kingdom acts that were enacted in 2010 include the Joint Court of Justice Kingdom Act, the Public Prosecution Service Kingdom Act for Curaçao, Sint Maarten and the BES islands, and the Financial Supervision of Curaçao and Sint Maarten Kingdom Act.

The first of these Kingdom acts regulate the judicial system of all Caribbean Islands. It establishes that the judicial authority in the Caribbean territories consists of the courts of first instance and the Joint Court of Justice. The Public Prosecution Service Kingdom Act sets out that each of the Caribbean countries involved has a public prosecutor's office of first instance and an office of the procurator general at the head of the public prosecution services of Curaçao, Sint Maarten and the three BES islands. The Financial Supervision Kingdom Act provides for the establishment of a financial supervision board, consisting of four members, appointed by royal decree, who advise the two countries involved in financial and budget matters. If in the view of this supervisory board, a budget fails to meet the applicable norms, the Council of Ministers of the Kingdom may then decide that the budget needs to be revised. In the recent past, the Government of the Kingdom has already intervened several times in the financial affairs of one of the Caribbean countries and issued instructions to bring its finances up to standard. This provision in the

Financial Supervision Kingdom Act illustrates that the 'autonomous' control of the countries over their internal affairs has lost some of its relevance with the enactment of these consensus Kingdom acts. The 'federal' construction of the Kingdom is clearly under pressure.

The three BES islands (Bonaire, Sint Eustatius and Saba) are part of the Dutch governmental structure since 10 October 2010. These islands have a form of government that is similar to that of Dutch municipalities. The merger of the BES islands with the Netherlands has far-reaching consequences for the way legislation operates on these three islands. In principle, the current Dutch-Antillean legislative system stays in effect. It is possible that Dutch legislation will apply in the BES islands.

In this context, Article 132a of the Constitution provides for the possibility of the Dutch legislature instituting rules for the BES islands involving customized rules concerning social, economic or geographic circumstances and the like. Finally, the inclusion of the BES islands in the Dutch governmental structure also has consequences for the exercise of voting rights by the citizens of these islands.

There is significant resistance on the three islands against the new status. Many islanders do not have the impression that the amalgamation with the Netherlands has benefited them in any significant way.

45. Furthermore, a reservation should be made in the field of foreign relations. As indicated above, foreign relations are a matter for the Kingdom. Under international law, it is the Kingdom which is a legal subject, not the states comprising the Kingdom. The Kingdom concludes treaties with other States. However, it is possible for treaties to apply only to parts of the Kingdom. The Dutch Constitution declares that the (Dutch) Government is to promote the development of international law. Dutch public authorities, including the Minister of Foreign Affairs, are authorized to represent the Kingdom when treaties are to be signed. If the treaties apply both in the Netherlands and Aruba, Curaçao and Sint Maarten, then in practice they will be approved by the legislature for the Kingdom. Furthermore, Aruba, Curaçao and Sint Maarten are involved in the preparation and implementation of treaties which affect them. Nevertheless, Dutch authorities, whether or not they are acting as authorities of the Kingdom, are sometimes able to exert considerable influence over government policy in the other states of the Kingdom through the power they have in making treaties.

§3. The Constitutional Law of Curaçao, Sint Maarten and Aruba

46. The constitutional law of Curaçao, Sint Maarten and Aruba is – apart from a few provisions in the Charter – mainly laid down in the three Constitutions (*Staatsregelingen*) of these countries. These Constitutions are laid down in legislative orders enacted at national level (*landsverordeningen*).

47. There are important areas of agreement with Dutch constitutional law, which are described in the following chapters. The Constitutions contain provisions for:

the governor as national authority, the government, the ministers and state secretaries, the Council of Ministers, the prime minister, the parliament (*Staten*) and the Advisory Council (*Raad van Advies*). On the whole, these bodies fulfil the same functions as are fulfilled in the Netherlands by the King, the government, the ministers and state secretaries, the Council of Ministers, the prime minister, the States General and the Council of State. Legislative orders enacted by the national government and parliament together (*landsverordeningen*) are comparable to Dutch Acts of Parliament. Legislative orders enacted by the national government (*landsbesluitenhoudendealgemenemaatregelen*) are comparable to the Dutch Orders in Council.

48. Alongside the legislative and executive powers, these constitutions also make provisions for a Judiciary. There is a Joint Court of Justice for all the Caribbean Islands together, as mentioned above. The administration of justice in the first instance and appeals are concentrated in this court. As we indicated above, the Dutch Supreme Court functions as court of cassation for these countries.

Chapter 2. Decentralized Authorities

§1. INTRODUCTION

49. For centuries, the Netherlands has shown a preference for spreading government power over a plurality of government bodies rather than concentrating it at central level. During the period of the Republic of the United Netherlands, the seven provinces considered themselves to be sovereign states. Together they made up a confederation of states. Within the provinces, furthermore, the cities enjoyed a large measure of autonomy.

50. The provinces lost their sovereignty in 1814 and a unitary state was formed. This drastic change in the form of state was expressed in the 1814 Constitution by, among other things, the provision that the States General henceforth represented all the Dutch people (Article 50 of the Constitution).

From then onwards, the provinces (*provincies*) were to be non-sovereign government entities within the Kingdom. Although they, and the municipalities (*gemeenten*), retained a certain amount of autonomy, their powers were for the first time considerably reduced during the reign of King William I and then King William II (1814–1849). Central authority – concentrated in the person of the King – had far-reaching powers over provincial and local governments. This concentration of power at the centre was brought to an end by the 1848 reform of the Constitution, and the enactment of the Provinces Act (1850) and the Municipalities Act (1851). The state structure created at this time, in particular through the efforts of the liberal statesman Thorbecke, can best be termed a decentralized unitary state. Its principal features still exist today, the most important of which is the existence of several layers of government in addition to the central authority. The organization of these various layers is regulated in the Constitution, which also assigns them legislative and executive powers. The administration of justice remains the exclusive power of the central government's judicial authorities.

The relationship between central government and the decentralized authorities is not hierarchical. Decentralized government authorities are autonomous public institutions with their own legal personality. Their functioning is, however, subject to various forms of central control, and their regulations are of a lower order than national legislation.

51. The Constitution does not guarantee the limits of the area of operation of the decentralized authorities. It does however state that certain subjects which are matters of government concern, fall outside the competence of the decentralized authorities. The Constitution declares that central government is solely competent on matters of defence, foreign affairs (the conclusion of treaties), the monetary system, the administration of justice and the regulation of civil law, criminal law (partially), and civil and criminal procedures. In addition, there are certain fundamental rights which can only be restricted by Act of Parliament.

52. With respect to the competence of the decentralized government authorities, Dutch constitutional law distinguishes between autonomous powers (*autonomie*) and shared powers (*medebewind*). Regarding the first category, Article 124 of the Constitution provides that the powers 'to regulate and administer their own affairs shall be left to' the decentralized authorities; with regard to the second, it states that they 'may be required by or pursuant to an Act of Parliament to provide regulation and administration'. In areas where it has autonomous powers, the decentralized authority conducts its own policies, deciding for itself its aims and means. In cases of shared powers, it cooperates in the implementation of policy which has been decided by other government institutions.

53. However, the designation of matters to be defined as their own affairs is not fixed. In the nineteenth century, the notion that the fields of activity of central government, provinces and municipalities were mutually exclusive more or less of their very nature was still defended in constitutional doctrine. However, this theory has not enjoyed support for a long time now. In practice, it is mainly political factors and considerations of expediency which determine the level of government which will take care of a particular government responsibility.

54. As the years have gone by, central government has taken over more and more policy areas which originally fell within the autonomous sphere of the provincial and municipal authorities. These shifts have usually been effected by means of central legislation. In some cases, regulations were drawn up which left no room for action by the decentralized authorities. In other cases, a central decision came into force requiring the local authorities to cooperate in the implementation of a policy, in the form of shared powers. Thus the autonomous competence which was taken away was returned as a shared power. Another possibility is that the decentralized authority has 'supplementary' powers.

Although the governing bodies of provinces and municipalities have relinquished their autonomous powers in many policy areas to central government, their administrative and rule-making activities have not been reduced in the least. On the contrary, their sphere of activity has been expanded considerably due to the assignment of all kinds of tasks in connection with the exercise of shared powers.

55. This development has had some influence on the organization of local government. In practice, the smaller municipalities proved unable to fulfil all the functions properly. At first, following the Second World War, this problem was mainly resolved by consolidating the smaller municipalities, by means of mergers. The number of municipalities was reduced in the post-war years from about 1,000 to about 340. In addition, in some policy areas, local authorities were given the possibility to cooperate and draw up joint regulations (*gemeenschappelijke regelingen*).

The 1960s and 1970s saw more far-reaching plans for increasing the scale of operations. Within the framework of a major local government reorganization, it was proposed that a new layer of government ('districts', *gewesten*) be introduced. When this plan proved not to be feasible, an attempt was made to increase the number of provinces drastically and reduce the number of municipalities. These plans also failed. After more than twenty years, attempts at local government reorganization largely ended in failure. At the moment, emphasis is once more on the consolidation of and (more especially) cooperation between municipalities. The Joint Regulations Act (1984) (*Wet gemeenschappelijkeregelingen*) offers ample opportunities for permanent, regional and cooperative schemes to be started in several policy areas. Furthermore, there has been a trend towards the formation of urban areas with their own form of local government.

56. So far, we have mentioned two forms of decentralized government, the provinces and municipalities, which together with central government possess general administrative and rule-making powers. This can be referred to as territorial decentralization. Within the boundaries of their own geographical areas, these public bodies have general administrative and rule-giving powers.

In addition, forms of 'functional' decentralization exist within the Dutch system of constitutional law. This term refers to the possibility that decentralized offices are authorized to represent particular interests. They possess rule-making and administrative powers connected with particular matters. Examples of this are the water boards (*waterschappen*) and the Social Economic Council (*Sociaal-Economische Raad*) (SER). Sections 6 and 7 of this chapter examine functional decentralization further.

§2. The Organization of the Provinces and Municipalities

57. The composition and organization of the institutions of the provinces and the municipalities are broadly similar. Articles 123–136 of the Constitution contain a number of basic provisions, and refer for the rest to the legislature, which may in turn delegate certain powers to other government institutions. In the 1980s, a start was made on a general revision of the Municipalities Act (*Gemeentewet*) and the Provinces Act (*Provinciewet*). It was agreed that this would not involve fundamental changes: modernization and adjustment to present-day requirements were felt to be sufficient. The system and terminology of the new Provinces Act and Municipalities Act are finely tuned to each other.

58. The provinces and municipalities are headed by the provincial states (*provinciale staten*) –'the states'– and the municipal council (*gemeenteraad*) –'the council'– respectively (Article 125 Constitution). One sees here a reflection of the republican tradition; there is no question of power being vested in one person at the top. The members of these representative bodies are directly elected, according to a system of proportional representation, for a period of four years, by Dutch nationals who are residents in the province or municipality. In 1983, the Constitution was amended to create the possibility for residents without Dutch nationality to vote in municipal elections. Subsequently, the Elections Act (*Kieswet*) made a provision to this effect.

59. The number of members in the provincial states and councils depends on the resident population. Membership varies from thirty-nine to fifty-five for the states,

and from nine to forty-five for the councils. There are certain public functions incompatible with membership of these bodies, such as minister, state secretary, Royal Commissioner, member of the Council of State or the General Chamber of Audit and (with some exceptions) civil servant in that same province or municipality.

60. The provincial states and municipal councils decide for themselves, in principle, how often they will meet. There are rules similar to the standing orders of the States General concerning conditions under which meetings are public or not, quorums, voting rules and political immunity of members.

61. The provincial executive (*gedeputeerde staten*) is the executive body for the provinces and comprises the Royal Commissioner (*Commissaris van de Koning*) and the 'deputies' (*gedeputeerden*). The executive body for the municipality is made up of the mayor and aldermen together (*college van burgemeester en wethouders*) (Article 125 of the Constitution). The deputies and the aldermen are appointed for four years, by the provincial states and the municipal councils, from among their members or from outside. Their term of office ends at the same time as that of members of the representative bodies.

The number of deputies is set at a minimum of three and no more than seven for each province. The number of aldermen may not exceed 20% of the number of municipal councillors, with a minimum of two. Deputies and aldermen are prohibited from holding certain other offices at the same time. An alderman is prohibited from holding at the same time certain public offices in provincial or central government, while a deputy serving in the provincial executive may not at the same time hold an office with a municipality or water board in his or her own province. An alderman cannot be a member of the municipal council at the same time. The office of deputy is incompatible with membership of the provincial states. In this aspect, separation of powers is a basic institutional principle for decentralized authorities as well.

62. In relation to the appointment of deputies and aldermen – the formation of the executive body – it has long been accepted practice that the composition of the executive should reflect as far as possible the political balance in the states or the municipal council. As far as possible, the political parties should be represented in the executive bodies in proportion to the number of seats held by members of these parties in the states and the council. More recently, however, the formation of the executive at provincial and municipal levels has undergone a development which is similar to that of cabinet formation at national level. Political groups within the council or the states currently strive, usually through a series of negotiations on a political programme, to create a majority coalition, with executive members belonging only to the political groups which form the majority. In this way, the executive body, supported by a permanent majority of elected members in the provincial states or municipal council, can push through a policy programme which is decided in advance, and against a minority opposition. This development illustrates that even at municipal and provincial levels, there is a continuing politicization of the executive.

63. The provincial and municipal executives are collegiate administrative bodies. Powers belong to the group, not to individual members. In practice, the activities of the executive are divided among the deputies and aldermen, so that each has a particular 'portfolio'. Thus, although in practice the members frequently take decisions in their own policy areas, the ultimate authority to take decisions is formally reserved to the collective body. The relationship between the executive and the representative bodies is one of responsibility. Members of the provincial and municipal executives are jointly and separately responsible to the provincial states and municipal councils respectively for the administrative activities which the executives carry out. It follows from this that they have a duty to supply information to the members of the provincial states and municipal councils unless this is against the public interest.

64. The Municipalities Act and Provinces Act also assume a 'confidence rule' between the executive and the representative bodies. The provincial states and municipal councils have the power to dismiss one or more deputies or aldermen respectively if these no longer enjoy the confidence of the states or council.

When the relevant statutory provisions were being drawn up, it was felt that the principles of collegiate administration and the primacy of the representative bodies logically meant that the representative body ought to have the authority to dismiss those members of the executive elected by them collectively. This possibility is a relatively new element in administrative relationships at provincial and local levels. Previously, the Municipalities Act had only provided for the dismissal of individual executive members due to loss of confidence. On this point, too, it is possible to perceive a movement towards greater similarity between central and local governments. Nevertheless, major differences remain. The confidence rule of the parliamentary system which regulates the relationship between the government and parliament does not give parliament any rights of dismissal. And at the local level, there is no power for the executive to dissolve the representative body in cases of conflict.

65. The Constitution mentions a third office for the provinces and municipalities which is, respectively, that of the Royal Commissioner (*Commissaris van de Koning*) and the mayor (*burgemeester*). Holders of these offices are appointed and reappointed, for six years at a time, by Royal Decree. The Provinces Act and the Municipalities Act contain provisions enabling the provincial states and municipal councils to make their opinion known about an appointment. They must set up a confidential committee from among their own members to assess candidates for these offices; the committee reports to the provincial states respectively the municipal council and the Minister for Home Affairs. The provincial states and the municipal council respectively propose two candidates, or in special circumstances one candidate, to the Minister, who nominates a candidate to the King for appointment by Royal Decree.

Over the last thirty years, repeated demands have been made for these two offices to be filled by election by the local electorates, instead of by appointment. . In 2018, Article 131 of the Constitution concerning the appointment of these two officials by Royal decree has been revised. The Constitution now states in Article 131 that appointment and dismissal of the Royal Commissioner and the mayor have to be regulated by Act of Parliament. However, there has not been a legislative initiative to change appointment procedures.

The holders of these two offices have a number of functions. They are chairpersons of the relevant representative body, as well as of the executive – and are also members of the latter. In addition, the office of mayor or Royal Commissioner may be regarded as a separate 'individual' office that is held by a single person. In this respect, the holders of these offices have their own additional powers, which will be discussed below. It is also important to note that the Royal Commissioner is not just a provincial official, but also a central government official, even though the latter role is of limited importance.

66. The Royal Commissioner and the mayor are responsible to the states and municipal councils, respectively. They have a duty to provide information to members of the representative bodies. In the case of the Royal Commissioner, this duty does not extend to the exercise of his or her authority as a central government official. In this function, he or she is only answerable to the Minister of the Interior and Kingdom Relations.

67. The Constitution provides that offices other than those it specifically mentions (those discussed up until now) may also be set up. Both the Provinces Act and the Municipalities Act make provision for committees to be created. The provincial states and the municipal councils can appoint committees, and also decide on their composition, tasks and powers. The committees may be granted limited rule-making and administrative powers. They may also fulfil an advisory role. The other offices discussed above, at both provincial and municipal levels, can also set up advisory committees.

68. The Municipalities Act and the Provinces Act authorize to establish a chamber of audit, to investigate the effectiveness and legitimacy of the policies of the municipalities or provinces.

69. Finally, both the Provinces Act and the Municipalities Act designate civil servants to assist the office mentioned above in carrying out their tasks. They are the secretary and the clerk (*Secretaris, Griffier*).

§3. POWERS

70. The Constitution contains a number of fundamental provisions on the allocation of powers and delegates the more detailed attribution of powers to the legislature.

71. There is no question of a complete division of powers according to the separation of powers (*triaspolitica*) principle at provincial and municipal levels. The judicial function is completely absent, and the legislative and executive powers are

not allocated to different, completely separate offices. This is made clear in the Constitution itself, since it assigns the regulatory and administrative powers, both autonomous and shared, to the 'provincial and municipal administrative organs', which includes all the offices discussed above (Article 124 of the Constitution).

While there is no division according to the *trias* principle, a different form of division of powers can be assumed, namely distinguishing general administration (*algemeenbestuur*) from day-to-day administration (*dagelijksbestuur*). The term administration here covers both regulatory and executive powers.

72. Under the Constitution, the provincial states and the municipal council are at the head of the province and municipality respectively. This means that, except where there are statutory provisions to the contrary, the states and council possess the full range of regulatory and administrative powers. The Constitution guarantees that it is the states and council which possess the competence to issue by-laws (*verordeningen*), under both autonomous powers and shared powers. Only if these powers have been allocated or transferred to other offices by Act of Parliament, or by by-laws issued by the local authority itself pursuant to an Act of Parliament, is this otherwise.

73. More detailed regulations on the powers of the states and council are contained in the Provinces Act and the Municipalities Act. These Acts contain the basic provision concerning the autonomous authority to issue by-laws: it states that the states and council issue by-laws which they consider to be in the interests of their province or municipality. The enactment of by-laws under shared powers is also, in principle, a matter for the states and council unless this power has been assigned by or pursuant to an Act of Parliament to the provincial executive or the Royal Commissioner in the case of the provinces, or the municipal executive or the mayor in the case of the municipality.

A question arises in connection with the power to issue by-laws as to the limits to this power. The basic provision just mentioned contains an element of subjectivity. The states and the council make the by-laws which they 'consider to be' necessary, not those which 'are' necessary. It does not follow from this wording that the judiciary must refrain from judging whether a by-law is in the interests of the province or municipality or not. The judge exercises a limited judicial review of the question of whether the states or the council have overstepped their powers by not confining themselves to the provincial or municipal interests, but by becoming involved in regulations relating to the private interests of their residents. By-laws must be concerned with the affairs of the province or municipality.

The power to enact by-laws is also limited by 'higher ranking rules'. Provincial and municipal by-laws may not conflict with the Constitution, Acts of Parliament, orders in Council or ministerial rules. In addition, provincial by-laws have the status of 'higher ranking rules' vis-à-vis municipal by-laws.

74. Provided they do not conflict with higher rules, provincial and municipal by-laws may contain supplementary provisions relating to a subject which is already regulated by an Act of Parliament or Order in Council (or, in the case of municipal by-laws, by a provincial by-law). However, if the higher rule in question is intended

to be exhaustive, then the power to issue rules at the decentralized level is cancelled. Moreover, the provisions in provincial and municipal by-laws cease to apply *ipso jure* if the matter is dealt with by a provision in a higher rule. In that case, it is still sometimes possible for the competent provincial or municipal authority to make supplementary rules.

75. The states and council may delegate their regulatory powers to the provincial or municipal executives or to committees, but this possibility is limited. For example, the power to issue by-laws which are to be enforced by means of criminal law or administrative coercion (*bestuursdwang*) can only be transferred if these concern further rules on subjects already regulated in by-laws.

76. The general administration is executed by the states and the council in the administrative as well as the regulatory fields. These bodies possess important powers, such as that of establishing the budget. An important power at the level of the provinces is that of setting up (or abolishing) water boards, and of regulating their powers and organization.

77. As we have shown, provincial and municipal executives may also have regulatory competence, either through shared powers or because it has been delegated to them. Even the statutory requirement to implement decisions of the states and council can imply regulatory competence, since rules may be needed to implement these decisions. The day-to-day administration of the province and municipality is primarily in the hands of the provincial and municipal executives. These bodies are charged with the preparation and execution of the decisions of the states and council respectively. The Provinces and Municipalities Acts do not specify what is included in day-to-day administration. Thus the provinces and municipalities are able, to some extent, to decide how to divide their powers.

What falls within day-to-day administration depends partly on the local situation. One important power which both executives have is the authority to apply administrative coercion (*bestuursdwang*). This covers the removal, prevention, restoration to its former state or carrying out of that which is, or has been, done, kept or neglected in contravention of an Act, Order in Council or provincial or municipal by-law, at the expense of the person who is in the wrong.

78. The Royal Commissioner and the mayor exercise in the first place their powers as chairpersons of the provincial states and the provincial executive, and the municipal council and municipal executive respectively. They can also be charged with executive powers by or pursuant to an Act of Parliament. They can apply administrative coercion to uphold rules they implement. In addition, they represent the province or municipality in and out of court.

As well as occupying an office at the level of the province, the Royal Commissioner is also an official of the central government. In this capacity, under rules laid down by an official instruction from the central government, he or she is charged with the coordination of civil defence, and with facilitating the cooperation of government civil servants working in the province. He or she also has to make regular visits to municipalities and recommend candidates to the Minister of the Interior for appointment as mayors.

79. The mayor has important powers in the sphere of maintenance of public order, through the police under his or her authority. Where public disturbances occur, or there is a serious fear that they will do so, he or she is authorized to give whatever orders are necessary to keep the peace. The mayor also has supreme command when there is a fire, and he or she supervises public meetings, public entertainment and buildings which are open to the public. The Municipalities Act furthermore includes certain emergency provisions which grant the mayor far-reaching powers. In the event of a riot, serious disorder or disaster, or a serious threat of one of these emergencies, the mayor is authorized to give any orders he or she deems necessary to maintain public order or limit the danger. In doing so, he or she may depart from all other regulations except those laid down in the Constitution. In such a situation, the mayor not only has the power to give concrete orders but he or she may also issue emergency by-laws. There are some conditions attached to the exercise of this power; these include the fact that the Royal Commissioner must be informed of the emergency by-laws, and these must be confirmed afterwards by the council.

80. Finally, it should be noted that provincial and municipal committees have certain regulatory, administrative and advisory powers both in the spheres of autonomous and shared power. They may exercise powers belonging to the provincial states and council, or the provincial and municipal executives.

§4. Finances

81. It was noted above that the provincial and municipal executives are charged with the management of provincial and municipal finances. The budget is set by the provincial states and the municipal council. Expenditure is partly funded by provincial and municipal taxes. The Constitution prescribes that the taxes which the provinces and municipalities may levy must be laid down in an Act of Parliament (Article 132 of the Constitution). The Provinces Act and Municipalities Act list the taxes which the provinces and municipalities may levy. The property tax is an important example of a municipal tax. In addition, special statutes may permit the provinces and municipalities to levy taxes.

82. In general, it can be stated that provincial and local taxes are of very limited importance now compared with central government taxes. Since the middle of the nineteenth century, there has been a gradual but large-scale centralization of taxation. As a result, the provinces and municipalities have to a large degree lost their financial independence. For many years now provinces and municipalities have had to turn to central government to finance their expenditure. Nevertheless, to guarantee some measure of financial independence, the Constitution lays down that the

financial relationship with central government must be regulated by Act of Parliament. The Provinces Act contains a rule on this point for the provinces, while an equivalent regulation for the municipalities is to be found in the Financial Relationships Act (*Financiële verhoudingswet*) of 1996. These Acts provide for a Provincial Fund and a Municipal Fund, which receive a certain percentage of almost all forms of central government taxation. The provinces and municipalities receive a general payment from these funds. In addition, they may be eligible for specific payments by virtue of special statutory provisions. These are contributions made by central government to help finance specific provincial or municipal tasks or activities, for example in the social or cultural fields. While the decentralized authority is free, in principle, to decide how to allocate the general payment, the specific payments must be used for the purpose for which they were made. Furthermore, of major importance is that it is central government that decides whether a specific payment will be made and if so how much it will be.

83. Over the last few decades, specific payments have become by far the most important source of income, especially for the municipalities. This development has restricted their financial independence even further. Its consequence is an ever-decreasing room for autonomous local policy.

§5. SUPERVISION OF THE PROVINCES AND MUNICIPALITIES

84. An essential characteristic of the decentralized unitary state is that the decentralized government bodies, while being autonomous, are not independent or sovereign in relation to central government. Decisions of a regulatory or administrative nature taken by provincial and municipal authorities must not conflict with central government policy. To ensure that this principle is upheld, the Constitution makes provision for the activities of the decentralized administrations to be supervised.

85. The first form of supervision is prior (preventive) supervision, which must be regulated by Act of Parliament. The best-known form of this is 'approval' (*goedkeuring*). The Provinces Act and the Municipalities Act and legislation governing shared powers – and in the case of municipalities, provincial by-laws pursuant to an Act of Parliament – lay down the circumstances where prior supervision is required. Also, the General Administrative Law Act contains general rules on approval.

Efforts have been made to minimize the use of prior supervision as far as possible. This can be illustrated in the case of the provincial and municipal budgets. Originally the provincial budget had to be approved by the government and the municipal budget by the provincial executive. Now, the Provinces Act and Municipalities Act take the line that the budgets only need to be approved if the minister – or on appeal of the government – or the provincial executive, respectively, consider that the budget does not balance and probably cannot be brought into balance in the short term.

86. The second form of supervision is supervision a posteriori or 'repressive' supervision, which involves the power of the central government to annul a decision (*vernietiging*). The Constitution lays down that this power may be exercised by Royal Decree where there is a conflict with the law (written or unwritten) or the public interest. The Provinces Act and Municipalities Act assume that all orders issued by provincial and municipal authorities are subject to annulment. In practice, the power is not frequently exercised although during the last years, the number of annulments is increasing, for example, in the field of town and country planning.

87. The so-called negligence rule (*verwaarlozingsregeling*) is a third special form of supervision. The Constitution lays down that provisions shall be regulated by Act of Parliament for situations where a decentralized authority has neglected its duty to carry out a task under shared powers (Article 132 of the Constitution). For example, the Municipalities Act makes the following provision for this situation: if the municipal executive does not (properly) take a decision required under shared powers, the provincial executive will provide for such a decision on behalf of the municipality, at the latter's expense.

The Constitution also makes provision for the situation where a decentralized authority neglects one of its autonomous functions. If it is a case of gross negligence, a measure can be taken by Act of Parliament which departs from the constitutional system of division of competences (Article 132 of the Constitution). There have been a few occasions in the past when a government commissioner has been appointed by Act of Parliament to exercise the powers of the council in a particular municipality when the council had been grossly negligent in its autonomous functions.

§6. THE WATER BOARDS

88. In the introduction to this chapter, a distinction was made between territorial and functional decentralization. The water boards are an important exponent of the latter category. Dykes and water management are vitally important for a low-lying country like the Netherlands. The water boards have fulfilled an important function in this area for centuries. The earliest water boards date from the beginning of the twelfth century.

While the provinces and municipalities have a general, regulatory and administrative role within their territorial boundaries, the water boards are only responsible for matters which fall within the sphere of the *waterstaat*, that is, water management of all kinds and related public works.

89. It must also be borne in mind that the water boards are not the only bodies which have responsibilities in this area. Central government, the provinces and the municipalities also function in this sphere. Furthermore, the water boards do not carry out water management tasks in general: each board has one or more specific functions which were laid down when the board was set up.

It is important to note that whereas in the case of provinces and municipalities, the whole territory of the Netherlands is divided up among them, this is not so for

the water boards. Some parts of the country situated on higher ground do not have
water boards at all, while in other areas several water boards (usually of varying
size) have developed specialized functions within the same geographical area. In
this sense, it is correct to speak of functional decentralization in the case of the water
boards, even though their operations are also divided up into geographical districts.
The Water Boards Act (*Waterschapswet 1991*) expresses both of these elements
when it defines a water board as a public institution, responsible for matters relating
to water management (*waterstaat*) in a particular geographical area.

90.   There are also noticeable differences between the organization and powers
of the water boards, and those of the provinces and municipalities. While the latter
were instituted as public bodies based on organic statutes (*see also* paragraph 26)
and following a uniform system, the water boards have always shown enormous
diversity. To a large extent, this is a consequence of the fact that, from 1814
onwards, the Constitution left the power to set up and organize water boards with
the provincial authorities, and until rather recently the legislature had laid down
very few rules in this area.

91.   However, this situation has changed gradually in recent years. In the first
place, the number of water boards has been drastically reduced as a result of
increases in the scale of operations. A few decades ago there were about 2,700 water
boards, now there are twenty-one water boards. In addition, the Water Boards Act
came into effect. This general statute governing the water boards contains a revision
of the existing water board legislation and lays down for the first time general principles for the structure of the water boards.
   The structure of the Water Boards Act – dealing in turn with the organization of
administrative bodies, powers, finance and supervision – is closely related to that of
the Provinces Act and Municipalities Act. However, there is an important difference
in the fundamental principles of water board structure. The legislature has not
assumed one single administrative model. Basically, rules are laid down governing
the exercise of powers by the provincial authorities with respect to the establishment and organization of water boards. Therefore, although, within certain boundaries, the provincial authorities retain their freedom, on essential points the Water
Boards Act now provides the framework for the organization of the water boards.
   On the basis of current legislation, the following broad picture of the organization and powers of the water boards and the administrative supervision to which
they are subject can be sketched.

92.   Article 133 of the Constitution lays down the basic arrangements. The main
powers to create and abolish water boards and to make standing orders for water
boards are granted to the provincial states, to be effected through provincial by-laws.
In addition, the Constitution confers the same powers on the legislature and other
offices that the legislature has delegated with these powers. The Water Boards Act
now also enables these powers to be exercised through an Order in Council in certain circumstances. With regard to the powers of the water board administrative
organs and supervision of them, the Constitution merely states that these will be
regulated by Act of Parliament.

93. The Water Boards Act, as we said earlier, lays down more concrete details relating to the powers of the provincial authorities with respect to the establishment and powers of water boards. The Act distinguishes between a general administrative committee, an executive committee and a chairperson. The general administrative committee is composed of members' representation concerning the various categories of stakeholders: landholders, leaseholders, owners of buildings, companies (industrial pollsters) and, since recently, all the residents as well. Certain stakeholders may be given the power to appoint members of the executive committees.

94. Members of the general administrative committee are elected. The election arrangements are determined by the provincial states in accordance with statutory regulations and are laid down in the water board standing orders.

95. The executive committee consists of the chairperson and other members, the number of which is laid down in the water board standing orders. Apart from the chairperson, the members are chosen from and by the general administrative committee. They should, as far as possible, reflect the various interest groups in the general administrative committee in the same proportions. The chairperson of the water board is appointed by Royal Decree based on the recommendation of the general administrative committee. The appointment is for a duration of six years.

96. There is a relationship of responsibility between the executive committee and the general administrative committee, which corresponds to that of members of the provincial and municipal executives. With regard to the powers of the water board administrative organs, a distinction is made between autonomous and shared powers, just as is made for the provinces and municipalities. The water board administrative organs are authorized to regulate and manage those functions which are assigned to it in the water board standing orders. In addition, rules and administrative arrangements may also be required by Act of Parliament, Orders in Council or provincial by-laws.

97. In principle both autonomous and shared powers are held by the general administrative committee unless they have been allocated to another office of the water board by the standing orders, a statute or an Order in Council. Certain powers are nevertheless reserved for the general administrative committee, such as fixing the budget, water taxes, and water board by-laws, which include orders and prohibitions enforceable through penalties or administrative coercion (*keuren*).

98. The executive committee is charged with the day-to-day management of the water board, and with the preparation and execution of the decisions of the general administrative committee. Subject to a number of exceptions, the power to apply administrative coercion is exercised by the executive committee. Finally, the chairperson chairs the meetings of both the general administrative and the executive committees, though he or she only has an advisory vote in the general administrative committee of which he or she is not a member. Furthermore, the chairperson holds an 'individual' single-headed office, and one of his or her roles in this capacity is to represent the water board in and out of court.

99. The finance and supervision of the water boards also merit attention. There is no central government funding for the water boards, as there is for the provinces and municipalities. A characteristic feature of the water boards is that their financing rests primarily upon an assessment of the costs of their operations, shared out over all those who have an interest in those operations. The general administrative committee lays down in a by-law how the costs are to be shared out among the different interest groups.

100. With respect to governmental control over the operations of the water boards, the Water Boards Act follows the line taken by the Provinces and Municipalities Acts in taking repressive supervision as the rule, and making preventive supervision the exception. Preventive supervision is the responsibility of the provincial executive. The provincial executive also has the authority to exercise repressive supervision over all decisions taken by the administrative organs of the water board. Decisions may be annulled if they are unlawful or against the public interest.

§7. PUBLIC-LEGAL INDUSTRIAL ORGANIZATION

101. The public legal industrial organization (*publiekrechtelijke bedrijfsorganisatie*) is another example of functional decentralization. The establishment of this type of organization dates from shortly after the Second World War.

102. In response to desires for a more corporatist organization of economic life, the Social and Economic Council (*Sociaal-Economische Raad*), commodity boards and industrial boards were established in several areas of the economy. In 2015, government and parliament decided to dissolve the commodity and industry boards. As such, the Social and Economic Council is nowadays the only institution in this decentralized organizational structure.

103. The statutory role of the Social and Economic Council is to promote business activities which serve the interests of the Dutch people, as well as to promote the interests of the business community and those involved in it. It also functions as one of the most important advisory bodies to the central government on social and economic issues.

104. In Article 134, the Constitution makes provision for public institutions for the professions or trades to be established by or pursuant to an Act of Parliament. The Industrial Organization Act establishes the SER.

105. The SER is made up of at least thirty and no more than forty-five members. At least two-thirds of the members are appointed on an equal basis by employers' and employees' organizations, designated for this task by the government. The remaining members (*kroonleden* – Crown members) are appointed by the government. The government also appoints the chairperson of the SER. The SER appoints an executive committee from within its own ranks.

106. With respect to the powers enjoyed by the administrative organs of these public bodies, Article 134 of the Constitution states that these will be regulated by Act of Parliament and that these may also be granted rule-making powers by or pursuant to an Act of Parliament. The Industrial Organization Act grants regulatory and executive powers to the SER. These powers may be exercised autonomously or as shared powers.

Part III. Form of Government

Chapter 1. General Information

§1. Introduction

107. In the third part of this analysis of Dutch constitutional law, the focus is on the central government institutions, and in particular on their composition, functions and powers. In the chapters which follow, we discuss in turn: the Head of State, legislature, executive, Judiciary and, finally, advisory bodies.

This division of chapters could suggest that Dutch constitutional law observes a strict separation of governmental activities in accordance with the separation of powers *(trias politica)* and that these activities are assigned to separate institutions of government. In reality, however, the situation is much more subtly differentiated. In general, it would be fair to say that the essence of the *trias* concept – namely that government powers are divided among various institutions of central government, each exercising its proper share of power – is realized in Dutch constitutional law to a large extent. Furthermore, there are controls built in against the expansion of government powers, insofar as the different institutions of government are able to control and influence each other (checks and balances). The division of powers over various institutions departs in several important respects from the strict *trias* scheme, in which the legislative, executive and judicial power belong to three, independently functioning government institutions. In particular, the distinction between legislative and executive power springs to mind in this context. In the Netherlands, legislative power is not exclusively, or even mainly, concentrated in the hands of parliament. Article 81 of the Constitution lays down that statutes are passed by the government (King and ministers) and the States General (parliament) together. Thus two separate institutions of government are involved in the creation of Acts of Parliament. Parliament can only be referred to as a legislative partner. As will become apparent in Chapter 3, the government which is in power at any one time plays a pre-eminent role in the legislative process in practice. In addition, Article 89 of the Constitution affords the government its own legislative powers.

108. Executive power belongs mainly to the government, but in this area too other institutions of government have some powers. For example, the budget is established by the legislature. In addition, in accordance with the principle of legality, the operations of the executive in many cases have to be based upon an Act of Parliament, which also contains general rules. Exercise of power without a specific foundation in the Constitution or an Act of Parliament occurs only rarely in the

Netherlands. The Constitution offers some clues for this. In a number of places, especially in the very first chapter, dealing with fundamental rights, the Constitution requires a statutory basis for government action.

In Dutch constitutional law, the *separation of powers* idea is probably most clearly expressed in the administration of justice. The Constitution assigns judicial power, in principle, exclusively to an independent Judiciary; within this, a distinction may be made between the so-called ordinary courts of the judiciary (*gewone rechter*) – traditionally concerned with civil and criminal law – and a number of specific, administrative courts. Nevertheless, there is an exception to this principle, in that certain forms of administrative litigation can be assigned to non-judicial administrative bodies (Article 112, paragraph 2 in connection with Article 115 of the Constitution). These issues will be examined further in Chapter 5 below.

109. We observed earlier that the separation of powers (*trias politica*) as it has developed in the Netherlands, in essence, implies both a division of powers and the presence of control mechanisms between the various institutions of government. Such checks and balances are plentiful in Dutch constitutional law and are effective not only between the different institutions of government but also between the different offices within one institution. Both the government and parliament provide illustrations of the existence of checks and balances within one and the same public body.

The government, as laid down in Article 42 of the Constitution, comprises the King and the ministers. A government order can only be enacted if both the King and a minister signal their agreement by signing (King) and countersigning (minister) it (Article 47 of the Constitution). Such a government order is termed a Royal Decree (*koninklijk besluit*). The King and the ministers are therefore in a position to influence and control each other, although, as we will see, the King nowadays has a limited advisory role in government.

The organization of parliament provides another example. The bicameral system assumes that each of the two Chambers controls the other.

110. The relations between the different institutions of government are – as in many other European countries – subject to well-known checks and balances. In the relationship between government and parliament, we see the principle of ministerial responsibility and the confidence rule, typical of the parliamentary system. The power to dissolve a Chamber of Parliament can be mentioned in this context too. Of course, these constitutional concepts have taken on their own specific significance in Dutch constitutional law, which will be looked at further in the following chapters. One can also point to checks and balances between the government on the one hand and the judiciary on the other hand. The Constitution and a number of Acts of Parliament lay down rules governing the institution, composition and powers of the judiciary. However, there are limits placed upon the decision-making powers of the political institutions in this respect, especially flowing from Article 6 ECHR, which contains guarantees that certain disputes will be judged by an independent and impartial court or tribunal.

111. The Judiciary exercises supervisory powers over the dealings of the other institutions of government with citizens. Both legislative and administrative decisions are in principle subject to judicial review, insofar as they affect individual citizens. One exception to this is the absence of the power of the courts to review the constitutionality of an Act of Parliament (Article 120 of the Constitution). Neither are courts empowered to judge the intrinsic value or reasonableness of an Act of Parliament (Article 11 General Provisions Act (*Wet algemene bepalingen*)).

This does not mean that Acts of Parliament are immune to judgment by the courts. The fact that the Act itself cannot be reviewed does not preclude the courts' right to test the compatibility of the application of national laws with certain provisions of treaties. This power has long been accepted in the Dutch case law. Article 94 of the Constitution nowadays states that statutory regulations are not applicable if their application turns out to be incompatible with any directly applicable treaty provision or decision by an international organization. Chapter 5 examines in more detail this particular possibility for the judiciary to review legislation, particularly in relation to the general prohibition on judicial review of Acts of Parliament mentioned earlier.

112. After this broad look at the operation of the principle of separation of powers in Dutch constitutional law, it now seems appropriate to give a more detailed description of the form of government in the Netherlands. This can best be described with the following three concepts: constitutional monarchy, representative democracy with a parliamentary system, and the rule of law.

These three concepts require some clarification. A constitutional monarchy requires the existence of a (hereditary) monarchy, whereby the power of government is divided between the King and other institutions of government by the Constitution. An essential feature is that the King's powers are limited and regulated by the Constitution.

Following currently accepted understanding, representative democracy with a parliamentary system means that government power – including, most importantly, legislative power – is exercised by representatives of the people, who are periodically elected through general elections. They have powers to control the government, the latter requiring the confidence of parliament.

Finally, the rule of law also assumes separation of powers, a division of powers over different institutions of government, including a democratically legitimated parliament, the latter exercising a share of the legislative power. There are other requirements too in the rule of law. First of all, there is the principle of legality: government action must be based on prior general rules laid down by a democratic legislature. In addition, independent judicial review of government activities is an important element. Finally, recognition of fundamental human rights is considered to be a requirement for the rule of law.

113. In order to analyse the development of central government institutions from 1814 onwards more closely, the three qualifying concepts of the Dutch form of government will be discussed in turn, in the order mentioned above.

114. In 1814–1815, the idea of establishing a constitutional monarchy (*constitutionele monarchie*) was predominant. The Constitution then in force was highly monarchical. A great many of its provisions dealt with the creation of the monarchy (succession and such-like) and the powers of the King.

Nevertheless, there were constraints upon the power of the King. Legislative power was conferred on the King and the States General jointly. Provision was made for the establishment of an independent Judiciary. Finally, it was the King who had the executive power. This division of powers lacked for the time being the most important of the checks and balances we have been discussing. The King was assisted by ministers who, as subordinate officials, were only accountable to him. There was no question of any relationship of responsibility or confidence between the government and parliament. In 1815, arguments were put forward on the part of the Belgians for ministerial responsibility to be adopted in the Constitution in line with the English example. King William I rejected this idea, speaking in this context of one of the most dangerous institutions for the orderly course of affairs.

Equally, it was not possible to speak of full judicial control over the government. In fact, under the rules contained in the Conflict Decree of 1822, the King was empowered to take disputes involving government authorities out of the hands of the judiciary in order to settle them himself. At the same time, the Constitution did not yet lay down an extensive catalogue of fundamental rights. The Constitution did contain some fundamental rights provisions, though these were scattered over various chapters.

115. In this perspective, it was not surprising that the King gradually emerged as the centre of power in the State, even more so since in these early decades of the Kingdom the political significance of the Dutch parliament was fairly limited. The way the two Chambers were composed undoubtedly played a significant part in this. The members of the First Chamber were appointed by the King, while the members of the Second Chamber were chosen by the provincial states, in which choice the King also exerted influence. Furthermore, there was as yet no trace of political parties or political groups being formed in parliament.

116. At first, parliament reconciled itself to the fact that the energetic King William I ruled more or less as an enlightened despot. Anything that the Constitution had not specifically reserved for the legislature, he considered to be the business of his government. For this reason, William I's rule is referred to as government by decree. Gradually, however, especially in the southern provinces, resistance to the King's authoritarian power grew. King William I did not even hesitate to become intensely involved in affairs of religion and language, and it was mainly this interference which drove the catholic and liberal opposition in the south to rebellion. The Belgian revolution resulted in the secession of the southern provinces in 1830. However, the King did not want to accept the establishment of an independent Belgian State. He conducted a policy of perseverance which put the country in a state of war for years. It brought the country to the brink of financial disaster.

This personal policy of the King met with increasing criticism in the States General. In 1839, parliamentary dissatisfaction came to a head when the Second Chamber rejected the budget and a bill concerning a government loan. The Ministers involved (of Finance and of the Colonies) offered their resignation over the issue. Although the parliamentary system was by no means established yet, these events constituted the first pre-sentiment of such a system. In the same year, a reform of the Constitution was pending, which was necessitated by the secession of the southern provinces. The Second Chamber urged the government to take this opportunity to anchor the principle of ministerial responsibility in the Constitution. At first, the government resisted, since such a proposal would lead to an encroachment on the personal powers of the King. But under pressure from the Second Chamber, which showed unwillingness to consider the newly presented budget, the government accommodated the wishes of parliament up to a point. With the reform of the Constitution in 1840, it was established that all Royal Decrees from then on must also be signed by a minister, who would thus be liable under criminal law in case the decrees breached the Constitution or an Act of Parliament. From 1840 onwards, therefore, it was no longer the King personally who functioned as part of the government, but the constitutional King (*constitutionele Koning*), which means the King plus one or more ministers or State secretaries.

117. Although this provision did not regulate political responsibility, but only liability under criminal law, it had far-reaching consequences for the relationship between the King and the ministers, and between the government and the States General. After all, giving ministers the power to countersign (*contraseign*) all the King's decrees, meant that the King was no longer able to take autonomous decisions without the cooperation of his ministers. The King thus lost his predominant position within the government. King William I, disappointed by these developments, abdicated in 1840.

At the same time, ministers could no longer take refuge behind the will of the monarch. The countersignature made them responsible for government decisions. Hence, the constitutional reform of 1840 paved the way for the arrival of political responsibility of ministers towards the States General. Throughout the 1840s, this responsibility really began to take shape, and time and again ministers whose proposals were rejected by the Second Chamber resigned. The constitutional reform of 1848 brought this development to its conclusion, enshrining the principle in the provision: 'The King is inviolable, the ministers shall be responsible' (now Article 42, paragraph 2 of the Constitution).

118. The 1848 reform of the Constitution strengthened the position of the States General in other ways too. There was a drastic change in the way the members of the two Chambers were chosen. Members of the First Chamber were no longer appointed by the King but chosen by the provincial states. Members of the Second Chamber were from then on to be elected directly. The Constitution granted both Chambers the right of interpellation. The Second Chamber acquired the power of amendment and of parliamentary enquiry. The 1848 Constitution also introduced the system of annual budgets. Before 1848, the budget was set partly for ten-year periods (fixed expenditure) and partly annually.

In connection with this strengthening of the position of the States General, the Constitution granted the government the power to dissolve parliament.

119. It can thus be concluded that the constitutional reforms of 1840 and 1848 formed a turning point in the relationship between the institutions of central government. From 1840 onwards, representative democracy with a parliamentary system developed step by step. The introduction of ministerial responsibility in the 1840s has been outlined above. This did not in itself result in the establishment of the parliamentary system, however. It was firmly established that ministers had to account for government policy in parliament, but their responsibility was not yet such that they were obliged to resign office if parliament denounced their policy, as the parliamentary system demands. It was important in this context that the Constitution at that time laid down that the King appointed ministers and dismissed them at his pleasure. On the government side, this provision was taken to mean that it was sufficient if the ministers had the confidence of the King. The appointment and dismissal of members of the government was the prerogative of the King, which the members of parliament might not encroach upon. However, in the years after 1848, resistance to this train of thought grew in parliament. Two events finally settled the matter in favour of the parliamentary system. In 1866, the Minister for the Colonies, Mijer, who was a leading figure in the government, resigned, so that he could be appointed Governor General of the Dutch Indies. This resignation caused great consternation in the Second Chamber. A motion by the Member of Parliament (MP) Keuchenius, condemning the conduct of the cabinet (which comprises all the members of government except the King), was passed after a fierce debate. The government, which considered this motion to be unconstitutional and revolutionary, did not hesitate to dissolve the Chamber. After the elections, the newly elected Chamber refrained from making a statement on the issue.

A year later, another serious conflict arose between the government and the States General about the Luxembourg question (*Luxemburgse kwestie*). The Grand Duchy of Luxembourg was joined in a Union with the Kingdom. When King William III revealed his willingness to hand the Duchy over to the French emperor Napoleon III in exchange for compensation, Prussia objected strongly. The international conflict was finally settled by the Treaty of London, which established the neutrality of Luxembourg for the future. The Second Chamber harboured serious objections to the policy of the government. In the autumn of 1867, it threw out the budget for the Ministry of Foreign Affairs. The cabinet offered to resign, but the King refused to accept its resignation, after which the Second Chamber was dissolved. This time the newly elected Chamber did not acquiesce in the government's action. In a motion introduced by Blussé, an MP, the Chamber declared that 'the most recent dissolution of the Chamber had not been necessary for any national interest'. At first, the cabinet ignored this pronouncement, but when the Chamber again rejected the foreign affairs budget, the cabinet tendered its resignation. The parliamentary system was thereby established.

Since then, the central element of the parliamentary system has been the confidence rule. It means that a minister, State secretary or even a whole cabinet is obliged to resign if it loses the confidence of one of the two Chambers. In this context, a negative formulation of the confidence rule is preferable: confidence is assumed until proven otherwise. A vote of confidence is very unusual in the Dutch parliament. One of the Chambers has to express disapproval of government policy.

120. The years following 1848 were characterized not just by the establishment of the parliamentary system, but also by the growth of representative democracy, although the latter development progressed much more slowly. It was mentioned above that the 1848 reform of the Constitution introduced direct election of the members of the Second Chamber. In these early years, the franchise was still very limited. It was conditional on a minimum tax assessment which was fairly high. In the following decades, an intense political struggle to expand the franchise ensued. The constitutional reform of 1887 opened up the possibility for widening the franchise with a provision which made the right to vote dependent upon 'criteria of suitability and social prosperity to be laid down in the Elections Act'. A new Elections Act in 1896 extended the franchise considerably, but there was still no question of universal suffrage. This was finally achieved with the 1917 reform of the Constitution. That year can therefore be said to represent the terminus of the development of the central institutions of government into a representative democracy with a parliamentary system.

121. Finally, the term rule of law (*rechtsstaat*) was mentioned above. In the first decades after 1814, this term was scarcely applicable to the Dutch form of government. As we have seen, King William I, the enlightened despot, ruled by decree. Furthermore, judicial control over government activity required the consent of the King, since he was able to take conflicts involving government authorities out of the hands of the judiciary by virtue of the Conflict Decree (*Conflictenbesluit*). Moreover, the Constitution of the time paid scant attention to the recognition of citizens' civil rights.

Gradually, bit by bit, Dutch constitutional law has developed over the years so as to now incorporate the various elements of the rule of law. A few important steps were taken in the 1840s. In 1844, the government revoked the Conflict Decree so that henceforth the judiciary could determine its own competence, within the boundaries laid down by the Constitution and Acts of Parliament. The 1848 revision of the Constitution introduced recognition of important fundamental rights, including the freedom of association and assembly and freedom of education. The separation of church and State was completed. Of course, the strengthening of the position of parliament through the constitutional reforms of 1840 and 1848 was also important for the development of the rule of law.

122. The period after 1848 witnessed a strong, development of the principle of legality (*legaliteitsbeginsel*) in the Dutch legal system. Since 1814, the King had been deemed to be able to issue so-called *algemene maatregelen van bestuur* (literally: general executive measures, but usually translated as 'orders in Council'), which were binding upon citizens, even when there was no basis in an Act of Parliament, provided the Constitution did not deny him this competence. The penalties for contravening provisions of these royal orders were laid down in an Act of Parliament of 1818 (the so-called *Blanketwet*).

In 1879, the Supreme Court (Supreme Court 13 June 1879 *Meerenberg*) turned against this system. The Supreme Court took the position that the King was only authorized to act in accordance with the powers granted to him by the Constitution.

Given that the Constitution only assigned executive power to the King and not legislative power, he did not have the authority to exercise legislative power autonomously. The King was only empowered to make legislation pursuant to delegation by the legislature.

When the Constitution was reformed in 1887, this view was elaborated and largely incorporated into the new Constitution. Since then, the Constitution has distinguished between orders in Council enforceable by penalties and other orders in Council (Article 89 of the Constitution). The first type must be based on delegation by the legislature.

123. The 1887 reform of the Constitution was important for the development of the rule of law in another respect too. On that occasion, a provision was adopted enabling the legislature to grant jurisdiction either to the ordinary judiciary or to special administrative courts, to settle disputes involving public authorities. However, in the years that followed, the legislature did not manage to create a uniform system of legal protection against government Acts. A number of special, administrative judicial procedures were created in specific areas of government activity. Examples could be found in: the Appeals Act (*Beroepswet*) of 1902, which created the right of appeal on social security matters to social security tribunals and (on final appeal) the Central Appeals Court (*Centrale Raad van Beroep*); the Civil Servants Act (*Ambtenarenwet*) of 1929 which opened the way for civil servants to appeal to the Civil Service Courts and the Central Appeals Court; and finally, the Act on Administrative Justice concerning government decisions on trade and industry (*Wet administratieve rechtspraak bedrijfsorganisatie*) of 1954, which instituted a right of appeal in the sphere of economic administrative law through the Regulatory Industrial Organization Appeals Court (*College van beroep voor het bedrijfsleven*).

This fragmented system of administrative jurisdiction underwent another important expansion in 1976 with the Administrative Decisions Appeals Act (*Wet administratieve rechtspraak overheidsbeschikkingen*). This Act introduced a general, supplementary right of appeal to the judicial division of the Council of State against, in principle, all government decisions against which no other administrative judicial procedure was available. In addition to these specific administrative courts, the ordinary Judiciary has offered legal protection to the citizen against the government since the beginning of the twentieth century (Supreme Court 10 May 1901 *Rotterdamse huizen*) especially against wrongful acts. Tax cases are also dealt with by ordinary courts.

124. At the end of the twentieth century, the legislature brought about a new structure for administrative review through a large-scale reorganization of the judiciary. Most of the specific administrative courts mentioned above have disappeared; jurisdiction in administrative matters is now, for the greater part, in the first instance concentrated in the district courts of the Judiciary. So it seems that an arrangement which was being championed from various sides over a century ago, on the occasion of the 1887 constitutional reform, has now been realized to a great extent. The Central Appeals Court still has appellate jurisdiction on social security matters and the Council of State now has appellate jurisdiction in cases concerning (other) administrative decisions.

125. After this outline of the development of judicial control over government activities, the final element of the rule of law which needs to be discussed consists of fundamental rights. Since the constitutional reform of 1848, for a long time, there were few developments in the sphere of fundamental rights apart from developments in case law. This changed after the Second World War when a number of international agreements came into force, in particular the ECHR and the ICCPR. These treaties added some new fundamental rights to Dutch constitutional law. Examples include the right to privacy (Article 8 ECHR), freedom of expression (Article 10 ECHR), which had a broader scope than the freedom of the press guaranteed in the Constitution, and the right to a fair and public hearing by an independent and impartial tribunal (Article 6 ECHR). The last-mentioned right had an especially important influence on developments in Dutch judicial organization, which will be examined in more detail in Chapter 5 below. These treaties also gave the Dutch courts, who were (and are) prohibited from reviewing the constitutionality of Acts of Parliament, the opportunity to review whether (the application of) such an Act was compatible with the fundamental rights protected in the treaties. Up to a point, therefore, this meant the arrival of constitutional review.

126. The complete revision of the Constitution in 1983 was another important step in the sphere of fundamental rights. As in some other modern European Constitutions, the fundamental rights are now set out together in the first chapter. This now comprises an extensive arsenal of classic fundamental rights (some new ones) and a number of social rights. Part IV will examine their significance, effects and limitations.

127. Insofar as it is possible, in general terms, to come to some sort of conclusion, on the basis of the three characteristics of the Dutch form of government dealt with here, one could cautiously say that as time has gone by, the tone has increasingly been set by the concept of rule of law. The elaboration of the principle of legality, the expansion and improvement of legal protection for citizens against government activities and the legal effect of fundamental rights have been the issues which have received most attention in both legal practice and theory in recent years. Whereas at the time the Constitution was enacted in 1814, the main issue was the establishment of a constitutional monarchy, this aspect has now receded to the background.

The development of the Netherlands as a representative democracy with a parliamentary system basically came to a halt with the introduction of universal franchise in 1917, even though proposals have been made regularly, in the subsequent course of parliamentary history, to modernize the political system. In the concluding part of this chapter, a number of these proposals will be examined.

§2. POLITICAL PARTIES

128. Political parties appeared rather late in the Netherlands. For much of the nineteenth century, there was a deep-rooted fear that the position of the States

General, in particular the independence of the members of both Chambers, and the unity of the state would be threatened by the existence of parties.

This negative attitude towards political parties is understandable if one looks at the historical development of the States General. During the period of the Republic of the United Netherlands (*Republiek der Verenigde Nederlanden*), this assembly could certainly not have been classified as a national representative body. It was far more like a congress of ambassadors. The States General at that time were no more than a meeting of the delegates of the sovereign states of the united provinces. Whenever any significant decision had to be taken by the States General, the regional delegates felt obliged to consult the states that they were representing. The decision-making process in the States General could be seriously impeded as a result.

129. The Constitution of 1814 aimed to end this system. The members of the 'new style' States General were to represent all the Dutch people and would therefore no longer occupy their positions as mandataries of the provinces. The relevant constitutional provision (now Article 50 of the Constitution) expressed the fact that the Kingdom was a unitary State. Voting based on binding mandate and instructions was ruled out by the Constitution (Article 67, paragraph 3 of the Constitution). It was commonly felt that the principle of a free mandate (*vrij mandaat*) for representatives of the people, which was thus guaranteed, could not be reconciled with the existence of close links between the individual members, or between members and political groups who could decide on the candidates.

Nevertheless, in the second half of the nineteenth century political parties gradually developed. After 1848, local political organizations grew up, which put up candidates in each district at elections. These 'electoral societies' (*kiesverenigingen*) began to cooperate more and more, basing themselves on common political convictions. When the franchise underwent a major expansion at the end of the nineteenth century, the need for this increased. As a result, the first national political parties were established in that period. The very first was the Anti-Revolutionary Party (ARP), established in 1879, a Protestant party led by A. Kuyper.

130. Before going on to discuss the position of political parties in constitutional law, we will briefly sketch the history of the party political scene in the Netherlands.

Two broad periods can be distinguished: 1848–1917, when the electoral system was an absolute majority system, combined with a constituency system; and 1917 to the present day, in which the system of proportional representation has been operating. The first period was characterized not only by the arrival of national political parties but also by the forming of two blocks of like-minded parties. The absolute majority system stimulated cooperation between parties at elections. A right wing was formed on the one side, consisting of Roman Catholic and Protestant parties, and a left wing on the other side comprising liberal parties and later on including socialists. At election time, these two blocks each tried to win a majority in parliament, which fluctuated from one side to the other. The resulting distribution of seats in parliament determined the political composition of the cabinet.

131. The introduction of proportional representation by the constitutional reform of 1917 ruptured these party political relations. Parties no longer needed to enter into electoral pacts. They entered the election contest on their own. The right and left wings fell apart. Although inter-party collaboration changed drastically after 1917, the party political scene as such remained broadly the same. Three main streams can still be distinguished: the religious denominational, social-democratic and liberal streams. Within the three main streams, there have been all kinds of developments, brought about by splits and unions. The Netherlands has also experienced the phenomenon of splinter parties, on the left and the right, which appear suddenly, and then (usually) disappear again after a few years. At this point in time, the Christian Democrats (*Christen-Democratisch Appel* (CDA)) are the most important exponents of the religious denominational parties. The social-democratic current is represented by the Labour Party (*Partij van de Arbeid*: PvdA) and the Socialist Party (*Socialistische partij*: SP), while the liberal line of thought is propagated mainly by the People's Party for Freedom and Democracy (*Volkspartij voor Vrijheid en Democratie*: VVD) and the Democrats 66 (*Democraten 66*: D66). A Green party (*GroenLinks*) is also a consistent part of the political scene. The Party for the Freedom (*Partij voor de vrijheid*: PVV) has a separate position in Dutch politics.

132. The parties' political situation has changed in the last few decades in one important respect. Until the mid-1960s, the largest parties and the three main streams could more or less count on the support of fixed groups of voters, resulting from a strong element of so-called pillarization (*verzuiling*) in Dutch society. As a general rule, elections only resulted in minor shifts in the balance between political parties. The secularization and breakdown of the traditional pillars, which took place in the 1960s and 1970s, has set the voters adrift. Voters' traditional bonds with a party, based on their religion or social position, have to a significant extent disappeared. The effect of this has been that election results have fluctuated more widely. For the political parties themselves, this has meant that they have to make more strenuous efforts to win votes. In addition, the personality of the political leader of the party, who heads the list of candidates and conducts the political campaign, has come to play an increasingly important role. Nowadays, the three traditional, large political parties (CDA, PvdA, VVD) have lost their dominant position in Dutch politics. The party political situation in the Netherlands is nowadays characterized by a substantial fragmentation of the political landscape. Several new parties have entered the political arena. Currently, the Second Chamber (150 seats) of the States General consists of members from twenty different smaller and medium-sized political parties. It goes without saying that the effective functioning of parliament is under tension because of this political fragmentation.

133. With respect to the position of political parties under constitutional law, the main point is that they are not part of the government organization. They are social organizations, just like any other private organization which sets itself certain goals. They are not therefore subject to any special legal requirements concerning their internal organization, democratic decision-making or statutory aims. The Constitution is silent on the subject of political parties. They are mentioned in a few Acts of

Parliament and regulations. In the Standing Orders of the Chambers of the States General, they are mentioned in the definition of the concept of a parliamentary group (*fractie*). Article 23 Standing Orders of The First Chamber states that MPs who are elected from the list of one political party are considered to be in the same parliamentary group.

134. The Elections Act contains some provisions relating to political parties. In particular, there are requirements relating to the registration of the name of a political party on the lists of candidates for elections. To be registered, the political party must be an incorporated association which has been established by notarial deed. To this extent, the freedom to form political parties is limited by constitutional law. It is also important to note in this context that civil law offers the possibility of (judicial) prohibition and dissolution of legal entities whose activities are contrary to public order. If a political party has such a measure imposed upon it, it no longer meets the registration requirements. Important lastly, for the functioning of political parties, is the Political Parties Financing Act. This law establishes rules for the granting of subsidies to political parties. Political parties that have a representation in parliament are entitled to substantial subsidy amounts, provided that they meet specified conditions. The law imposes the obligation on political parties to record subsidies and gifts received and to publish these under specific circumstances. In addition, the law establishes supervision of compliance with the provisions governing financial contributions. The law sets no limits on the number of gifts to political parties. In fact, the rules regarding financial contributions are not very strict. However, despite this and a few other regulations, Dutch constitutional law assumes a large measure of freedom to form, organize and run political parties. Proposals for a statutory Charter for political parties, guaranteeing internal party democracy, have not been realized in the Netherlands. In 2022, the government initiated a new bill in Parliament concerning political parties. The bill mostly brings together existing regulations on political parties. It does not present rules on internal party democracy.

135. The fact that political parties are merely private law organizations, does not prevent them from getting intensely involved with the functioning of public authorities. Of course, they play a decisive role in putting up candidates for election. They also exert influence on the appointment of other political officials, such as ministers, Royal Commissioners and mayors. And, naturally, their activities include the composition of policy programmes, which aim to influence the direction of government policy.

From a constitutional law perspective, the relationship between members of parliament and political parties is especially important. There tends to be a fairly strong link between them. Party membership is usually a necessary requirement for candidates for parliament. Several parties also require that members resign their seats in parliament if they lose their party membership. Sometimes party charters also include requirements that candidate members cooperate in parliamentary groups, and resign their seats if they lose their places in a parliamentary group. Party charters also prescribe that members must endorse the principles and election programme of the party and that they are responsible to the party executives.

136. Taking all these obligations into account, one might consider that the autonomy and independence of members of parliament are no more than a constitutional fiction, taking no account of political reality, in which party and group discipline determine the political actions of the members. However, such party dominance does not exist, either in constitutional law or in fact. From the point of view of constitutional law, the provision guaranteeing the free mandate (Article 67, paragraph 3 of the Constitution) effectively prevents the voting behaviour of members from being determined by party executives. If a member votes contrary to an instruction from his or her party or parliamentary group, the legal validity of his or her vote cannot be called into question. Non-fulfilment of obligations laid down by parties in private law cannot have any consequence in public law for the validity of the voting in parliament. The same applies to party-imposed obligations to resign a seat. These cannot detract from the guaranteed term of office for members which is laid down in the Constitution and in the Elections Act. Members may be expelled from their party or parliamentary political group, but this does not affect their autonomous and independent position as an MP either. In this context, the Supreme Court (Supreme Court 18 November 1988 *Arubaanse verkiezingsafspraak*) judged that such agreements are null and void because they conflict with the principle of a free mandate.

137. There are thus constitutional law barriers to dominance by political parties of members of parliament. Moreover, such dominance does not actually occur in practice. When the cabinet is formed, it is usually only the parliamentary groups in the Second Chamber which have a say in appointing members of the cabinet. The PvdA is the only party whose party conference consistently insists on passing judgment on the end result of the cabinet formation process. Likewise, for the work of the parliament in session, there is no question of party dominance. The parliamentary groups have a large measure of freedom in the implementation of party programmes. There is a general refusal to identify the party with the parliamentary group; this is apparent, for instance, from the fact that party rules lay down the incompatibility of membership of parliament with various party offices.

138. From the above, it may be concluded that despite strong ties between political parties and their members of parliament – and these are most prominent when candidates are being selected – members of parliament and the parliamentary groups enjoy a large measure of independence from party executives.

§3. SUPPLEMENTS TO THE REPRESENTATIVE SYSTEM

139. The Dutch form of government has been defined as a representative democracy with a parliamentary system. Through periodic elections, citizens who are eligible to vote decide on the composition of the representative body (the States General), which plays a part in legislating and controlling the government. Ministers have to enjoy the confidence of (or at least be tolerated by) the States General.

140. A representative system constructed in this way certainly offers important guarantees for popular influence on legislation and administration. But there are other ways in which democracy can be given shape. One may think in this context of aspects of direct democracy like referenda, and of the possibility of political officials other than members of parliament being elected by the citizens. Dutch constitutional law is not very highly developed in this sphere. The representative system has the monopoly for the time being.

141. In the past, repeated proposals have been made to supplement the representative system. Twice at the beginning of the past century (in 1903 and 1922), arguments were advanced in favour of introducing the possibility of referenda, but to no avail. In the 1960s, the idea of strengthening representative democracy with a number of new elements was again debated, the emphasis in the first instance being on the introduction of a directly elected prime minister. An Advisory Committee, which was charged with the preparation of a general reform of the Constitution, rejected this proposal, but then came up with the idea of electing the so-called *kabinetsformateur*, that is the person entrusted with the task of forming the cabinet. Objections to both these proposals were that they would impair the Dutch parliamentary system. After all, if there was a confrontation with the States General where the confidence question arose, an elected prime minister (or a prime minister who had been elected as *kabinetsformateur*) could invoke the fact that he had been directly elected. There was a real danger that the confidence rule of the parliamentary system could thus be undermined.

Despite repeated attempts, the proposals never got anywhere. The general revision of the Constitution in 1983 did not involve any fundamental constitutional innovation.

142. The idea that Dutch representative democracy was in need of improvement remained current among constitutional academics and practitioners. In 1982, even before the general constitutional revision had been enacted, a new Advisory Committee was set up to make proposals on the relationship between the electorate and policy-making. This committee elaborated proposals for the introduction of certain forms of referenda.

Once again, however, the legislature turned out to be unwilling to respond to appeals for elements of direct democracy to be added to the representative system. The theme of constitutional renewal was not removed from the agenda, though. In 1996, the government put a bill before Parliament for an amendment of the Constitution to permit the introduction of a so-called corrective legislative referendum. The First Chamber rejected the bill in 1999 in the second reading. A new attempt to introduce such a referendum was rejected by the Second Chamber in 2004. The consultative referendum of 1 June 2005 on the treaty establishing a Constitution for Europe was based on an Act ad hoc. As we know, the voters voted against the ratification of this treaty. Nevertheless, attempts to introduce the referendum in Netherlands' constitutional law continued.

Since 2015, the Advisory Referendum Act determined that laws that are adopted by the States General could be subjected to an advisory (non-binding) referendum. Certain laws, such as budget laws or laws regarding the monarchy, were excluded from such advisory referendums. Citizens could submit an introductory request for a referendum when having obtained 10,000 signatures. A definitive request required 300,000 signatures, after which an advisory referendum would be held. A compulsory attendance threshold applied for referenda. The law that the referendum related to did not take effect so long as the outcome of the referendum was still pending. As mentioned above, a referendum was not binding, but political parties can declare in advance that they will respect the outcome of the referendum. The Advisory Referendum Act was applied in 2016 with regard to the Act approving the EU association treaty with Ukraine. A majority of participants in the referendum, which had sufficient attendance, voted against the approval Act. A majority of the members of both Chambers nonetheless ruled that the treaty involved needed to be ratified. The Advisory Referendum Act was applied again in 2018 with regard to a new Act on intelligence and security services. The outcome of the referendum was not favourable for the Intelligence Act, but it nevertheless came into effect with minor alterations. Because of these disappointing experiences with non-binding advisory referenda, the Advisory Referendum Act was repealed in 2018.

In the meantime, an amendment is still pending in parliament for revision of the Constitution and introduction of a binding corrective legislation referendum. Several initiatives to introduce a corrective legislation referendum in the Constitution have failed between 2004 and 2022, but some political parties never give up and keep promoting this element of direct democracy.

143. Should the conclusion be drawn from the above that the Dutch form of government suffers from a democratic deficit because Dutch citizens have relatively little say over the choice of those governing them and because of the lack of direct democracy? Such a conclusion seems exaggerated. In the first place, the importance of a representative system must not be underestimated. It is also important to recall that democracy is also expressed in other ways, especially through the operation of fundamental rights such as freedom of expression and freedom of association and assembly, through the realization of open government, and through legislation and policies which respect the rights of minorities.

144. It should also be mentioned here that citizens have various possibilities for participating in the decision-making process of public authorities. In a number of areas, such as town and country planning, a participation procedure is prescribed by law. Then, there are the hearings before parliamentary committees. Another factor which is relevant in this context is advice given to government bodies in the area of policy-making. Especially since the Second World War, in numerous spheres of government concern, permanent and temporary advisory bodies have been created in which experts and representatives of public interest groups can give advice on proposed legislation and policy plans.

Nevertheless, a binding referendum on legislation could be a desirable addition to the representative system in the Netherlands.

Chapter 2. Head of State

§1. THE KING

145. In a constitutional monarchy, the King (*Koning*) is Head of State. What this position involves legally and practically, and the special position of the King in constitutional law will be discussed in the following paragraphs.

First consideration must be given to the succession to the throne. The Constitution contains exhaustive, compulsory rules on this. First of all, it states that the monarchy is hereditary and that the throne is inherited by the legitimate heirs of the constitutional primogenitor of the Royal House, King William I, Prince of Orange-Nassau (Article 24 of the Constitution). The rules of succession follow the Castilian system, except for the priority of sons over daughters, which was scrapped when the Constitution was revised in 1983.

146. In essence the system of succession, which is formulated concisely in Article 25 of the Constitution, means that the eldest, legitimate heir of the King succeeds upon the King's death, with substitution following the same rule. Thus, if the King's oldest child dies before the King, his own oldest child succeeds to the throne. If the King has no descendants, succession passes to the oldest descendant of his parent. If there are no descendants there either, then the oldest descendant of his grandparents in the line of succession becomes King. To inherit the throne, an individual may not be further removed from the King than the third degree of consanguinity.

In addition, Article 26 of the Constitution provides that if a woman is pregnant when the King dies, the child is considered already to have been born for the purposes of succession. If the child is subsequently stillborn, it is deemed never to have existed.

147. Kingship does not only end through death, it may also be ended through abdication. The same rules of succession apply in cases of abdication (Article 27 of the Constitution). Children born after the abdication and their descendants are excluded from the succession, except if Article 26 is applicable. Abdication of the monarchy is effected by means of a unilateral statement (Act of abdication) on the part of the King. In addition, if the King marries without the consent of the legislature he is deemed to have abdicated (Article 28 of the Constitution).

Potential heirs to the throne cannot abdicate their right of succession. They may, however, lose their right to succeed to the throne under certain constitutional provisions. Entering into a marriage without the consent of the legislature would result in exclusion from future succession to the throne. The legislature may also exclude one or more potential successors if exceptional circumstances make this necessary (Article 29 of the Constitution).

148. In order to give assent to the marriage of the King or an heir to the throne, or to effect the exclusion of an heir in exceptional circumstances, the States General (being part of the legislature) meet in joint session. This avoids the possibility of the two Chambers reaching a different decision. With respect to the proposed exclusion of an heir, such a proposal must be submitted by or on behalf of the King, and it can only be adopted if there is a two-thirds majority vote in the States General.

149. The rules discussed so far relate to the succession to the throne on a hereditary title. It is also possible for the throne to be transferred to an appointed successor. The Constitution makes provision for two sets of circumstances in which this may take place. First, a successor may be appointed by Act of Parliament if it appears that there will be no hereditary successor. Such an Act requires a special procedure. The proposal is submitted by or on behalf of the King. Then both Chambers of the States General are dissolved. After the elections, the new Chambers discuss and decide upon the matter in joint session. Once again, for the proposal to be accepted, a qualified majority is required (Article 30, paragraph 1 of the Constitution).

Second, a successor may be appointed if, upon the King's death or abdication, there is no hereditary successor. The procedure is as follows: The Chambers are dissolved. The new Chambers meet in joint session within four months of the death or abdication to make a decision on the appointment of a King. As before, the appointment must have a qualified majority in the Chambers of the States General (Article 30, paragraph 2 of the Constitution). An appointed King may only be succeeded by his legitimate heirs (Article 31 of the Constitution).

150. With respect to the two provisions contained in Article 30 of the Constitution, one should note that the Constitution does not make the appointment of a successor compulsory. If no such order is made, then of course a revision of the Constitution would be necessary whereby the monarchy would disappear and a Republic (with an elected president) could be installed in the Netherlands. Another conspicuous feature in the arrangements is the fact that both Chambers must be re-elected before such a decision is made. For the rest, all that remains to be said is that given the size of the royal family at present, neither of these arrangements is likely to be applied within the near future.

151. One question which needs to be answered is: when exactly does a successor to the throne become King following the death or abdication of the former King? The Constitution assumes continuity. The successor becomes King immediately. The saying 'The King never dies' is applicable in this context. The swearing-in of the new King in the capital Amsterdam, which is prescribed in the Constitution (Article 32) has no juridical significance. At this ceremony, the King swears or promises allegiance to the Constitution, and that he will faithfully fulfil his office.

152. To conclude this section, some consideration should be given to the incapacity of the King. The Constitution distinguishes three circumstances in which the King does not exercise his royal authority. First of all, during his minority, the Constitution states that the King exercises his royal authority for the first time upon reaching the age of 18 (Article 33).

The second case concerns the King's power to temporarily relinquish exercising his authority. Both the relinquishing and resumption of royal authority are effected through an Act of Parliament upon the King's own initiative. The States General discuss and decide on the matter in joint session (Article 36 of the Constitution).

The third case concerns the so-called statement of incapability (Article 35 of the Constitution). The procedure is as follows: If the Council of Ministers is of the opinion that the King is incapable of exercising his authority, it will, after first having obtained the advice of the Council of State, inform the States General of this, who will meet in joint session on the matter. If parliament agrees with the judgment of the Council of Ministers, it will declare the King incapable. The declaration takes immediate effect. It is important to realize in this context that the King does not lose his throne, but only the power to exercise his authority. As soon as he is again able to do so, his powers are restored by Act of Parliament following another joint session of the Chambers of the States General. The Constitution does not lay down the circumstances for a declaration of incapacity. It is likely that this would come about in cases of physical or mental illness or long-term absence from the country. However, it is also possible that political considerations could play a part.

153. If one of the three above-mentioned circumstances arise, royal functions are exercised by a regent (Article 37 of the Constitution) appointed by Act of Parliament. In the case of a declaration of incapacity, or temporary relinquishment of royal authority, the heir to the throne automatically becomes regent provided he has reached the age of 18. In the absence of both King and regent, the Council of State exercises royal authority (Article 38 of the Constitution).

§2. LEGAL STATUS

154. The King appears in various capacities in the Dutch constitutional law. In general terms, a distinction can be made between the King personally and the King as part of the government, who is functioning jointly with one or more ministers or State secretaries. The concept of the King personally relates to his functioning as Head of State or in private matters. Examples of the appearance of the King in a private capacity can be found in Articles 33 and 34 of the Constitution concerning a King who is a minor and (partly) in Article 41 of the Constitution relating to the organization of the Royal Court. This provision also partly concerns the King as Head of State.

155. It is not expressed in so many words in the Constitution that the King is Head of State. However, on the basis of a historical interpretation of Article 24 and the various explanatory notes on the Constitution, it can be concluded that the King does fulfil this function. Under this provision, the throne is inherited by the legitimate descendants of King William I. The original Constitution of 1814 assumed that the King was Head of State. The new 1983 Constitution did not bring any changes to the monarchical structure of the form of government, which is confirmed in the explanatory memorandum to the Constitution. It is expressly stated in the Constitution that the King forms a constituent part of the government. Article 42, paragraph 1, declares that the government is made up of the King and the ministers.

Through this membership, the monarchical element in the Dutch system of government remains relatively strongly preserved. However, the relationship between the King and the ministers is not hierarchical. The King is not the head of the government.

156. To deal with the different capacities in which the King functions, the drafters of the 1983 Constitution aimed to use a consistent and clearer terminology. The intention was to reserve the term King for the King personally, while the words 'Royal Decree' and 'government' would be used to relate to decisions by the King and (one or more) ministers (or State secretaries). However, the 1983 revision did not entirely succeed in this aim. The term King is still used with different meanings. In the context of the succession to the throne, for example, it means the King personally. However, where the Constitution employs the term King in connection with legislative procedure, it means the King as a part of the government (Articles 82 and 87 of the Constitution).

The Constitution is equally inconsistent in its use of the term Royal Decree. For example, the Constitution speaks of the ratification of bills by the King (Article 87), although, in fact, in this case, it is a countersigned (Royal) Decree.

157. Despite the somewhat confusing terminology, it can be asserted in general terms that the constitutional regulations governing the functions of the King personally are to be found in the provisions on succession, incapacity and the King's personal rights (Chapter 2, section 1 of the Constitution), while other references in the Constitution usually mean the King as part of the government.

158. The King has various personal rights. The most important is his immunity, currently expressed in Article 42, paragraph 2 of the Constitution: the King is inviolable (immune), and the ministers are responsible. Royal immunity has been an intrinsic aspect of kingship from time immemorial. It means that no institution of government can exercise compulsory power over the King. The King cannot be called to account: neither by the ministers, nor by parliament, nor by a criminal court. This immunity does not exclude liability in civil law cases at the expense of the King's property (Articles 48 and 77 of the Civil Procedure Code). Immunity is applicable to all the King's acts in whatever capacity: within the government, as Head of State and also in his personal capacity. Of course, in a constitutional monarchy, immunity does not mean that the King is not subject to the law. On the contrary, its very basis is the assumption that the King will conduct himself in accordance with the law. The King's inaugural oath is a testimony to this.

159. The granting of immunity to the King, who fulfils an important function in the state, is problematic in itself. First of all, it contains the risk of misuse of power. Royal immunity does not mean unassailability, in as much as it is possible to declare a King who seriously disregards the law 'incapable', whereby he is no longer empowered to exercise royal authority. However, an intervention of this kind by the States General should be regarded as a last resort.

Besides, although constitutional practice shows the risk of misuse of power to be hypothetical, the absence of political and judicial controls on such a holder of office is in principle hardly acceptable in a modern State with a representative democracy. In order to overcome these objections, bearing in mind the existence of royal immunity in constitutional law, ministerial responsibility and the countersignature were adopted. The birth and development of these two legal institutions were discussed in Chapter 1 above.

160. The countersignature requirement (Article 47 of the Constitution) ensures that the King cannot carry out acts of government autonomously. In order to act as a member of government, he needs the cooperation of a minister or State secretary. Thus the King's power and the possibility of misuse of power are limited. The minister (or State secretary) is responsible to the Chambers of the States General for his own actions and those of the King within the government. Furthermore, ministerial responsibility also extends to the King's actions outside the government that is as Head of State and in his personal capacity. Ministerial responsibility thus extends over the whole range of royal immunity.

161. There is a difference between ministerial responsibility for acts in the government sphere and for the King's actions outside government since in the former case, the prior cooperation of a minister is required. In the latter case, the minister is not legally empowered to prevent personal acts by the King, but can only try to influence them before or after the event. In this context, one may think of official speeches given by the King on State visits, for instance. In such situations, ministers cannot prevent the Head of State from expressing a view which may be unwelcome to the cabinet. They may *request* the King to refrain from so doing. Nevertheless, they are still responsible for the King's actions in this respect. If they feel unable to accept this responsibility, they must resign. There has been one occasion in constitutional history when a cabinet (the Thorbecke cabinet in 1853) found reason to tender its resignation on account of the public utterances of the King.

162. Apart from immunity, the Constitution lays down a number of other personal rights that the King enjoys. Under Article 41 of the Constitution, the King may organize his own court (household), taking due account of the public interest. This means that the King may himself decide upon the organization and composition of the Royal Court. He does not need to involve a minister in decisions relating to members of the court. The additional requirement of taking due account of the public interest expresses the fact that here too, ministerial responsibility applies.

163. Article 40 of the Constitution provides that the King shall receive annual payments at the expense of the State, following rules to be laid down by Act of Parliament (*Wet financieel statuut Koninklijk Huis*). Under this funding system, dating from 1972, the King (or reigning Queen) is entitled to an annual, indexed personal income and an annual, indexed remuneration of personal and substantive expenses. The personal income is not subject to personal taxation. These payments represent only a limited part of the costs of the monarchy. Aside from this, other significant personal and substantive expenses are separately included in the budgets of various ministries. The funding system has hereby become a complex set of expenditures, partly based on fixed payments, and partly on all sorts of budget items.

164. Since the reform of 1972, the funding of the monarchy has increasingly come under public scrutiny and become the subject of criticism. In recent decades, complaints are voiced practically every year in parliament about the lack of transparency and the significant increase in the expenses for the royal house. As of 2021, total expenses, including for security, amount to roughly EUR 100 million. Public opinion also reflects scepticism in recent years about the high level of expenses. The funding of the Dutch monarchy has thus become a thorny political issue, one that comes up each year during budgetary debates. Until now, successive cabinets have withstood the urge to reform the funding system. However, such reform appears only as a matter of time. In Dutch society, there is at present clearly less sympathy for the exceptional funding status of the King and members of the royal house. Other members of the Royal House may also receive payments under this constitutional provision. In this context, it is important that the Constitution provides (in Article 39) that membership of the Royal House will be regulated by Act of Parliament. The Membership of the Royal House Act (*Wet lidmaatschap koninklijk huis*) states that, in addition to the King who is head of the Royal House, those – up to the second degree of kinship – who could succeed to the throne under the provisions of the Constitution, a former monarch who has abdicated, and the spouses of the above, are all members of the Royal House. At present, three members of the Royal House are entitled to personal income and remunerations. One of them, Crown Princess Amalia, has waived her allowance temporarily.

165. The Membership of the Royal House Act could also possibly be significant from the point of view of ministerial responsibility. The fact that the other members of the Royal House do not enjoy immunity and do not exercise any constitutional powers is not disputed. Nevertheless, their actions can affect the public interest, by damaging the prestige of the monarchy, for example. In this context, reference is sometimes made to 'derived ministerial responsibility' (*afgeleide verantwoordelijkheid*). Ministers have to ensure that the position of the King is not damaged by activities of members of the Royal House. Their action as ministers in relation to this falls within the scope of their ministerial responsibility. For example, contacts between members of the Royal House and the media go through the Netherlands Government Information Service (*Rijksvoorlichtingsdienst*), which comes within the prime minister's sphere of responsibility. The problem however is that the statutory definition of the members of the Royal House does not mark a boundary in this respect; the activities of members of the royal family who are not members of the Royal House could also bring the monarchy into disrepute and activate ministerial responsibility. Moreover, it is difficult to understand why and how a minister can be held responsible for acts of persons in relation to whom he or she has (nearly) no competencies. The concept of 'derived ministerial competence' seems to be a more political than constitutional one.

§3. COMPETENCE

166. When discussing the powers of the King, a distinction can be made between the King as Head of State and the King as a part of the government. There is very little in the Constitution itself which is relevant to the powers of the Head of State. Two examples are Article 27 on abdication and Article 41 on the organization of the Royal Court.

Legal doctrine generally assumes that the King as Head of State represents the country in external matters. He makes State visits and receives foreign Heads of State and diplomats. In his position as Head of State, the King is considered under international law (Article 7 Vienna Convention on the Law of Treaties) to act as the representative of the State for the conclusion of treaties.

Within the Kingdom, the role of the Head of State is primarily symbolic. The King represents the unity of the State. He makes working visits and attends important events. Every year, a number of traditional events with a royal character take place, where the King is the central figure. These are the 'frills' of the monarchy under the House of Orange.

167. The King's functions as Head of State within the Kingdom used to be not just symbolic: he played an important role in the formation of the cabinet. The King obtained the advice of a number of people, including the chairpersons of the parliamentary groups in the Second Chamber. He appointed a person, who is charged with forming a cabinet (*formateur*) or someone who should investigate the possibilities of cabinet formation (*informateur*). The King took these decisions on his own without involving ministers. In 2012, the King's position in the formation process changed. Nowadays, the Second Chamber itself appoints a formateur or informateur. In Chapter 4 below, the process of cabinet formation will be examined more closely.

168. Given that the King is a member of the government, he is involved in the exercise of all the powers that belong to the government. The substance and extent of these powers will also be dealt with in Chapter 4 below. The important question here is: what is the King's role within the government? What personal power does he have in relation to ministers?

Constitutional law does not, in itself, offer any definite answers to this. The Constitution merely states that the King and the ministers form the government (Article 42) and that an order of the government – a Royal Decree – needs the signature of the King and one or more ministers or State secretaries (Article 47). It can be assumed from these provisions that the relationship is one of coordination, equality and mutual dependence. Central to this traditional vision is the idea that the King cannot operate in the government without the ministers, but also that the ministers cannot operate without the King. In the constitutional doctrine, however, a position which is quite frequently defended these days is that, in practice, in a modern parliamentary democracy, the King has very little or no constitutional power. In this view, his role is merely to 'be sympathetic to, to show interest in and to stimulate' the ministers.

169. In the explanatory notes on the 1983 Constitution, the government emphasized that the minister, by countersigning a Royal Decree, accepts the responsibility for it – to the exclusion of the King, who enjoys immunity. The King will constantly be aware of the fact that only the ministers are responsible and will act

accordingly. This awareness will determine the relationships within the government. The King will confine himself to carrying out his role, in accordance with the rights formulated by Bagehot for the English sovereign: 'the right to be consulted, the right to encourage, the right to warn'. This position taken by the government when the Constitution was revised clearly emphasizes that the responsibility of ministers to parliament necessarily involves the King's role within government being rather restricted. At the same time, this must mean that ministers occupy a pre-eminent position in the government.

170. Constitutional practice confirms this picture. Since ministerial responsibility was introduced and the parliamentary system established, ministers have no longer functioned as servants of the Crown. Their main function is to represent a parliamentary majority which has entered into a government coalition in order to put into effect a particular government policy. They are the ministers – together constituting the Council of Ministers – who are charged with forming general government policy.

This appears, for instance, from the decision-making on the statement which is made when a new cabinet makes its first appearance in parliament, and on the annual speech from the throne (*troonrede*) in which the government, through the King's speech, outlines government policy to parliament (Article 65 of the Constitution). It should moreover be recalled that the parliamentary groups are also strongly involved in drawing up government policy.

Finally, in this context, it is also important to note that in practice, ministers take the initiative in the drafting of a Royal Decree, although the King is free to make suggestions.

171. Although according to current opinion and practice the King's role in government is limited, the Constitution does not limit his powers within the government, so in theory, the possibility that under certain circumstances he might take more prominence and try to impose his will upon the ministers is not ruled out. Several examples of this can be found during the reigns of the former Queens Wilhelmina and Juliana in the twentieth century. In most Western European monarchies, including the Netherlands, the power of the monarch steadily declined during the 1900s as modern parliamentary democracy took shape. The so-called Royal Prerogatives, such as in international affairs and war powers, have passed to the prime minister and ministers, even if the constitution may suggest otherwise. In a modern parliamentary democracy, the hereditary and inviolable King has no say over national government matters. The prime minister and ministers are expected to set policy in a democracy. The question rises whether the Constitution should be revised, in order to clarify the position of the King in a modern parliamentary democracy.

172. It is reasonable to assume that the personal power of the King is limited, but it cannot be asserted with certainty, since the unity of the government, the immunity of the King and ministerial responsibility together oblige ministers not to communicate the personal views and input of the King in connection with government policy. The discussions between the King and ministers within the government are secret. This avoids the King being drawn into party political discussions. The observation of this 'Crown secret' is an indispensable condition for the preservation of the monarchy.

Chapter 3. The Legislature

§1. THE STATES GENERAL

173. In the provisions on the organization and composition of the States General (*Staten-Generaal*), the Constitution declares first and foremost (Article 50) that the States General represent the entire Dutch people. As was shown in Chapter 1 above, this provision is of special historical significance. It expresses the choice which was made for the establishment of a unitary state. The members of the States General do not occupy their seats as representatives of sovereign provinces, as was the case in the sixteenth to eighteenth centuries in the Republic of the United Netherlands. They now represent all the Dutch people. Thus the States General are to be considered as the representation of the national people: as the Dutch Parliament. It can also be inferred from Article 50 of the Constitution that the members of the States General may not, under the present structure, behave in such a way as to promote only local, regional or other group interests.

The States General consist of the Second Chamber (*Tweede Kamer*) and the First Chamber (*Eerste Kamer*) (Article 51, paragraph 1 of the Constitution). The bicameral system dates from 1815. At the instigation of the Belgians, the drafters of the Constitution opted to split the States General into two separate Chambers. The Second Chamber (Lower House) consisted of elected members, and the First Chamber of members appointed by the King. Proponents of the bicameral system aimed to follow the example of the British Parliament by creating a separate Chamber for the nobility who would be able to support the King against the common people's Chamber.

As time passed, however, the bicameral system developed in an entirely different direction. Formal representation of the nobility in parliament never came about. Since 1848, the trend of parliamentary development has been towards representative democracy with a parliamentary system. Since that date, members of the Second Chamber have been directly elected, while members of the First Chamber have been indirectly elected, by the members of the provincial states. So both Chambers are constituted on a democratic footing.

174. If the Dutch bicameral system cannot be compared with the British, comparisons with the French or German systems do not work either. As has been stated already, both Chambers of the States General represent the entire Dutch population. There is no representation of federal or regional government bodies in a separate Chamber. The Dutch bicameral system may be considered sui generis. In principle, both Chambers fulfil the same function. It is not surprising therefore that several attempts have been made in the past to abolish the First Chamber on the grounds that it is a superfluous duplication.

175. The question arises as to the position of each Chamber in parliament. In the first place, each fulfils a self-contained and (in important respects) equally valuable role in parliament. This is clear in particular from the allocation of powers to them under constitutional law. Both form part of the legislature. Both have been given important parliamentary rights, such as the right of parliamentary enquiry, the right of interpellation and the right of questioning, and since the budget is enacted by Act of Parliament both Chambers share in 'the power of the purse'. Ministerial responsibility and the confidence rule of the parliamentary system apply to both Chambers.

Nevertheless, the two Chambers do fulfil different roles in some areas, and this can be seen in both constitutional law and parliamentary practice. When legislation is being prepared, bills are always debated in the Second Chamber first. Only the Second Chamber has the right of initiative and amendment. In the legislative process, therefore, the First Chamber only has the opportunity to accept or reject in its entirety a bill which has been passed by the Second Chamber. Also, recommendations to the government on certain appointments, such as appointments to the Supreme Court, are exclusively the power of the Second Chamber (Articles 77, 108, 118 of the Constitution).

176. Probably even more important than the differences in constitutional law are the differences in the relationships which have evolved in parliamentary practice. In general terms, the Second Chamber has, in the course of time, gained political primacy in parliament – especially in the sphere of ministerial responsibility and the confidence rule. It is the Second Chamber which is more prominent in the relationship between government and parliament. The formation of a cabinet is based on the political make-up of this Chamber. The presentation and defence of government policy take place primarily, and sometimes exclusively, in the Second Chamber. The First Chamber is not in the limelight. On the whole, it has developed into a 'chamber for reconsideration'. Its work is valued nowadays in the sphere of the legislative process in particular. It is assumed to guard against unconstitutional or imprudent legislation.

The composition of and procedures in the two Chambers are related to their historical development. The Second Chamber now consists mainly of professional politicians. The frequency of meetings (plenary sittings and committee meetings) is high and virtually takes up a whole working week. There are regular meetings with members of the government. The First Chamber, however, is made up of members whose main occupation is outside parliament. They usually only meet once a week, and consultation with members of the government is much less frequent.

177. Although the First Chamber recognizes the political primacy of the Second Chamber in practice, and in general, observes restraint, it is certainly not obliged to give way if it has a different opinion from the Second Chamber. On the contrary, it is quite conceivable that the First Chamber occasionally rejects a bill that has been passed by the Second Chamber. Dutch constitutional law does not have any arrangement for resolving such differences of opinion between the two Chambers. In recent years, the idea of a constitutional arrangement whereby the Second Chamber would be given the final say has been urged from various quarters.

178. Confrontations with the cabinet are not ruled out either. On more than one occasion in recent years, the First Chamber has stubbornly resisted government proposals which enjoyed widespread support in the Second Chamber. Only the threat of a cabinet crisis made the First Chamber give in. This development is partly explained by the workings of the parliamentary system in the two Chambers. As we have shown, a cabinet is formed in the Netherlands on the basis of the political balance in the Second Chamber. The cabinet has close links with the parliamentary groups representing the majority. The distance maintained by the parliamentary groups in the First Chamber from the process of cabinet formation means that they are more ready to be critical of government policy.

179. Even under a bicameral system, the two Chambers meet together on occasion to discuss and decide matters in joint session. In such a joint session, which is presided over by the Speaker (*voorzitter*) of the First Chamber, the Chambers are deemed to be one entity (Article 51, paragraph 3 of the Constitution). This prevents them from arriving at different decisions. The Constitution lists all the circumstances when the States General meet in joint session for consideration and decision. We have seen above that, in Chapter 2, the Constitution prescribes a joint session on several occasions concerning the King (Articles 28, 29, 30, 32, 34, 35, 36 and 37 of the Constitution). Additional examples are the annual speech from the throne (*troonrede*) upon the opening of the parliamentary year (Article 65 of the Constitution) and in order to consent to a declaration that the Kingdom is at war (Article 96 of the Constitution).

180. Compared to other western European countries, the Dutch parliament has relatively few members. Under Article 51 of the Constitution, the Second Chamber consists of a hundred and fifty members and the First Chamber of seventy-five. The following observations concern the election of members of both Chambers (*Kamerleden*).

181. Article 4 of the Constitution guarantees to each Dutch citizen the right to elect the members of the general representative bodies, among which the States General, and also the right to stand for election. The Constitution and the Elections Act (*Kieswet*) contain a number of restrictions. Dutch nationals who have attained the age of 18 and are not disqualified from voting (Article 54 of the Constitution) have the right to vote for members of the Second Chamber. The Act of the Kingdom on Dutch nationality (*Rijkswet op het Nederlanderschap*) determines who is a Dutch national. In principle, a person does not have to be a resident of the Netherlands to exercise the right to vote.

Article 54 of the Constitution deals with exclusion from the franchise. Anyone who, on account of an offence designated by Act of Parliament, has been sentenced by an irrevocable judgment in a court of law to a prison sentence of one year or more, and additionally has been deprived at the same time of his or her active and passive voting rights, is excluded from active and passive voting rights.

182. We have indicated the electorate of the Second Chamber. In principle, the members of this same group of people are eligible to be elected as members of the First or Second Chamber (Article 56 of the Constitution). The members of the provincial states make up the electorate of the First Chamber (Article 55 of the Constitution). Requirements which must be met by these members are laid down in Article 129 of the Constitution. They must be Dutch, resident of the province, and they must also fulfil the requirements which must be met for persons to be elected to the Second Chamber. As has been indicated above, members of the provincial states are directly elected by Dutch citizens living in the province. Since the partial revision of the Constitution of 2022 Dutch nationals, not being resident in the Netherlands, can vote for a special electoral college for the election of members of the First Chamber (Article 55 Constitution).

183. Next, some consideration should be given to the elections themselves. In principle, elections to both Chambers take place every four years. The Constitution lays down that the duration of both Chambers is four years (Article 52). These four-yearly elections are known as 'periodic' elections. Elections can also take place at another moment if one or both Chambers are dissolved. In both types of elections, all seats in the Chamber are up for re-election.

184. The arrival of universal suffrage through the constitutional reform of 1917 (universal suffrage for men in 1917, universal suffrage for women in 1922) was accompanied by a fundamental change in the electoral system. Before 1917, an absolute majority system, organized on a constituency basis, operated in the Netherlands. This electoral system promoted cooperation between political parties at election time. Two major political blocks, consisting of coalitions of like-minded parties, competed for a parliamentary majority. The outcome of the election determined the political composition of the cabinet. Since 1917, a system of proportional representation has been in operation, whereby the country is treated as a single electoral territory. Under this system, a candidate is elected if he or she wins 1/150 (Second Chamber) or 1/75 (First Chamber) of the number of valid votes cast.

The Dutch system of proportional representation is known as a list system. The voter votes for a particular (party) list, upon which he or she is able to express a single 'preference'.

185. The system of proportional representation has undeniable advantages. Scarcely any votes are lost; the composition of the Chamber reflects the wishes of the whole electorate and there is no risk of 'gerrymandering'. There are also certain disadvantages to this system. There is no incentive for political parties to work together. The parties enter the election separately. The election result determines the party's political balance in parliament, but it is not in the least decisive for the political make-up of the cabinet. The voter has no opportunity to express his or her views about the government coalition. Furthermore, because of the absence of a constituency system, the bond between the voter and the elected member is weak. In practice, the voter votes for a list of unknown names. Finally, as said, the electoral system of proportional representation promotes a multi-party system in parliament. The parties' political situation in the Netherlands is characterized by fragmentation of the political landscape. Currently, the Second Chamber of the States General consists of members from twenty different smaller and medium-sized political parties. It goes without saying that the effective functioning of parliament is under tension because of this political fragmentation.

186. The procedure for electing members of the Second Chamber can be summarized as follows: It begins with the nomination of candidates, on a date which is laid down in the Elections Act. As we explained in Chapter 1 above, the nominations are controlled in practice by the political parties. Nomination takes place when lists of candidates are submitted to the presiding officer of one of the main polling stations. The lists have to be supported by at least ten voters. A deposit has to be paid for each list unless the list is from a party which already has a seat in the Chamber. The deposit is surrendered to the State if the list wins less than 75% of the 'electoral quotient' (*kiesdeler* – *see* below). On the ballot paper, the lists are numbered in the order of the size of the parties (i.e., the number of seats held in the Second Chamber).

187. Voting takes place forty-three days after nomination. The voter presents himself or herself at the polling station with the polling card which has been sent to him or her. He or she is given a ballot paper on which the lists of candidates are printed. Article 53 of the Constitution lays down that voting shall be secret. The Elections Act allows postal voting and proxy voting. Electronic voting is more and more current.

188. The establishment of the election result is a typically arithmetical business. All the votes on the lists are compiled together by the central voting office, which then establishes the electoral quotient. This is the number of votes cast divided by the total number of seats (150). Each list which achieves the quotient one or more times over gets a corresponding number of seats. The remaining seats are shared according to the D'Hondt system (greatest averages), which is to the advantage of the large parties. The Elections Act also enables combined lists to be drawn up at nomination time, which can be advantageous when the remaining seats are being shared out. Finally, the seats allocated to each list have to be shared out among the candidates on those lists. The available seats are first allocated to those candidates who won more than 25% of the quotient. The order of priority among them is determined by the number of votes they received. If there are still seats left over to be allocated, this is done according to the order in which candidates are listed on the list of candidates.

189. Election of the members of the First Chamber also takes place following a system of proportional representation. Except in cases where the Chamber has been dissolved, elections take place three months after the election of the members of the provincial states. Thus the provincial elections have an almost immediate effect on the composition of the First Chamber.

190. Nomination takes place on a date which is fixed by the Elections Act. Then the lists of candidates are submitted to the Royal Commissioner. Here too, the numbering of the lists corresponds to the order of size of the parties in the First Chamber.

191. Election takes place thirty-four days after nomination. The Royal Commissioner establishes the outcome of the voting and sends it to the central voting office which establishes the total result of the voting. It is important to note in this context that not every vote carries the same weight. The more inhabitants a province has, the more value is attached to a vote cast by a member of the provincial states. Apart from that, the result is established in virtually the same manner as with the Second Chamber.

192. Following this discussion of the franchise, the electoral system and elections, some observations should be made on the admission to membership of the States General. Basically, the following arrangement applies to both Chambers. Once the election result has been determined, the central voting office informs the person elected in writing. Within a fixed period, the elected candidate has to inform the Chamber concerned whether he or she accepts his or her 'appointment'. This does not yet make him or her a member of the Chamber. An order of admission from the Chamber is required. Admission takes place after the newly elected candidate's credentials (geloofsbrieven) have been examined by the Chamber in its old composition. The Speaker of the Chamber sets up a credentials committee. Provided no problems arise in connection with his or her credentials, the elected member is admitted to the Chamber. It is open to question whether he or she becomes a member from that moment. In fact, in parliamentary practice, the start of membership is considered to be not admission but the swearing of allegiance (Article 60 of the Constitution). However, the explanatory notes in Article 49 of the Constitution on the swearing-in of ministers and state secretaries, as well as the text of the Elections Act, which only lays down rules for admission as far as the start of membership is concerned, imply that swearing-in is not a constitutive requirement for parliamentary membership.

§2. LEGAL STATUS

193. Chapter 1 above demonstrated that the essence of the *trias politica* – separation of powers and checks and balances within central institutions of government – is realized in Dutch constitutional law to a significant extent. In this context, it is very important that the government institutions occupy separate and independent positions in relation to each other. This means that there are no hierarchical relationships whereby one organization of government receives orders or instructions from another to which it is responsible. It is not possible to indicate one national body which is the highest authority under Dutch constitutional law. Meanwhile, however, the autonomy and independence of the central government institutions do not result in a complete separation between them. We have already shown how constitutional law contains checks and balances, which introduces some control mechanisms between government institutions. These checks and balances may infringe on their autonomy and independence to some extent. However, they do not create a hierarchical relationship, but rather aim to facilitate cooperation between central government organizations.

194. When we look at the legal status of the States General, the concepts of autonomy and independence can serve as a central theme. They are the concepts

which form the background to the constitutional provisions concerning the legal status of the States General. In addition, certain checks and balances can be found elsewhere in constitutional law.

195. The way in which the States General is formed provides the first example of its autonomy and independence. Since 1848, when the King lost his power to appoint members of the First Chamber, the members of both Chambers have been elected. Other central government institutions have no say in the matter apart from the fact that the legislature provides for general rules governing the elections in the Elections Act and in the Constitution. The same applies to the manner of admitting members to the Chamber. The Chambers themselves examine the credentials and decide any disputes which may arise in connection with the credentials or the election (Article 58 of the Constitution).

196. These days, the States General are considered to be permanently in session. Before the constitutional reform of 1983, the situation as a matter of law was different. Then, the Constitution provided that the King opened and closed both the normal, yearly sessions and extraordinary sessions. However, this did not entail any infringement of parliament's autonomy in practice. Even before 1983, parliament was as a matter of fact permanently in session. Now, the Constitution merely speaks of the 'duration', which is fixed at four years for both Chambers (Article 52 of the Constitution). The two Chambers use the term 'year of sitting' (*vergaderjaar*). This begins on the third Tuesday in September with a declaration of government policy, given by the King – the speech from the throne (*troonrede*) – in a joint session of the States General (Article 65 of the Constitution).

197. The government's exercise of its power to dissolve Chambers of Parliament (Article 64 of the Constitution) may be considered an infringement of the aforementioned autonomy and independence, insofar as it interrupts the session of one or both Chambers with a view to terminating a particular composition of the Chamber(s). The power to dissolve the Chambers should be regarded as one of the checks and balances in Dutch constitutional law. For the time being, the role of dissolution in the parliamentary system will be left aside. It will be given further consideration in the next chapter as part of the discussion of the confidence rule with which it is closely linked.

198. At this stage, it can be stated that dissolution does not infringe upon the permanence of the States General. It does not lead to a period without a parliament. Article 64 of the Constitution prescribes that a decision to dissolve a Chamber involves a duty to hold elections for the Chamber that is to be dissolved. The newly elected Chamber has to meet within three months. Dissolution occurs on the same day as the newly elected Chamber comes together. Thus, the old Chamber stays in operation until the new Chamber meets.

As for the organization and procedure of the States General, the Constitution also contains provisions which point to autonomy and independence. First, there is Article 72 which empowers the two Chambers to draw up Standing Orders (*Reglement van Orde*) separately or jointly. The Standing Orders of the First and Second

Chamber are very important for the functioning of parliament. On the basis of these Standing Orders, the Chambers are free to make their own decisions on internal structural matters and on the manner in which they carry out their supervisory and shared legislative activities, taking into consideration constitutional and statutory provisions.

Standing Orders are internal orders which are only binding upon the members of the Chamber concerned. Ministers and state secretaries cannot derive any rights or obligations from Standing Orders. When Standing Orders are drawn up or changed, they do not intervene in the process.

In addition to Article 72, Article 61 of the Constitution also expresses parliament's autonomy and independence. Each of the Chambers appoints its own Speaker (*Kamervoorzitter*). Before 1983, the Constitution still granted the King this power, although it was already accepted practice that he would conform to the wishes of parliament.

199. Autonomy and independence are key concepts not just as far as the legal status of the Chambers of the States General is concerned, but also with respect to their individual members. They are expressed in the following regulations governing the legal status of members of parliament.

200. The first point to be made in this context concerns the beginning and end of membership of parliament. The arrangements for admitting members to the Chamber have already been discussed. Apart from the collective termination of membership through a general election, membership ceases in four cases: death, resignation, if it is established that an individual member lacks one of the requirements for membership, or if he or she occupies a post which is incompatible with being an MP. In the latter two cases, the Chamber has the last word if disputes arise. Dutch constitutional law does not make provision for parliamentary membership to be terminated, for example by judicial verdict. Temporary replacement of a member of the States General is possible for reasons of pregnancy and childbearing, as well as for reasons of illness (Article 57a of the Constitution).

201. Second, there are rules that membership in one of the Chambers cannot be combined with certain other functions. This is referred to as incompatibility. Article 57, paragraph 1 of the Constitution first of all excludes the possibility that anyone can be a member of both Chambers at the same time, a necessary prerequisite of the bicameral system. Paragraph 2 of this Article lists a number of offices which disqualify from membership of parliament. These are the posts of minister, state secretary, member of the Supreme Court, and Attorney General or Advocate General at the Supreme Court. In general, these incompatibilities may be deemed to be founded on the principle of separation of powers.

202. The incompatibility between being an MP and being a minister or state secretary deserves special attention. It typifies the relationship between the government and the States General. Dutch constitutional law assumes that the government and parliament are two separate and distinct government institutions. In practice, this is referred to as a 'dualistic' relationship.

Ministers and state secretaries are not appointed by parliament and do not have to come from its midst. The above-mentioned incompatibility of functions accentuates the separation between these institutions of government. The Constitution does make provision for an exception to this in Article 57, paragraph 3. If a minister or state secretary has tendered his or her resignation, he or she may combine his or her outgoing office with membership of the States General. In practice, it frequently happens that outgoing ministers and state secretaries combine both functions while a new cabinet is being formed.

Article 57 of the Constitution states furthermore that membership of parliament cannot be combined with membership of the Supreme Court or the office of Attorney General or Advocate General at the Supreme Court. It is surprising that this incompatibility only extends to the Supreme Court. Following the principle of separation of powers, the combination of functions in parliament and in the judiciary should be banned altogether. The Dutch Constitution unfortunately does not ensure this separation between parliament and the judiciary. In the past especially, members of the first Chamber (often a part-time function) occasionally were judges at the same time. Nowadays, it is considered unacceptable in the judiciary to have a political office in parliament at the same time. In 2022, the government finally presented a bill with a general ban on this combination of functions.

203. There are a few other provisions in the Constitution concerning the incompatibility of certain offices with parliamentary membership (Article 61, paragraph 2). The clerk and other civil servants working in the Chambers cannot at the same time be members of the States General. In addition, in 1983 the Constitution created the possibility for the legislature to declare other public offices to be incompatible with membership.

204. Article 67, paragraph 3 of the Constitution is also significant in relation to the autonomy and independence of members of parliament: members are not bound by a mandate or instructions when voting. Chapter 1 has already dealt with the significance of the principle of the free mandate in the relationship between MPs and political parties. This principle does not mean that MPs cannot be guided by the wishes and opinions of their own parties in the decision-making process. In practice, political discipline within parliamentary groups is not unusual in the Dutch parliament.

205. In itself, the acceptance by individual MPs of decisions made by their parliamentary group does not need to be objectionable. The Standing Orders assume that MPs will work together in parliamentary groups. It is obvious that within such groups, agreements on common positions will be made. Furthermore, this kind of cooperation strengthens the position of parliament. It facilitates the formation of opinions and decision-making in the Chamber and steers this process.

The free mandate plays a part in as much as ultimately the MP is free to exercise his or her own will. If he or she votes against an instruction from his or her party or parliamentary group, the legality and validity of his or her vote remain intact. In practice, dissident voting is not unusual. If, however, political conflicts within a parliamentary group become more or less permanent, cooperation may come to an end.

Dutch parliamentary history offers numerous examples of resultant splits in parliamentary groups. In Chapter 1, we noted that dissident behaviour by an MP only has internal party consequences. MPs may lose their party membership or membership of the parliamentary group, but they cannot be forced to relinquish their seat.

206. The autonomy and independence of members of parliament are furthermore guaranteed by the creation of a measure of immunity. This is not comparable with royal immunity. While the King cannot be held to account before any other institutions of government, an MP is, in principle, subject to the normal proceedings within the Judiciary just like any other citizen. There are only very minor exceptions to this, concerning certain activities within parliament itself.

One of the provisions of Article 71 of the Constitution states that members of the States General cannot be sued or prosecuted for anything which they say in parliament, or in a parliamentary committee, or for anything which they communicate to parliament or a parliamentary committee in writing. Parliamentary immunity does not only affect criminal prosecution and disciplinary matters, it extends to accountability under civil law as well. It only covers the spoken and written word. It is not a licence to insult or commit other criminal offences. Parliament itself must guard against misuse of immunity. In particular, this is a function of the Speakers of the Chambers who are empowered by the standing orders to take disciplinary measures. The Chambers and their Speakers can take action against unacceptable written remarks by deciding not to make the documents concerned public. There are a number of possible responses to verbal remarks. The MP can be admonished, closured, or he or she can be excluded from the meeting. In actual practice, these measures of order are seldom applied.

207. With the exception of the written and spoken word inside parliament, an MP is responsible under criminal and civil law just like any other citizen. With regard to certain criminal offences, there has long been a special legal procedure to protect members of parliament against rash prosecution. Article 119 of the Constitution lays down the following procedure. Only the Second Chamber and the government may order members to be prosecuted for certain offences committed in the exercise of their office. The prosecution is conducted by the Attorney General of the Supreme Court. Members of parliament are tried in first and final instance by the Supreme Court. Thus, the decision to prosecute rests with a political body. The fact that the case is heard in only one court means that the MP is not at the centre of a political upheaval for too long and political life is not unduly disturbed. This procedure has up to now been applied only once, in 2015, although the proceedings, in this case, ended without a trial by the Supreme Court. There was not enough evidence to start a prosecution against an MP. To promote integrity in parliament and prevent conflicts of interest (corruption) both Chambers of Parliament adopted a code of standards in recent years. For a long time, the leading consideration in the Dutch parliament has been that the furtherance and enforcement of integrity should be a matter to be addressed by the political parties. Neither the Second Chamber nor the First Chamber felt the need to establish a code of conduct. However, a few limited standards of conduct for Dutch MPs have been enacted. In 2003, the Second Chamber decided to include in its Standing Orders the requirement that MPs report their functions outside the parliament. This provision has gradually been expanded with registration requirements for outside activities, side income, interests and gifts. There was no requirement to monitor compliance with these provisions. In the First Chamber, similar provisions were included in the Standing Orders. In 2013, a working group of the Council of Europe, called GRECO (Group of States against Corruption), issued a critical evaluation report concerning the Dutch parliament. GRECO was quite negative about the fact that enforcement of integrity was regarded as strictly a matter for political parties. These parties could address integrity issues in widely varying ways, which impaired the trustworthiness and credibility of parliament. GRECO strongly urged the introduction of a code of conduct and an enforcement mechanism in parliament. In 2020, the First Chamber established a code of conduct. The Second Chamber followed soon after.

According to these codes of conduct, MPs have to act independently in the public interest. They are not allowed to represent personal interests. No MP shall act as a paid advocate in any proceeding of the Chamber. In the Second Chamber, an independent committee has exclusive powers to investigate complaints against MPs. The committee reports to the Second Chamber. MPs in violation with the code of conduct can be admonished or suspended for maximum one month. The First Chamber unfortunately lacks a similar enforcement system.

208. To conclude this section, a few words must be said about the financial position of members of the States General. Article 63 of the Constitution provides that financial provisions for members and former members of the States General, and for the surviving relatives of deceased members, shall be regulated by Act of Parliament. The Chambers may not pass a bill pertaining to this subject unless there is a majority of two-thirds of the votes in favour. It follows from this that it is not parliament itself, but the legislature (including the government) which makes the rules on this matter. In practice, however, the government adopts a low profile. Through its use of the term 'financial remuneration', the Constitution leaves the way open for all kinds of financial facilities, distinguishing between members of the First and Second Chambers and between different members of each Chamber.

209. Current statutory provisions assume that membership of the Second Chamber is a full-time occupation, whereas for members of the First Chamber their main occupation lies elsewhere. The former receive an income which is linked to a particular civil service pay scale. There are also provisions for the reimbursement of expenses, a pension scheme and the right to (reduced) pay for a certain period after membership has ceased. Certain members, such as the chairmen of parliamentary groups, receive additional payment in connection with their function. Compared with MPs' salaries in neighbouring countries, the financial remuneration of Second Chamber members is quite generous. Certainly, there is no need for them to take on additional functions on a large scale to keep their income up to a certain level. In this respect, the current arrangements probably encourage the independence of members. Members of the First Chamber only receive attendance fees and expense allowances.

§3. COMPETENCE

210. Broadly speaking the Chambers of the States General have two main areas of competence: a shared role in the legislative process, and a role to control the government in its exercise of powers. These two aspects will be dealt with in turn below.

211. Under Article 81 of the Constitution, the power to make Acts of Parliament (*wetten*) is assigned to the government and the States General acting jointly. Neither the Constitution itself nor any other constitutional rule, determines what the content of an Act of Parliament must or may be. In principle, the legislature is free to draft an Act as it desires. But one must not consider the legislature to be sovereign. There are some limits as to what an Act of Parliament may contain. Thus, Chapter 8 of the Constitution lays down the special procedure for revising the Constitution which was discussed earlier. In addition, the legislature may not act in conflict with fundamental rights or other constitutional provisions. For example, certain powers are attributed under the Constitution to institutions other than legislature, such as the government or the judiciary. Moreover, it is also assumed these days that the legislature must take general legal principles into consideration, even though there is as yet no judicial review of this.

212. In addition to prohibiting the legislature from making regulations on certain issues, constitutional law also orders to make regulations on certain topics. In several places, the Constitution and the Charter refer to the legislature (or the legislature of the Kingdom) as the body to set norms. This is true, for example, in the case of many fundamental rights, of the provisions concerning the organization and powers of central government institutions, and in the case of financial provisions (budget, taxes and the money system). We shall return later to the question of when the legislature is free to delegate its legislative powers. First, the legislative procedure itself will be described.

213. Under Article 81 of the Constitution, the power to make statutes rests with the government and the States General jointly. The initiative for legislation may come from the government or from one or more members of the Second Chamber. In practice, the majority of Acts come about at the government's initiative. That is to be expected, given that they have an extensive civil service machinery at their disposal. We shall therefore also concentrate on government bills.

Bills are prepared by civil servants in a particular ministry, possibly working in cooperation with other ministries. During the preparatory stages, consultations are usually held with the representatives of social groups and with experts. Advice is also frequently sought from one or more of the various advisory bodies which exist in the Netherlands. There are extensive, official instructions (*Aanwijzingen voor de regelgeving*) for the drafting of bills which are enacted by the prime minister. These aim to bring consistency into legislation and to reduce the enormous flood of rules. Once the bill with its explanatory memorandum is prepared, then the Council of Ministers must come to a decision on it, in accordance with Article 4, paragraph 2 of the Standing Orders for the Council of Ministers. If the Council of Ministers decides in favour of the bill, it will be sent to the Council of State for its advice (Article 73 of the Constitution). The relevant minister responds to this advice in a so-called further report, and if required amends the bill. Then it is ready to be put before the Second Chamber. The advice from the Council of State, the further report and the reports from any other consultations are submitted at the same time.

214. Next, the bill is referred to a permanent or temporary committee. The committee's investigations are usually conducted in writing, unlike the procedure in many other countries. The committee produces a report, consisting of the written comments on the bill provided by the various parliamentary groups within the committee. The government responds with a memorandum of reply. Sometimes the committee and the government produce more than one report and memorandum. The government may make changes to the bill at this stage.

After these investigations have been completed, which sometimes takes years, the plenary discussion of the bill begins. The bill is promoted in the Second Chamber by one or more ministers or state secretaries. In principle, a bill is debated in two phases. In the first phase, the bill is debated as a whole; the second phase deals with separate articles. The second phase is important in connection with the Second Chamber's power to make amendments. The government can also introduce changes to its bill during the plenary debate.

215. The handling of a bill in the First Chamber proceeds rather differently because the First Chamber has no power to amend bills. It can only accept or reject a bill. Moreover, once the bill has passed to the First Chamber, the government is no longer able to introduce changes. What the government can do, upon the instigation of the First Chamber or on its own initiative, is to decide to submit an amending Act (*novelle*) to the Second Chamber. This is in fact a bill to change a bill which is pending before the First Chamber.

The committee stage of investigations proceeds in the same way as in the Second Chamber. After the committee stage, a plenary debate takes place and a vote is held on the complete bill. The government may still withdraw the bill before the vote. It is able to do this at any stage as of the moment that the bill is first put before the Second Chamber.

216. Once the First Chamber has accepted a bill – rejection does not occur frequently – it still has to be ratified by the government, that is to say by the King with the countersignature of one or more ministers or state secretaries (Article 87 of the Constitution). Once it is ratified, it becomes an Act of Parliament. However, this does not mean that the Act comes into force. Under Article 88 of the Constitution, the legislature is required to draw up rules governing the publication of Acts of Parliament and their coming into force, and it adds that an Act cannot come into force before it has been published. The Publication Act (*Bekendmakingswet*) implements Article 88 of the Constitution. Article 3 of the Publication Act requires that Acts of Parliament be published in an official journal, called the *Staatsblad*. The Minister of Justice is responsible for the publication of Acts of Parliament.

Article 7 of the Publication Act concerns the procedures whereby legislation comes into force. Unless a particular Act provides otherwise, an Act comes into force on the first day of the second month following the date of publication. The date of the *Staatsblad* in which the Act is (nowadays digital) published is accepted as the date of publication.

217. As well as their shared legislative powers, the Chambers of the States General also have an important role in controlling the government. The most important element here, from the point of view of constitutional law, is ministerial responsibility, which is regulated in Article 42 and Article 68 of the Constitution. Under these provisions, ministers and state secretaries are obliged to supply information requested by one or more members of parliament, provided that the provision of such information does not conflict with the interests of the State. There are various procedures for such provision of information. Obvious examples are through interpellation and the right of questioning. These will be looked at in more detail in Chapter 4.

218. However, this is by no means the only way in which the Chambers control the government. In the first place, mention should be made of the right of parliamentary enquiry (*enquêterecht*), enjoyed by both Chambers (Article 70 of the Constitution). In principle, this grants the Chambers power to conduct investigations – without hindrance – into abuses or any other matters on which they consider that they need information. The right of parliamentary enquiry is further regulated in the Act on Parliamentary Enquiry (*Wet op de parlementaire enquête*). Up to the present date, about twenty enquiries have been carried out, a number of which resulted in the resignation of a member of the government.

219. One important control mechanism, which is not regulated in constitutional law, is cabinet formation; this will also be dealt with in more detail later. The government programme of a newly formed cabinet tends to be an almost exact copy of the coalition agreement concluded by the parliamentary groups which support the cabinet. Thus, at least initially, these groups have a great influence on cabinet policy. In addition, each year the government makes a government policy statement and presents a budget. This gives the Chambers ample opportunity to consider the policies which the government intends to carry out. Through motions and amendments to the budget bills, parliament can make its views known.

220. Supervision and controlling government also take place regularly in committee meetings, where members of parliament can consult or interrogate a minister or state secretary. There are also informal contacts between members of the government and members of the States General. It goes without saying that ministers and state secretaries regularly consult the chairmen of the political groups which support the government and, where it is felt desirable, other members of those groups too. Sometimes the groups making up the opposition are also consulted.

221. There are some special forms of control, where the government may not decide without the prior assent of the legislature or the Chambers of the States General. For instance, the conclusion of treaties and the declaration of war must, in principle, be approved by the States General. In other cases, the States General are empowered to put an end to an order made by the government. This is the case if the government has declared a state of emergency: the States General are empowered to decide whether this should continue or not (Article 103, paragraph 3 of the Constitution).

222. In practice, controlling government has its political limits, especially in the Second Chamber. The parliamentary majority which supports the cabinet often avoids making life too difficult for that cabinet. The close link between the cabinet and the majority coalition in parliament often proves so strong that government mistakes have few or no consequences. The relationship between the First Chamber and the cabinet is not so close, partly because this Chamber is not involved in the formation of the cabinet. Its position *vis-à-vis* the cabinet is therefore often more detached, but this does not mean that it can easily force a minister or cabinet to resign. In actual fact, that is the political prerogative of the Second Chamber.

223. In addition to the shared legislative and controlling functions discussed, there are a number of specific tasks which one or both Chambers fulfil. For example, the Second Chamber appoints the National Ombudsman (Article 78a of the Constitution), and it draws up a list of three persons for the appointment of a member of the Supreme Court (Article 118 of the Constitution) and the General Chamber of Audit (Article 77 of the Constitution). Also, each of the Chambers has a petitions committee which handles incoming petitions.

224. The budget has already been mentioned several times. As in many other West European countries, it is adopted by Act of Parliament (Article 105 of the Constitution). Each ministry has its own budget, which underlines the responsibility of the individual minister. The budgets cover one calendar year. The budget bills are submitted to the Second Chamber on the third Tuesday in September, the day the King makes the speech from the throne. Unlike many other West European countries, the Netherlands does not have a rule that the budget must balance. The Budget bills are dealt with in more or less the same way as other legislative proposals, which means that the Second Chamber can amend them freely. The First Chamber may only accept or reject. It is rare for a budget bill to be rejected by either Chamber.

225. In Dutch constitutional law, a Budget Act merely authorizes expenditure. It does not impose an obligation on the ministers actually to make that expenditure. A Budget Act includes estimates of government revenues but does not authorize the levying of taxes or other income. That is regulated by other legislation, concerning (changes in) tax laws, loans and the like.

Frequently, the Budget Acts for a particular year are not ready by 1 January of that year. The Government Accounts Act (*Comptabiliteitswet*) provides a solution for that situation. It authorizes a minister to incur expenditure up to a maximum of four-twelfths of the total annual sum for the previous year for the budget item concerned. The Minister for Finance may authorize higher sums. Finally, at some time during the first five months of each year, the Minister for Finance must send a memorandum to the States General summarizing the changes to the original budget which are considered to be necessary.

226. The adoption of the budget is not the only task which the Constitution assigns to the legislature. As has been shown above, there are many subjects for which the Constitution leaves it up to the legislature to draw up further regulations; and the latter is sometimes authorized to delegate, and sometimes not. We must mention here just a few of these subjects. In many cases, restrictions on the exercise of fundamental rights may only be imposed by Act of Parliament. The organization and granting of further powers to many offices such as the Council of State, the General Chamber of Audit, the judicial offices, the National Ombudsman and the decentralized authorities require Acts of Parliament. The legislature is also charged with regulating electoral law, national taxation and the money system.

Article 107 of the Constitution is especially important for guaranteeing legal uniformity. It instructs the legislature to compile general codes to regulate civil law, criminal law, and civil and criminal procedural law. The same Article also requires the legislature to lay down general rules of administrative law. Finally, the legislature must regulate the legal position of civil servants.

One should not think that the Constitution, with its frequent references to the legislature, gives an exhaustive picture of the latter's activities. Many subjects which are not mentioned at all in the Constitution are regulated in Acts of Parliament, or in orders which are based on Acts of Parliament.

There has been a good deal of criticism of the legislature in past decades, though. According to the critics, there are far too many rules, they are insufficiently harmonized, changed far too often, and in practice often unworkable. Attempts are made at deregulation and other methods of improvement in the quality of legislation, but the results so far are unimpressive. The pace of the legislative process also causes concern, especially in the case of the implementation of the EU directives. Again and again, time limits are exceeded.

§4. PROCEDURES

227. In order to describe how parliament works, it is important to look both at its internal organization and at the procedures of the two Chambers. The Constitution has little to say on these matters. It merely gives a few general rules. The Chambers are empowered to determine for themselves, to a large extent, their organization and working methods (Article 72 of the Constitution). The Standing Orders give detailed rules on these matters. In the following paragraphs, the working of the Second Chamber is taken as a starting point.

228. For the main part, the work of parliament is conducted in the plenary sittings of the Chamber and in the parliamentary committees. The plenary sittings are chaired by the Speaker. Under the Standing Orders, he or she is assigned numerous chairman-like functions. He or she convenes sittings. A sitting may also be convened at the request of a certain number of members or following a decision of the

Chamber itself. The Speaker makes proposals to the Chamber regarding the organization of work in hand; he or she calls members to speak; he or she maintains order; he or she is empowered to take disciplinary measures; and he or she formulates the points upon which the Chamber has to make a decision. In exercising his or her function, the Speaker must maintain strict impartiality. The Standing Orders make provision for offices to be set up to assist the Speaker in conducting the activities of the Chamber. The Presidium (made up of the Speaker and Deputy Speakers) fulfils this role in the Second Chamber. In the First Chamber, there is a committee made up of the Speaker and the chairmen of the political groups.

229. The Constitution lays down the principle that the meetings of the States General are public (Article 66 of the Constitution). The Chamber may, however, decide to meet behind closed doors. It is not only the plenary sittings of the Chamber which are held in public as a general rule but also the numerous meetings of the Second Chamber committees.

An official verbatim report of each sitting is made by the clerk (*griffier*) of the Chamber, which is published as the Proceedings of the States General (*Handelingen der Staten-Generaal*). The deliberations and decisions of the Chamber are only valid if more than half of the members are present (Article 67 of the Constitution). Decisions are taken by majority vote, except on matters where the Constitution requires a qualified majority. Despite this constitutional requirement, it is possible for discussions to be held and decisions taken without the quorum being physically present. The standing orders take the number of signatures on the attendance list as the criterion for presence at the meeting. The only exception to this is if one or more members request voting by roll call. Then the quorum must be present in person. In practice, voting by roll call does not often happen.

The Standing Orders enable decisions to be taken via a number of different procedures. Decisions can be taken without a vote, and votes can be held by show of hands, or by standing or remaining seated. The Dutch parliament does not have electronic voting.

230. In the first paragraph of this chapter, it was noted that the Second Chamber (the Chamber of professional politicians) meets far more frequently than the First Chamber (the Chamber of part-timers). The First Chamber concentrates its activities on one working day per week, while the Second Chamber usually holds plenary sittings three days a week. The sittings tend to proceed along established lines. After the opening, the Speaker makes known what papers have been submitted and raises the matter of the business in hand, at which point members can bring up any points they wish to have discussed. After this, the debate on a particular subject can begin, often involving discussion with one or more ministers or state secretaries. The Speaker calls the members to speak who have requested to do so, after which the relevant member of the government replies. After one such 'first exchange' others can follow. The time allowed to an individual member may be limited. The Speaker may also allow interruptions. It is helpful to repeat in this context that the provisions of the standing orders only concern the conduct of members of parliament.

They are strictly internal and are thus not binding upon ministers and state secretaries. Of course, as 'guests' of parliament, the latter are subject to the authority of the Speaker.

231. As we have shown, members of parliament tend to work together in parliamentary groups (*fracties*). This is emphasized in the plenary sittings of the Second Chamber by the fact that members of the same group sit together. Under the standing orders, a group is deemed to comprise those members who were elected from a list of the same political party. Parliamentary groups should not be considered offices of the Chamber. They do not have any powers with respect to the functioning of the Chamber. They are informal groups of members committed to working together. Their internal organization is strongly reminiscent of that of an association. The highest authority of a parliamentary political group is the general meeting of members; in addition, there is generally an executive committee and a chairman, who is the political leader of the group.

The organization of the parliamentary group and allocation of powers to its different organs aims to determine to a great extent the behaviour of individual members, both within the context of the group and outside it. The group strives to ensure that its members act as a unity in the Chamber. This is referred to as group discipline. Any action taken in the Chamber by individual members is usually based on a decision of the group. Although the parliamentary group has little significance in constitutional terms, it is very important indeed in day-to-day political life. In the First Chamber, political groups occupy a much less prominent position. Members enjoy a much greater degree of individual freedom.

232. A significant proportion of parliament's work takes place in committees. There are different kinds of committees: First, some committees are instituted by the standing orders themselves, others by decision of the Chamber. In the Second Chamber, for example, there is a committee for investigating the credentials of elected members, a national expenditure committee, a petitions committee, and a procedural committee. A distinction can also be made between permanent and temporary committees (*vaste, en tijdelijke Kamercommissies*). In principle, the Chamber sets up a permanent committee parallel to each ministry. Temporary committees are not set up for the duration of a session. They simply exist until their work is completed.

233. The Speaker plays an important part in setting up a committee. In principle, it is he or she who decides how many members will sit on a committee, although the Chamber has power to decide otherwise. In practice, committees comprise twenty-three members on average. The Speaker appoints the members and their deputies. In practice, he or she tends to consult the Presidium, and usually the parliamentary groups too, on the composition of committees. He or she thus strives to reflect the political balance in the Chamber as closely as possible.

Each committee appoints its own chairman, following intensive consultations between the political groups. The chairmanship of an important committee, for example, the permanent foreign affairs committee, has become a sought-after parliamentary post.

234. The Speaker and the first and second Deputy Speakers play an important role in allocating work among the various committees in the Second Chamber. In the First Chamber, the Speaker decides. The Speakers (and the first and second Deputy Speakers) decide, for example, whether a bill should be sent to a permanent or a general committee for scrutiny.

The committees fulfil a dual function: First, they carry out the (oral or written) preparatory work on government bills which have been sent to the Chamber for debate. The role of committees in the legislative process was discussed in the preceding section. Second, they play an important part in promoting the exchange of views with the government. This second function has become more and more significant in recent years, especially in the Second Chamber. Ministers and state secretaries frequently appear in committees nowadays to explain government policy.

235. Finally, committees are empowered to hold public or private hearings. These may be to allow for participation, enabling interested private citizens to express their views; or they may be to gather information, to hear the opinions of learned experts, for example.

Chapter 4. The Executive

§1. THE GOVERNMENT

236. Before the constitutional reform of 1983, the Constitution assigned executive power to the King. The introduction of the countersignature (*contraseign*) in 1840 meant that as of then the term 'King' had to be taken to mean the constitutional King, that is the government (King and ministers) (*regering*). Since 1983, there has been no explicit provision in the Constitution relating to the executive power of the government. Article 42, paragraph 1, of the Constitution, merely states that the government is made up of the King and the ministers. Constitutional history shows, however, that this provision does not just give an indication of the composition of the government but also of its function. Thus it can be assumed that basically, it is still the government which possesses executive power.

237. When discussing the government, a number of institutions spring to mind. In Article 42 of the Constitution, it appears that the government comprises the King and all the ministers together. However, if one reads this provision in conjunction with Article 47 and Articles 81–89 of the Constitution (on the procedure for enacting Royal Decrees and Acts of Parliament), and bearing in mind constitutional history, the conclusion must be that it is also possible to speak of the government when the King acts with one or several ministers or state secretaries. Three offices have been mentioned already in the context of the government: the King, who was the subject of Chapter 2 above, the ministers and the state secretaries. In addition, the Council of Ministers, and the Prime Minister should be mentioned (Article 45 of the Constitution).

238. We begin with a few observations about ministers. The Constitution distinguishes in Article 44 between ministers who head a ministry (*ministerie*) – sometimes referred to as a department – and ministers who do not have this task, known as ministers without portfolio. The number of ministers and the number of ministries under them is not laid down in the Constitution. Ministries can be instituted by Royal Decree, and over the course of constitutional history, their number has greatly increased. Most ministers are responsible for a ministry and each looks after a package of government duties. In his or her capacity as head of a ministry, each minister takes a share of government responsibility upon himself or herself and exercises a number of powers accordingly. Sometimes he or she acts by ministerial decree; sometimes he or she operates within the framework of the government, composed of the King and the minister(s) (Article 42 of the Constitution). The allocation of the national budget links in with this. Each ministry is allocated a share of the budget. Each ministry has its own budget Act. The responsibility for financial administration is thus shared between the different ministers.

239. The ministers without portfolio, who, as was said, do not head a ministry, do not have their own budgets, nor do they have management powers over staff and material resources. Apart from this; however, they occupy the same constitutional position as the heads of ministries. In practice, ministers without portfolios are appointed in order to emphasize a politically important policy area. Sometimes a minister without a portfolio is appointed to achieve political balance within a coalition cabinet.

Apart from those named in the Constitution, there are two other kinds of ministers in Dutch constitutional law: First, there are the plenipotentiary ministers who represent the governments of the overseas territories of Aruba, Curaçao and Sint Maarten in the government of the Kingdom. Second, there are the ministers of State, an honorary title conferred upon former politicians for outstanding service. A minister of State does not have any constitutional powers. His or her role is to offer wise advice to the government or the King in certain situations, such as cabinet formation.

240. As has been stated, in their role as heads of ministries, ministers each take on a share of the responsibility for governing the country. However, this does not mean that they work in total isolation from each other, developing the policies in their own areas according to their own wishes. On the contrary, the division of work along departmental lines does not detract from the fact that they are obliged to cooperate with each other. The Council of Ministers (*ministerraad*) is important in this context. Given that the significance of the Council of Ministers has long been a controversial issue in Dutch constitutional law, we shall examine this government institution more in-depth.

241. Since its institution in 1823, the Council of Ministers has gradually come to play an important role. Initially, it was merely an advisory body to the King, who at that time was the centre of government. The introduction of the countersignature and ministerial responsibility changed this situation. Ministers acquired powers of co-decision within the institution of the Crown. The King lost his authority as head of the government. Henceforth, the ministers themselves had to achieve a unified government policy. This unity was achieved through the Council of Ministers. In 1850, Standing Orders for the Council of Ministers were drawn up, which laid down that decisions would be taken in the Council by majority voting, and that no individual minister might act contrary to a decision taken by the Council. Thus, the guarantee of a consistent policy was shifted from the King to the ministers united in the Council of Ministers.

242. For a long time this strengthening of the position of the Council of Ministers was not coupled with any definition in the Constitution of its functions and powers. The development of the Council's role took place completely outside the Constitution. It is true that as early as 1887 the Constitution stated in Article 28, paragraph 1, that the ministers in joint council must decide whether the King is not competent to function, but that article cannot be taken to mean that the Council had a permanent role within the government in ensuring the consistency of government policy. Nonetheless, as the years went by, the Council of Ministers was increasingly recognized as an important State institution.

In this context, it was also relevant that, as of the end of the nineteenth century, cabinets could much less be considered a hotchpotch of professional ministers and members of the elite than had been the case in earlier decades. The arrival of the

243-245Part III, Ch. 4, The Executive

party system and changes in political relationships – the formation of coalitions on the right and the left – also had repercussions on the relationships within the cabinet, and the latter began to operate as a more coherent whole. Furthermore, the expansion of government activities increased the need for consistency in government policy. The position of the Council of Ministers in determining policy became more and more important. One constitutionalist even concluded at the end of the 1960s that one could speak of the 'supremacy of the Council of Ministers'.

243. Since the reform of 1983, the Constitution has included a separate provision on the Council of Ministers. Article 45 now provides that the Council of Ministers is composed of the ministers (paragraph 1), under the chairmanship of the prime minister (paragraph 2), and that it has a particular function and specific powers (paragraph 3): the Council of Ministers shall 'consider and decide upon general government policy and promote its coherence'. According to the Explanatory Notes, the government held the view that the Council of Ministers 'is a fundamental element in our system of government'. Moreover, this provision in the Constitution expresses the notion that the Council of Ministers is an independent government institution, 'with collective external responsibility, and with powers of its own in relation to individual ministers'.

244. This last excerpt from the explanatory notes requires some qualification. First and foremost, insofar as the Council of Ministers can be said to be independent, this means that it does not stand in a hierarchical relationship with other State institutions such as the King, the government composed of King and ministers (Article 42 of the Constitution) or the States General. However, the question arises whether the Council of Ministers is independent in the sense that it possesses exclusive decision-making powers in relation to other State institutions or in relation to citizens. For the reasons given below, it is likely that such a question would be answered in the negative.

The Council of Ministers' power to discuss and decide on matters of general government policy is not an exclusive power. During the preparation of the new Constitution of 1983, it was emphasized that State institutions, such as the States General, are also involved in policy-making. So it is not possible to say that the Council of Ministers determines overall government policy. In the discussion on cabinet formation below, we shall show that nowadays political groups in the Second Chamber also play an important part in determining the main features of government policy. Moreover, in terms of constitutional law, the Council of Ministers really only has a part to play with respect to internal relationships, that is: between individual ministers. In external relationships, for example with the States General or the citizens, it is not the Council of Ministers that acts, but individual ministers or the government. Ministers are responsible for the Chambers. Orders binding upon citizens come from the legislature, the government or an individual minister, not from the Council of Ministers.

245. Therefore, it can be concluded that it is the individual authority and responsibility of ministers which is of primary importance within the government. The Council of Ministers has no autonomous decision-making powers in relation to

other state institutions or citizens. The Council's sole function is an internal one in relation to its members. The function and power laid down in Article 45, paragraph 3, of the Constitution refer to its role in promoting the consistency of government policy, and it is in this context that the Council discusses and decides on overall government policy.

246. Regarding the question of consistency of government policy, the concept of homogeneity in the Council of Ministers (*homogeniteit van de ministerraad*) is frequently used in the constitutional doctrine. In the Dutch system, homogeneity definitely does not imply unity of political principles within the cabinet, as is usually the case in cabinets in the UK, for example. The Netherlands has, for a long time, had multi-party or coalition cabinets. In such cabinets, political unity is by no means a foregone conclusion. Therefore, it is not without reason that Article 45 of the Constitution speaks of the promotion of a coherent government policy. The emphasis is on the effort to achieve unity. In practice, this is shaped by the setting out of a government programme, to which ministers commit themselves when they are appointed. In addition, the Standing Orders for the Council of Ministers (*Reglement van Orde voor de ministerraad*) contain a number of provisions which guarantee a certain measure of unity. For instance, Article 26 states that members of the Council must maintain secrecy with regard to the decision-making of the Council. Articles 11 and 12 of the Standing Orders are also important in connection with homogeneity. They provide that decisions in the Council of Ministers shall be taken, where necessary, by majority voting, whereby each member present has one vote.

A member of the Council of Ministers may not act in conflict with a decision of the Council. If he or she considers that a particular decision conflicts with his or her ministerial responsibility, he or she must inform the Council of this. In that case, there are three possibilities. The Council may revise its decision, thus re-establishing its own unity. The individual minister may tender his or her resignation if his or her colleagues are not prepared to make concessions, resulting in a ministerial crisis. Finally, all the ministers involved in the conflict which has arisen within the Council of Ministers may tender their resignation, resulting in a cabinet crisis.

247. The unity of the Council of Ministers relies to a great extent on Articles 11 and 12 of the Standing Orders. Ministers may not act contrary to the Council's decisions. It would go too far, however, to deduce a relationship of subordination from this. These provisions aim to bring about a form of collegiate government, where subordination would be inappropriate. Ministers cannot be forced to act in accordance with the Council's decisions. They always have the choice between conforming to the Council's resolutions or resigning. In the latter case, the duty to implement the Council's decision lapses.

248. The word subordinate is equally inappropriate in the context of the relationship between the prime minister (*minister-president*) and the ministers. Article 45, paragraph 2, of the Constitution, states that the prime minister is chairman of the Council of Ministers. His or her position in constitutional law is determined by this function. The Standing Orders for the Council of Ministers provide him or her

with numerous relevant powers, such as convening meetings of the Council, setting the agenda and deciding on the order of business. He or she also has some special powers, usually powers of coordination. Thus, where there is a difference of opinion between ministers as to which minister is competent in a particular matter, the prime minister takes the decision.

249. Even though his or her powers are limited, the position of the prime minister has become more and more important in practice in recent decades. He or she is seen as the political leader of the cabinet, especially in the media. The fact that the prime minister usually is the political leader of the largest government party has contributed to this development. Usually, he or she has the role of *formateur* in cabinet formation and therefore is intensely involved in putting the cabinet together. His or her coordinating activities have increased considerably. He or she makes public statements in many cases on the position taken by the Council of Ministers: for example, at the annual general debates (*algemene beschouwingen*) in parliament, and at the weekly press conferences held after meetings of the Council of Ministers. His or her activities in the European Council, where he or she has a seat alongside the French Head of State and the heads of government of other European countries, strengthen the impression that the Dutch Prime Minister is a head of government too. In law, and in fact, he or she is not. The Prime Minister has no hierarchical executive powers over the other ministers. Nor does he or she occupy a central position in relation to parliament – with respect to ministerial responsibility, the confidence rule or the dissolution of parliament. In Dutch constitutional law, powers and responsibilities are shared among all the ministers individually and administration takes a collegiate form through the Council of Ministers. There is no place for power concentrated in the hands of an individual officer in this system.

250. There is, however, a relationship of subordination between ministers and state secretaries (*staatssecretarissen*). Nonetheless, state secretaries certainly cannot be put on par with civil servants working in the ministries under the leadership of a minister. In the first place, the Constitution provides that ministers and state secretaries are appointed and dismissed following the same procedure (Articles 46 and 48 of the Constitution). Furthermore, state secretaries in many respects do the same job as ministers. They have the same powers and duties as ministers under the Constitution, except that they do not have responsibility for ministries, and they are not members of the Council of Ministers. A state secretary is also a member of the government. He or she is empowered to pass Royal Decrees in conjunction with the King (Article 47 of the Constitution), and he or she is responsible to the Chambers of the States General (Article 46 of the Constitution).

There are some limitations on his or her exercise of these powers and duties. Article 46 of the Constitution (which contains the main provisions concerning state secretaries) assumes that the minister to whom the state secretary is attached decides in which circumstances the state secretary will take his or her place as minister, acting in accordance with his or her instructions. Thus, the Constitution assumes that a system of substitution will operate. Either the minister or the state secretary will appear in a given situation, but the minister decides in what area the state secretary is to function and can give him or her instructions. The state secretary is responsible, but this does not diminish the minister's responsibility for the operations of the state secretary. In the meantime, practice has shown that a strictly hierarchical relationship is not usual. Since the office was instituted by the 1948 reform of the Constitution, the role of state secretary has gradually evolved into that of a full political office. The appointment of a state secretary and establishment of his or her duties is no longer simply a matter for the minister concerned but is negotiated during cabinet formation. As a rule, the state secretary is given more or less sole responsibility for a significant and defined part of the work of the department. His or her day-to-day relationship with the minister is one of equal status, even though he or she may always be given instructions by the minister.

251. Following this discussion of the various offices relating to the government, the question of the appointment and dismissal of ministers and state secretaries is now given closer attention.

252. The Constitution gives particularly concise rules on this point. Article 43 states that the prime minister and the other ministers are appointed and dismissed by Royal Decree. Article 46 extends the same arrangement to state secretaries. Article 48 requires that the prime minister countersign the relevant Royal Decrees. Finally, Article 49 regulates the swearing-in of ministers and state secretaries in the presence of the King.

253. There are no rules laid down either in the Constitution or in any other written law on who may be appointed as a minister or state secretary, and when they may or must be appointed or dismissed. However, an established practice developed in relation to the appointment and dismissal of members of the cabinet. Usually, they all resign at the same time when the process of cabinet formation after general elections for the Second Chamber has been completed, in order to make way for the new team. However, individual appointments do occur in between; for example, where there has been a death or a resignation, which may happen for a number of reasons, such as disagreement within the cabinet or between the minister and one of the Chambers or a political group. We confine ourselves below to a discussion of cabinet formation.

254. The process of cabinet formation begins when the ministers tender their joint resignation to the King. Written constitutional law does not lay down when that must happen. There is no fixed term of office for a minister or cabinet.

In general, it can be said that joint resignation occurs for one of four reasons. First, a conflict with the King can result in a cabinet crisis. This has only happened once in constitutional history, in 1853. This nowadays is a purely theoretical ground for a cabinet crisis.

Second, internal conflict within the Council of Ministers may lead to a cabinet crisis. There are numerous examples of this in constitutional history. Since the Second World War, there have been internal cabinet crises in 1965, 1972, 1977, 1982, 1999, 2002 and 2010.

Third, a cabinet may have to resign as a result of the working of the confidence rule, if one of the Chambers ceases to have confidence in the cabinet. This will be dealt with further in the following section.

Finally, a general election is a reason for the collective resignation of a cabinet. This requires some further explanation. Actually, there is no obligation laid down in either written or unwritten law requiring a cabinet to resign when there is an election. In principle, it is conceivable that a cabinet could wait for the outcome of the election, and only resign if it lost its majority in the Second Chamber. This was accepted practice in the period between 1887 and 1917 when the absolute majority system in elections was in operation. However, since the system of proportional representation was introduced, elections never result in an overall majority. Parties do not enter the election in coalitions; coalitions come into being after the election during the formation of a new cabinet. Therefore, a cabinet will logically tender its resignation when an election is called. Since 1922, cabinets have followed this practice, usually referred to as the 1922 convention. Of course, it is not out of the question that the tide might turn, insofar as a government coalition might go into the election as a coalition at some time in the future. In that case, a revival of nineteenth century practice would be possible. However, at this point in time, such a development does not seem likely.

255. Two general conditions need to be taken into consideration when a new cabinet is being formed. First, account needs to be taken of the political balance in parliament. Because of the confidence rule, the cabinet to be formed must be able to count on the support, or at least acceptance, of a majority in the Second Chamber. Second, when a cabinet is being formed, account must be taken of the need for a measure of unity amongst ministers. Indeed, as was shown above, a certain level of homogeneity is assumed within the context of the Council of Ministers.

256. With these general principles in the background, a more or less constant practice for the formation of a new cabinet developed over the years. This practice is followed, not only when a new cabinet is formed following a general election, but also on the occasion of cabinet crises between elections. It should be understood that one cannot speak of a formation procedure determined by written or unwritten law. Departures from established practice are possible and occur quite regularly.

257. The cabinet formation process is set in motion by the submission of the existing cabinet's resignation. The King considers the resignation request and asks the ministers to stay in office and continue all government policies which they consider necessary in the interest of the Kingdom. The outgoing ministers usually confine themselves to concluding matters already in hand, though this does not have to be the case. The longer the situation carries on with the outgoing cabinet still in post, the more likely cabinets are to be able to effect even important policy changes.

For a long time the King had a central position in the cabinet formation process. In his capacity as Head of State, he would take the lead in forming a new cabinet. After the elections, the King would consult the vice-president of the Council of State, the Speakers of the two Chambers of Parliament and the chairpersons of all parliamentary groups in the Second Chamber. On the basis of their advice, the King would appoint an 'informateur' or a 'formateur' (sometimes more than one) to conduct negotiations with the chairpersons of the parliamentary groups to form a new government.

This longstanding practice, with the King in a central position, ended in 2012. The Second Chamber of the States General decided to reform its Standing Orders. Since that time, Article 139a of the Standing Orders of the Second Chamber of the States General states that the Second Chamber itself decides on the appointment of an 'informateur' or 'formateur'. The King no longer has the initiative in forming a new government. This new provision in the Standing Orders of the Second Chamber was successfully applied after the elections of 2012, 2017 and 2021.

258. There are points of agreement as well as differences between the constitutional position of the *informateur* and the *formateur*. Both office holders used to be advisers to the King but are nowadays advisers to the Second Chamber. They preside over the day-to-day work involved in the cabinet formation process, which is concluded when they present a final report to the Second Chamber, which is published.

The *informateur* investigates the possibilities of forming a cabinet. He or she accepts his or her mandate immediately. The *formateur* is assigned the task of forming a cabinet. He or she only accepts this task when he or she is certain that it is possible to draw up a list of nominations for ministers.

The content of an assignment may be worded in great detail, or it may be left very open. The first assignment is usually given to a representative of the biggest parliamentary group in the Second Chamber. In practice, there is no clear demarcation of roles between the *informateur* and the *formateur*. As the years have gone by, *informateurs* have been given more and more of the work involved in cabinet formation. At present time, the *formateur*, who is often also the intended Prime Minister, only makes his or her appearance after an agreement has been reached on almost all aspects. It is his or her task then to conclude the cabinet formation successfully.

259. In principle, the *(in)formateur* must take into account the wishes of the parliamentary groups who are considered likely participants in the government coalition. The way he or she sets about his or her task is determined to a large extent by the question of whether and to what extent the chairmen of the parliamentary groups and the groups themselves are to be involved in the cabinet formation process. The main aim is to form a cabinet which can count on the firm support and cooperation of a majority in the Second Chamber, or at least one which will not be rejected by the parliamentary majority straight away. It is conceivable that the *(in)formateur* might restrict himself or herself to some general discussions with chairmen of the parliamentary groups, to be certain of a minimum level of support for the new cabinet. This is referred to as the extra-parliamentary formation method in the literature, and a cabinet formed in this way is known as an extra-parliamentary cabinet. Alternatively, the *(in)formateur* may enter into intense negotiations with parliamentary political groups and their chairmen in an effort to form a cabinet. This is known as the parliamentary formation method, and a cabinet so formed is referred to as a parliamentary cabinet. In the last forty years, the latter method has been followed virtually always, so that the influence of the parliamentary political groups on the cabinet formation process has increased continually.

260. The decision as to which political groups are to form the government coalition has to be taken during these discussions. In the Netherlands, there is a definite preference for a majority cabinet; that is a cabinet made up of representatives of political parties which together form a parliamentary majority in the Second Chamber.

261. The drafting of a coalition agreement plays an important part in the intensive discussions over the formation of a parliamentary cabinet. The coalition agreement is a political agreement between the parliamentary groups involved in the future government coalition on a programme outlining government policy for the coming cabinet period. The groups have to refrain from supporting a motion of no confidence in the new cabinet, and also to act in accordance with the agreed programme while it is being implemented during the course of the cabinet period. While the coalition agreement is of limited significance in terms of constitutional law – it is no more than a political agreement- its political importance has increased considerably in recent decades.

Coalition agreements have become increasingly voluminous and detailed. An advantage of this is that parliament has become more involved in the establishment of government policy. From a democratic viewpoint, it is to be applauded when the government governs on the basis of agreements made by the parliamentary groups in a majority coalition. But there are also disadvantages to coalition agreements. They restrict the government's independence and scope for policy-making, especially now that they are intended to remain valid for the whole four-year cabinet period. Experience has shown that it is untenably pretentious to set out government policy in detail for such a long period. Furthermore, it means that the parties commit themselves to the policy of the cabinet to such an extent that the scrutiny function of parliament, at least the Second Chamber, suffers. Against this background, it seems advisable to work towards a concise coalition agreement, in which inter-party agreement is only specified on a few essential elements.

262. Once the coalition agreement has been concluded, negotiations usually proceed to the question of the composition of the cabinet. Here too, the participation of the parliamentary groups and their chairmen is more or less indispensable. Agreement has to be reached on the allocation of the posts of minister or state secretary to the various parties in the coalition, and also on the candidates themselves. Once this obstacle has been negotiated, the *formateur* can offer the posts to the proposed candidate ministers in the concluding phase of the cabinet formation. Finally, the *formateur* and the candidate ministers hold a constituent meeting, where they endorse the coalition agreement and examine whether they will be able to pursue a joint policy. In effect, thus, the composition of the Council of Ministers could be said to be laid down in the constituent meeting.

263. At the end of this meeting, the *formateur* accepts his or her assignment and presents a final report to the Second Chamber, which contains a proposal on the appointment of the new ministers and, mostly, state secretaries. Finally, the resignation of the outgoing ministers and state secretaries is accepted, and the new government is appointed. As stated earlier, the new prime minister countersigns the relevant Royal Decrees (Article 48 of the Constitution). Then the swearing-in takes place in the presence of the King (Article 49 of the Constitution). After a few weeks, the new cabinet makes its appearance in the Second Chamber to present the government policy statement, in which it unveils the main points of the policy it intends to pursue.

264. The formation of a new cabinet is a complicated and often time-consuming business in the Netherlands. The formation of a new cabinet following the elections of 2021 took almost a year, a new record in Dutch politics. The members of the new cabinet are responsible to the States General for their appointment. With regard to either the process or result of the cabinet formation, the Chamber could find reason to adopt a no confidence vote immediately upon the first appearance of the cabinet. Only once in Dutch parliamentary history has this happened. In 1939, Colijn's brand new fifth cabinet, which had been formed without the cooperation of the parliamentary political groups, was rejected immediately by a parliamentary majority (the Deckers motion).

§2. LEGAL STATUS

265. Following the separation of powers principle the government has an independent position vis-à-vis the States General and the judiciary. It does not occupy a hierarchical position with respect to other state institutions. Within the government too, the relationships between the various offices are characterized by the same principle of independence. The relationships between King and ministers, prime minister and ministers, Council of Ministers and ministers are all non-hierarchical. The only exception to this is the relationship between a minister and a state secretary.

266. As we have shown already, this independence and autonomy do not result in a complete separation between the various offices. Constitutional law provides for numerous checks and balances enabling the offices of government to operate in conjunction with one another. The functions and powers of the Council of Ministers with respect to ministers, discussed in the previous section, provide an example of this. Another example which can be given in this context is the position of the King within the government, which was discussed in Chapter 2 above.

There are two checks and balances operating in the relationship between the government and parliament which dominate the legal status of ministers and state secretaries. They are ministerial responsibility and the confidence rule of the parliamentary system. These are considered next, together with a discussion of the power to dissolve parliament.

267. First of all, we need to consider a number of special constitutional provisions concerning the legal status of ministers, in which their independent and autonomous position is expressed. In principle, the same rules apply to state secretaries. The Constitution states that the office of MP cannot be combined with the office of minister, at least not unless the minister has tendered his or her resignation (Article 57 of the Constitution). In addition, other offices which cannot be combined with being a minister are laid down in organic laws. Members of the Council of State and the General Chamber of Audit cannot at the same time hold the office of minister. Apart from these and a few other specific situations, the Constitution does not prohibit a minister from combining his or her office with one or more public or private functions. In practice, however, the office of minister has long been a full-time occupation which allows no time for additional offices. Occasionally, a minister may retain certain business interests while he or she is a minister, but it goes without saying that this situation must be handled extremely carefully.

268. Ministers are independent and autonomous but not impartial since they do not fulfil their political office in isolation from party politics. As a general rule, ministers can be seen as representatives of the political parties which make up the government coalition in the Chamber. In practice, ministers' party political allegiances have become much more significant in recent decades. Ministers are often drawn from the men and women who headed the party list of candidates in a general election or who occupied a prominent position on the list. During their period in office, they maintain close and frequent contact with their party and parliamentary group, especially in the Second Chamber. Nevertheless, it would be wrong to conclude that ministers operate as a kind of delegate for their party in the cabinet. It is usual for them to maintain a certain distance from their party and parliamentary group. This is why ministers do not usually occupy any executive positions within their parties.

269. There are two constitutional provisions on the legal status of members of parliament which also apply to ministers: First, there is parliamentary immunity (Article 71 of the Constitution). Ministers cannot be sued or prosecuted for anything that they have said or submitted in meetings of the States General or parliamentary committees. Second, the special criminal law procedure laid down in Article 119 of the Constitution is applicable in the case of ministers who have committed certain offences while in office.

270. In certain respects, the latter procedure is linked with ministerial responsibility. In general, in constitutional doctrine, a distinction is made between four kinds of ministerial responsibility: civil law, financial, criminal law and political.

The first kind of responsibility concerns responsibility or accountability in private law for the actions and omissions of ministers. Common civil law is applicable. The State as a legal person can be held liable for the operations of its organs, which includes ministers.

With regard to financial responsibility, the Government Accounts Act (*Comptabiliteitswet*) contains a number of provisions. The basic starting point is that ministers may only authorize payments which were covered by the budget. If these are exceeded, it is possible for the minister to be held personally and financially responsible. However, in practice financial responsibility is absorbed into political responsibility, to be discussed below.

271. The origins of criminal and political responsibility were discussed in Chapter 1 above. The introduction of criminal responsibility in 1840 was coupled with the granting of the power of ministers to sign all Royal Decrees (the countersignature). The introduction of the countersignature altered the minister's position within the government. The King could no longer issue orders without the cooperation of a minister. The minister was made responsible for orders of the government.

Criminal responsibility as such is of little significance in practice. It is true that there is an Act on Ministerial Accountability (*Wet op de ministeriële verant-woordelijkheid*) which makes ministers criminally responsible if they wilfully act in contravention of the Constitution or Acts of Parliament, but this Act has never been applied to ministers. The current Constitution provides a general provision on the responsibility of ministers in criminal law for offences committed while in office in Article 119. Also as far as criminal responsibility is concerned, it can be stated that this is completely eclipsed by political responsibility.

272. Political ministerial responsibility is founded on Article 42, paragraph 2, of the Constitution: the King is inviolable; the ministers are responsible. It is not clear from this provision what this responsibility entails, or to whom ministers are responsible. The answer to these questions can be found in Constitution. According to Article 68 of the Constitution ministers are required to provide the Chambers information, orally or in writing, if requested to do so by one or more members of parliament, provided that the provision of such information does not conflict with the interests of the State. This provision reveals that ministerial responsibility concerns the relationship between ministers and parliament. The minister's responsibility to parliament does not arise out of a hierarchical relationship, but from a provision in constitutional law. The extent of ministerial responsibility is (no more and no less) that the minister must answer to the Chambers.

273. This duty to answer parliament is worked out in more detail in the Standing Orders of the Chambers since these contain parliamentary powers relating to the duty to answer. A distinction can be made between the right of interpellation and the right of questioning.

The former is a right enjoyed by (the majority in) the Chamber. A member can ask leave of the Chamber to hold an interpellation. If the Chamber agrees, a date is fixed and the minister concerned is invited to attend the Chamber on that date. The member concerned (the interpellant) hands in his or her questions to the Speaker, who ensures that they are sent on to the minister. During the interpellation, the minister answers the questions, and the interpellant has the opportunity to speak (twice) as do other members (once). Interpellation is a fairly weighty political instrument for obtaining information from ministers.

Each MP individually has the right of questioning. He or she does not need leave from the Chamber. The minister may answer the questions verbally, during the weekly question time, or in writing.

The right of interpellation and the right of questioning are included in the standing orders of both Chambers. The right of questioning is frequently used in the Second Chamber and occasionally in the First.

274. The duty to answer parliament is not confined to interpellation and the right of questioning. It also applies when members question a minister during the course of discussions on a certain subject, such as a bill or policy document. It is also conceivable that a minister might supply information to the Chamber on his or her own initiative in the context of his or her ministerial responsibility.

275. There is a limit placed upon the duty to answer. The minister may refuse to provide requested information on the grounds of the State's interest. He or she decides for himself or herself whether the State's interest is at stake. If he or she takes this position, then the Chamber does not get the information it requested. Of course, the Chamber may see this as cause for withdrawing its confidence in the minister. Even then, though, it cannot be certain of an answer; that depends on whether the new member of the government is prepared to supply the information.

276. The next question is: what is covered by ministerial responsibility to the Chambers? As a general rule, the extent of a minister's responsibility corresponds to the extent of his or her powers. In concrete terms, the extent of ministerial responsibility amounts to the following. In the first place, the minister is responsible for the actions and omissions of the government, his or her own actions and omissions and those of the King within the government. In addition, he or she is also responsible for the King's actions when he is acting as Head of State.

Second, of course, the minister is responsible for the exercise (or not) of his or her own ministerial powers based on numerous Acts of Parliament and other regulations.

Third, ministers are responsible for decisions of the Council of Ministers. This is known as collective ministerial responsibility. This need not mean that the Council of Ministers has a duty to answer as a body. We have already seen that the Council of Ministers is an internal structure which does not act in relation to parliament. Collective responsibility means therefore the duty upon ministers to answer to parliament for decisions taken by the Council as a body. In this context, the responsibility of ministers for their operations in the EU Council of Ministers can also be mentioned. The minister acts in that Council as a representative of his or her national government. He or she is responsible to his or her national parliament. There is no relationship of responsibility vis-à-vis the European Parliament because of the intergovernmental nature of the Council of Ministers of the EU.

277. Finally, there is the question of the minister's responsibility as head of a ministry for his or her exercise of authority over subordinates. The minister is authorized to give orders to civil servants in his or her ministry. These civil servants are usually following instructions. On this assumption, the minister is responsible for everything that takes place, or fails to take place, within his or her ministry. On several occasions in the recent past, often within the framework of parliamentary enquiries, ministers have been called to account for serious shortcomings in departmental organization. The question arose in this context as to whether a minister could be held responsible if he or she was completely uninformed about the conduct of his or her subordinates. This approach would make the existence of ministerial responsibility dependent upon the culpability of the minister, but that does not conform to constitutional law. It is a requirement for the proper functioning of democratic control of governmental action that parliament can call someone to account – and constitutionally that can only be the minister – for the policy being implemented, even if he or she had no knowledge of it.

Another question, a political question, is whether the minister's lack of culpability has any consequences with respect to whether or not he or she remains in office. In the political culture of the Netherlands, it is by no means certain that a minister will tender his or her resignation if the civil service department under his or her control has committed serious errors.

278. Separate mention must be made in this context of ministerial responsibility with regard to civil servants who possess independent powers pursuant to Act of Parliament. Tax inspectors who are empowered independently to impose tax assessments, and members of the Public Prosecution Service (*Openbaar ministerie*) who have powers of prosecution provide examples. These civil servants are nevertheless under the authority of the minister. The minister is responsible to parliament for the exercise (or not) of his or her authority to give them instructions and for their content.

279. Within the framework of the checks and balances between the government and parliament, and alongside ministerial responsibility, the confidence rule of the parliamentary system is important. The confidence rule (*vertrouwensregel*) can in some ways be linked with ministerial responsibility. It is the sanction for the latter. If a minister fails in his or her responsibilities, the Chamber may decide that it no longer has confidence in him of her. The confidence rule then obliges the minister (or the state secretary or the whole cabinet) to tender his or her resignation to the King if the Chamber has passed a motion of no confidence.

280. In the first chapter, we showed how the confidence rule arose in the second half of the nineteenth century. It was then and still remains, even after the constitutional reform of 1983, an unwritten law: a convention. Its validity is generally accepted. Its content and scope are to a certain extent undefined. There are no formal requirements for the confidence rule to come into operation. The Constitution gives no detailed rules on this, unlike Belgian, French, German and Spanish constitutional law. Nevertheless, one thing that is more or less certain is that the main concern of the confidence rule is its effect in bringing about the resignation of members of the government. Indirectly it also plays a part in their appointment, as was demonstrated earlier in our discussion on the formation of cabinets.

The confidence rule can best be described in negative terms. It is not parliament's confidence in a minister or cabinet that must be demonstrated, but the absence of such confidence. As long as there has not been a vote of no confidence, confidence is assumed. Motions of confidence are unusual occurrences in the Dutch parliamentary system.

281. In the absence of fixed further rules, the unwritten confidence rule leaves enough scope for developments to take place in the relationship between the government and parliament. There is ample opportunity for varied interpretations of the confidence question in the Dutch parliamentary system.

Against this background, the main points concerning the functioning of the confidence rule in the relationship between the government and parliament can be summarized as follows: During the lifetime of a cabinet, differences of opinion between the government and parliament on government policy may crop up several times. The ministers, although they represent different political parties, are required to strive to achieve coherence in government policy. However, there is no such obligation upon the political groups in parliament which make up the government coalition. It is easy to conceive, therefore, that agreement might be achieved between ministers in the Council of Ministers, but not with and between the majority political groups. This may lead to political conflicts in parliament, a confrontation between the government and parliament, the outcome of which would be uncertain. This begs the question of what the balance of power is between the government and the representative body in the Dutch parliamentary system.

282. The main point is that parliament has the last word. By expressing a lack of confidence, a Chamber can force a cabinet to resign. Votes of no confidence are rare in the Dutch parliament, however. The last unmistakable vote of no confidence was in 1939. The Second Chamber adopted a resolution of no confidence (motie-Deckers) against the new cabinet, in its first appearance in parliament. The last time that the Second Chamber expressed its disapproval of government policy by rejecting a budget occurred in 1919. This reluctance on the part of parliament to provoke a cabinet crisis can be explained by the political relationships in the Dutch system. A great deal of effort is usually put into creating government coalitions so that there is considerable apprehension about risking an irrevocable break-up of the coalition without there being any alternative in sight.

283. As a result of this reticence, the government may gain a certain ascendancy. It may then try to impose its will upon the Chamber by declaring a motion, amendment or rejection of a bill to be unacceptable, in the sense that a minister informs the Chamber that he or she attaches political consequences – his or her resignation – to an unfavourable motion by the Chamber. It is also possible for the whole cabinet to threaten to attach consequences to a decision of the Chamber, a point of view which is usually announced by the Prime Minister. This puts the Chamber in a spot. They can persist, and risk a cabinet crisis with all its attendant complications, or they can make the best of a bad job and concur with the wishes of the government. In the first case, one can identify an ascendancy of the Chamber, and in the second, an ascendancy of the government. This illustrates that it is not only the judgment of parliament which plays a role in the interpretation of the confidence question: the view adopted by the government has a part to play too. The government may decide that a decision taken in parliament, which is not explicitly a vote of no confidence, implies such a degree of lack of confidence in government policy that the minister or cabinet may wish to attach political consequences to it. The cabinet will give due consideration to whether it is worth putting its political survival in the balance. This frequently results in cabinets and parliament finding some means of upholding political consensus at the eleventh hour. It is also possible that the cabinet finally acquiesces, and parliament insists on its own wishes, against those of the cabinet.

284. Thus ministers have an important role in the working of the confidence rule. They determine to an important extent whether the continued existence of the cabinet will be at stake when a dispute with parliament is being settled. That the emphasis is on the ministers and not on the Chamber, results partly from the fact that the government coalition takes shape mainly in the cabinet through cooperation between ministers. In the Chamber, the bond between the different political groups which represent the government is weaker, especially when general elections are at hand. Furthermore, the political leaders of the government coalition usually have seats in the cabinet, which also helps to explain the dominant role of ministers.

285. The question has been repeatedly asked in the Netherlands as to whether a minister should not also resign if not the Chamber as such, but his or her own political colleagues lose confidence in him or her. Of course, it may be completely desirable from a political point of view for a minister to go if he or she no longer enjoys the support of his or her own group in parliament. His or her position in the cabinet or in the Chamber may become untenable through the loss of this support. Whether he or she has a legal duty to resign is another question, however. We answer this question in the negative. The confidence rule requires a decision by a majority in the Chamber. It would be a breach of this rule if a minister who had the support of a parliamentary majority was forced to resign because he or she no longer had the support of a political group which only represented a minority.

286. The division of powers between the government and parliament makes close cooperation necessary. The need for close cooperation between these two equal institutions of government entails a delicate balance. If the cooperative relationship stagnates, every attempt to find a solution must take account of their independent and equal positions. The role fulfilled by the unwritten confidence rule of the parliamentary system has already been discussed. A conflict between the government and parliament may lead a minister or a cabinet to tender its resignation. In addition, the confidence rule can be used to put pressure on both sides in order to achieve cooperation. By declaring something to be unacceptable, or by threatening a vote of no confidence, the institution concerned is put under pressure to cooperate.

287. In addition to the confidence rule, the power to dissolve (a chamber of) parliament (*Kamerontbinding*) also plays a role in Dutch law in resolving serious deadlocks in the cooperation between the government and parliament. Once again, when this power is used, it is very important to preserve the constitutional balance. Unlike the confidence rule, the power to dissolve parliament is based on a written provision in the Constitution. Article 64, paragraph 1 of the Constitution states that either of the Chambers may be dissolved by Royal Decree. Paragraph 2 further states that the dissolution of parliament must be immediately followed by an election and that the newly elected Chamber must assemble within three months. Paragraph 3 of Article 64 states that dissolution shall take effect on the day on which the newly elected Chamber meets. Thus to a certain extent, the Constitution sets boundaries for the exercise of the power of dissolution; however, it does not indicate the circumstances in which the government may dissolve parliament. The exercise of the power of dissolution is governed to an important extent by customs which have developed in the course of parliamentary history. Occasionally, such customs may be considered rules of unwritten law.

288. The power to dissolve parliament was enshrined in the Constitution in 1848. Its introduction was closely linked with the strengthening of the position of parliament brought about by the important constitutional reform of that year. After 1848, the government was far more dependent on the cooperation of parliament for the implementation of its policies than it had been previously.

If a conflict came up between the government and parliament which could not be solved, there were two possible solutions. First, the cabinet could offer to resign, thus yielding to parliament's views. Second, the cabinet could use the conflict with the Chamber as a reason for provoking a dissolution. In that case, the cabinet claimed the right to stay in power and parliament had to give in. The government needed the possibility of appealing to the electorate to find out whether parliament still represented its wishes. In the case of this kind of 'conflict dissolution,' the government would 'appeal to the sensible majority of the population' to support it by electing a Chamber whose composition favoured the cabinet. It has always been generally accepted that dissolution should only take place as a last resort. Throughout the history of parliament, the Second Chamber has been dissolved sixteen times and the First Chamber three times, but these have not always been conflict dissolutions.

289. There have been a number of developments in the exercise of the power of dissolution over the years. The dissolutions of the Second Chamber in 1866 and 1868, which were discussed in Chapter 1 above, and which were highly significant for the establishment of the parliamentary system, deserve to be considered first. There is a rule of unwritten law concerning the exercise of the power of dissolution which can be traced back to the events of these years, and which is known as the convention of 1868. It is very closely linked with the parliamentary system and it holds that the government may not dissolve parliament more than once for the same reason. Ultimately, therefore, a cabinet must bow to the wishes of parliament, if parliament has withdrawn its confidence, and the government has not been able to regain that confidence through the dissolution process.

290. Second, the constitutional reform of 1917 was highly significant in relation to the exercise of the power of the government to dissolve parliament. In our earlier discussion of cabinet formation, the point was made that the introduction of proportional representation in 1917 meant that elections no longer produced a majority verdict. Since that date, coalitions do not enter the elections as such but come about afterwards during the formation of a new cabinet.

This change to the electoral system and the political balances which have resulted from it have had radical consequences for the exercise of the power of dissolution. Since then, there have been no more conflict dissolutions, since there is no point in a cabinet putting the conflict before the electorate if the election cannot produce a majority for or against the cabinet. Nevertheless, the Chamber has been dissolved several times since 1917; however, as a means of resolving conflicts between the government and the Chamber, these dissolutions had a quite different function. The cabinet was no longer faced with the choice between resigning or dissolving parliament, and in the latter case appealing to the electorate in its existing form. Henceforth, a dissolution decree was a death sentence both for the Chambers and for the cabinet. The only purpose behind a dissolution was to bring forward the date of a general election and thus enable a new cabinet to be formed.

291. The third development to be considered is one which has taken place since the Second World War. Since 1958, it has been the custom that the resignation request of the cabinet and the recommendations of the leaders of the parliamentary groups in the Second Chamber should always be put before the King before the dissolution decree is issued. The cabinet no longer decides independently whether a conflict with the Chamber should be resolved through early elections followed by the formation of a new cabinet. This decision is now taken on the basis of the opinions of a majority of the leaders of the parliamentary groups.

This practice has led to the conclusion being drawn in Dutch constitutional doctrine that parliament cannot be dissolved unless there is a majority in favour of dissolution in the Chamber, because the right to dissolve parliament may not impinge upon the confidence rule of the parliamentary system. A 'conflict dissolution' would be unacceptable according to this view. This would mean at the same time that the government would no longer be empowered to dissolve parliament on its own if it were confronted with a vote of no confidence. In that case, the cabinet would always have to tender its resignation.

292. It would not be appropriate in a work of this nature to go into too much detail on this interpretation of the power of dissolution. An important objection is that it damages the constitutional relationship between the executive and parliament, which has been characterized from way back by balance, independence and equal status. If one assumes that the consent of a majority in parliament is needed for parliament to be dissolved, then the primacy of government power comes to belong to parliament. The balance is disturbed. The cabinet loses an important means of exerting pressure on the Chamber and loses the element of choice in how to resolve conflicts. Indirectly, the Chamber decides on its own dissolution. However, this interpretation does not square with the constitutional rules on dissolution, given that Article 64 of the Constitution grants this power to the government. Furthermore, the constitutional reform of 1983 confirmed that the power to dissolve parliament must still be considered an autonomous power of the government. So it seems reasonable to assume that a 'conflict dissolution' is acceptable in constitutional law, despite the developments in practice, as is a dissolution initiated by the cabinet in order to bring about an early election.

293. Finally, as far as the dissolution of the First Chamber is concerned, some remarks are appropriate. This Chamber has only been dissolved three times in the history of parliament, which corresponds with the fact that it is the Second Chamber which has political primacy. On two of these occasions, this was in connection with a change in the electoral system. In addition, the system of indirect elections for the First Chamber can mean that its composition hardly changes following dissolution. As long as the members of the First Chamber are not directly elected, and unless the provincial states are dissolved at the same time, the dissolution of this Chamber will probably continue to be a rare event in the foreseeable future.

§3. COMPETENCE

294. It is difficult to define the powers of the government. A reading of the Constitution can easily lead to misunderstandings because it contains so few provisions explicitly granting power to the government. There are a number of places where government powers are couched in rather misleading terminology: everywhere where the Constitution refers to a Royal Decree (*koninklijk besluit*), it means an order of the government, that is to say, the King and one or more ministers. The text of the pre-1983 Constitution was rather more clear on the subject of government powers. As has already been pointed out, it assigned executive power to the government. While it is true that the 1983 Constitution no longer contains this provision, the fact that the government still wields the executive power is undisputed. However, anyone who thinks that the government's power is limited to the executive is way off target.

295. We have already indicated that the overwhelming majority of Acts of Parliament are a result of government initiatives. It would not be going too far to say that, without the continuous initiating activity of the government, the legislature would be more or less impotent. Furthermore, the government largely determines the content of Acts of Parliament. Notwithstanding the powers of the Second Chamber to amend legislative proposals, most of them pass through parliament essentially unchanged.

296. As in other western countries, the phenomenon of rule-making by government authorities other than parliament, or parliament and the government together, is also encountered in the Netherlands. We will confine ourselves here to rule-making at central government level. Rule-making by the executives of the decentralized authorities has been dealt with elsewhere.

297. The question of whether the legislature is competent to delegate rule-making powers to other offices, such as the government or a minister, is answered in principle in the Constitution. Where the Constitution assigns competence to the legislature or instructs the legislature to regulate a certain matter, it uses fixed terminology. If a form of the verb 'regulate' (*regelen*) is used, or the noun 'rule' (*regel*), or if the expression 'by or pursuant to an Act of Parliament' (*bij of krachtens de wet*) is used, then the legislature is authorized to instruct or allow another office to make further rules. If the Constitution does not use any of these terms, then the legislature must handle the matter itself, though the regulation of details may be left to others. In that case, it is not a question of delegation but of execution. It will be clear that the question of whether there has been unauthorized delegation or authorized execution is not always easy to answer. After all, what are details?

298. In connection with the problem of rule-making by offices other than the legislature, Article 89 of the Constitution merits attention. The most important part of that article lays down that rules or regulations issued by the government or a minister which can be enforced by penalties must be based on an Act of Parliament. Furthermore, the penalties to be imposed must be laid down in the Act of Parliament itself. Thus, according to this article, rules to which penalties are attached cannot be decreed by the government or a minister autonomously, without delegation by Act of Parliament.

299. In fact, delegated rules issued by the government or a minister are extremely common. Those issued by the government are usually called Orders in Council (*algemene maatregel van bestuur*), those issued by a minister, ministerial rules (*ministeriële regelingen*). The legislature is not able to deal with everything itself and the legislative process is too cumbersome to meet the requirements of flexibility and speed. The need to implement EU directives quickly has also led to a large number of broad delegation provisions in Acts of Parliament.

The delegation of rule-making powers to the government or a minister does not mean that parliament is excluded altogether, however. In the first place, the minister or cabinet remains responsible for the orders they issue. In the second place, several Acts of Parliament which delegate rule-making powers also include constructions which guarantee a measure of parliamentary influence upon the delegated rule-giving.

300. Policy rules (*beleidsregels*), sometimes also known as quasi-legislation, are a special phenomenon. These are rules that an administrative body lays down as a form of self-regulation over the exercise of its administrative powers. One area where policy rules operate widely is that of subsidies. In strict doctrinal terms, they only operate internally and do not create any rights or duties for citizens. Nevertheless, the courts have assumed that certain provisions contained in policy rules may furnish the citizen with a claim against the government (Supreme Court 28 March 1990 *Leidraad administratieve boeten*). This means that rules can have external effect without being based upon attribution or delegation by the Constitution or an Act of Parliament.

301. The above leads to the conclusion that the government is not only an executive authority, it also has a very important rule-making role. However, having said that, this is still an incomplete representation of government powers.

During the debate on the constitutional reform of 1983, the government was described as 'the engine of the state'. Although there is no question here of a typical juridical designation of powers, it does indicate the important function fulfilled by the government in the state. The government has a clear role of initiative: it prepares most bills and draws up plans in all kinds of areas, develops new forms of policy, negotiates with groups in society, deals with national finance, and manages the increasingly important foreign relations (EU), to name just a few of the salient points, some of which are not mentioned in the Constitution.

The fundamental social rights contained in Chapter 1 of the Constitution also give an indication of the many activities of the government. It is not going too far to state that the government, with its army of civil servants, runs the country. . There is little difference in this respect between the Netherlands and other West European countries.

§4. PROCEDURES

302. Formally speaking, the various government powers belong to the King cooperating with one or more ministers. In practice these powers are exercised by a single minister, a number of ministers, or all the ministers acting jointly in the Council of Ministers. It is usually assumed that the King's role is confined to the giving and receiving of advice. Bearing this in mind, government policy rests in principle with individual ministers running their own departments. However, we have shown already that individual policy areas have to be coordinated, because so many matters are now interdependent. With a view to achieving this coordination, Article 45 of the Constitution states that the Council of Ministers discusses and decides about government policy in general and promotes the coherence of that policy. The Standing Orders for the Council of Ministers work out this provision in more detail and prescribe that certain orders must pass through the Council of Ministers. These include bills for Acts of Parliament, proposals for Orders in Council, treaties, important government memoranda and a number of appointments. To prevent the Council of Ministers from becoming overburdened with work, a number of subsidiary councils (*onderraden*) have been set up which do some of the preparatory work. The prime minister chairs the meetings of the subsidiary councils. As well as the subsidiary councils there are also ministerial committees.

303. Unless there are special circumstances, the Council of Ministers meets weekly on Fridays, after which the Prime Minister holds a press conference. Decision-making is not always quick and easy in the Council meetings, partly due to the fact that the Netherlands always has coalition cabinets.

304. We stated earlier that the Dutch Prime Minister does not have any special powers vis-à-vis the other ministers, even though he or she chairs the Council of Ministers. However, his or her political authority has increased in recent years. He or she is increasingly charged with the coordination of government policy, and he or she is becoming more and more prominent in foreign affairs, especially in connection with the EU. However, it is doubtful whether this will be expressed in his or her constitutional status or in the way decisions are taken in the government. Dutch constitutional and political tradition has always preferred a collegiate form of administration. People are not keen on 'the strong man'. While this sometimes hinders the decision-making process, it is also a guarantee against absolutist and oligarchical developments. The fact that cabinets are always coalitions also obstructs such developments.

§5. The Role of the Administration and Administrative Agencies, the Bureaucracy

305. It goes without saying that a government or minister cannot carry out the work of government without the support of a large number of services. Constitutional law refers occasionally to the existence of these services. Article 44 of the Constitution makes provision for ministries to be set up by Royal Decree, and for them to be headed by a minister. Article 109 of the Constitution presupposes the existence of civil servants. At the time of writing (2023), the Netherlands has the following ministries:

– the Ministry of General Affairs (*Algemene Zaken*) is responsible for matters relating to the general government policy. It is headed by the Prime Minister who is at the same time Minister for General Affairs. The Netherlands Government Information Service and the Advisory Council on Government Policy come under this ministry;
– the Ministry of Foreign Affairs (*Buitenlandse Zaken*) is responsible for foreign relations. There is a Minister for Foreign Affairs and in addition a Minister for foreign trade and development cooperation issues;
– the Ministry of Public Safety and Justice (*Veiligheid en Justitie*) is responsible for the organization of the legal system in the broadest sense;
– the Ministry of the Interior and Kingdom Relations (*Binnenlandse Zaken en Koninkrijksrelaties*) is responsible for the organization of internal administration and the civil service;
– the Ministry of Education, Culture and Science (*Onderwijs, Cultuur en Wetenschappen*) is responsible for education and research as well as cultural affairs;
– the Ministry of Defence (*Defensie*) is responsible for national defence and for defence activities undertaken in the international sphere;
– the Ministry of Infrastructure and Water Management (*Infrastructuur en water management*) is concerned with the infrastructure, and the protection of the environment, among other matters;
– the Ministry of Finance is responsible for fiscal legislation and for collecting taxes. It also monitors responsible and efficient expenditure of government funds and safeguards budgetary rules;
– the Ministry of Economic Affairs and climate policy (*Economische zaken en Klimaat*) is responsible for national economic growth in a sustainable country.;
– the Ministry of Social Affairs and Employment (*Sociale Zaken en Werkgelegenheid*) deals, among other things, with wages policy, social services and employment;

- the Ministry of Health, Welfare and Sports (*Volksgezondheid, Welzijn en Sport*) is responsible, on the one hand, for the health service in the Netherlands, and on the other hand for many matters which can contribute to the physical and mental well-being of citizens;
- the Ministry of Agriculture, Nature and Food Quality (Landbouw, Natuur en Voedselkwaliteit) is responsible for strengthening the link between nature and agriculture, and improving farmers' economic situation.

In addition, it should be noted that there are large differences between the ministries in terms of size, organization and location. At one end of the scale, the Ministry of General Affairs is small, has a simple organizational structure and is located entirely in The Hague. At the other end of the scale, the Ministry of Infrastructure and Water Management is large, has a complex organization and has many so-called external services spread out throughout the country.

306. In a description of central government, it is not enough simply to mention the ministries. There are many institutions which operate more or less independently from the minister and which possess powers which are quite often directly derived from Acts of Parliament. The Public Prosecution Service which is responsible for detecting and prosecuting criminal offences is one example, the tax inspectorate is another. In recent decades, there has been a trend toward giving certain branches of ministries greater independence from the minister.

Aside from the ministries, there are more or less independent institutions of central government in the form of companies in which the State has a major interest. There are also many independent agencies (*zelfstandige bestuursorganen*) and funds such as the General Civil Servants Pension Fund and other financial institutions such as the Dutch National Bank. All in all, the work of central government is carried out by an amazingly complicated conglomerate of organizations, institutions and services.

As in most West European countries, there are hardly any constitutional regulations governing State bureaucracy. This does not mean that the political role of the bureaucracy is a minor one, however. The government and ministers are to a great degree dependent upon the advice and insights of civil servants when carrying out their policies. They are also forced to leave much of the actual work involved in decision-making to the civil servants. Many decisions are taken by mandate, therefore, on behalf of the minister.

Chapter 5. The Judiciary and Judicial Independence

§1. JUDICIAL ORGANIZATION

307. Reading the Dutch Constitution one could easily get the impression that the structure of judicial organization is simple. Chapter 6 of the Constitution is based on the principle that there is a single type of judicial institution – the Judiciary (*rechterlijke macht*) – which is competent to decide on all kinds of disputes and to impose penalties (Article 112 paragraph 1 of The Constitution). However, closer examination reveals that the legislature may institute administrative and disciplinary courts (Articles 112 paragraphs 2 and 113 of the Constitution).

An analysis of legislation and case law in the sphere of the administration of justice reveals a complicated state of affairs, both in the area of organization and with regard to the division of competence between the various judicial institutions. This complex system has evolved over the last hundred years or so.

Apart from the national system, one must also refer to the EU treaty under which the European Court of Justice exercises binding jurisdiction over the Netherlands, and to the ECtHR. However, these two courts remain outside the scope of this work.

308. Chapter 6 of the Constitution deals, as we have said, with the administration of justice. Under Article 112, this can be exercised by the Judiciary and by courts which do not form part of the Judiciary. Article 116 of the Constitution states that the legislature shall specify which courts form part of the Judiciary, although the requirements of Article 117 must also be taken into account. We shall return to this point later.

309. In principle, the administration of justice by the Judiciary is carried out by lawyers who fulfil the requirements to become members of the judiciary. However, Article 116 of the Constitution opens up the possibility for people who are not members of the Judiciary to participate in the administration of justice. These are the lay judges. We emphasize the word participate: trial by jury alone is thus excluded. Only in a few specialized courts, do lay judges participate in the administration of justice.

310. Up to the present time, courts of the Judiciary as intended in the Constitution have been regulated by the Act on Judicial Organization (*Wet op de rechterlijke organisatie*). According to Article 2 of this Act, the Judiciary comprises the Supreme Court (*Hoge Raad*) – also named in the Constitution – the courts of appeal (*gerechtshoven*) and the district courts (*rechtbanken*). The wording of the Constitution and the Act on Judicial Organization reveal that officers at the Public Prosecution Service (*openbaar ministerie*) may also be counted as members of the Judiciary. However, the Prosecution Service does not administer justice, in the sense of making judicial decisions; it is part of the executive and is responsible for tracking down and prosecuting criminal offences.

311. Members of the Supreme Court are appointed for life by Royal Decree (Article 117 of the Constitution); this means until they reach the age of 70. A particular feature is that the appointment is made on the basis of a list of three persons, drawn up by the Second Chamber of the States General. The government may choose out of this list of three. The involvement of the Second Chamber can be explained by the fact that the Supreme Court is responsible for passing judgment when, among others, ministers have committed an offence while in office (Article 119 of the Constitution). In practice, the Second Chamber places on its list the three names which are highest on a list of six candidates recommended by the Supreme Court itself. Current practice is that the Supreme Court plays a decisive role itself in the selection of candidates for membership of the Supreme Court. Nearly always the first candidate recommended by the Supreme Court is ultimately appointed by the government. So political involvement in the composition of the Supreme Court does not exist in the Netherlands to this day.

The Supreme Court consists of three permanent chambers, one for private law cases, one for criminal law cases and one for tax law cases. Each chamber has twelve to fifteen justices. According to the Judiciary (Organization) Act, most judgments are passed by a team of five justices. But in reality, the full chamber of twelve to fifteen justices will discuss each case before judgment is passed.

312. The Netherlands has four courts of appeal, which also have chambers. In principle, judgment is passed by three judges.

There are eleven district courts also with Chambers. Most judgments in the district courts are made by a single judge, some by three judges.

The district court functions as the court in the first instance depending upon the relevant statutory regulations. The courts of appeal adjudicate cases on appeal, and the Supreme Court is the court of cassation.

Judges at district courts and courts of appeal are also appointed for life by royal decree (Article 117 of the Constitution). These judges are appointed on recommendation of the Court. In practice, the recommendation is decisive for the selection of judges for these courts.

313. As the preceding paragraphs have shown, the organization of the Judiciary is reasonably simple and uniform. The administrative courts present a different picture, though. There is more diversity of administrative courts, which in turn are organized differently. This diversity can partly be explained by the gradual introduction of administrative courts into areas of public law. Over time, the following administrative courts have come into being:

- The Central Appeals Court (*Centrale Raad van Beroep*), which is established pursuant to the Appeals Act (*Beroepswet*). Judgments are handed down by three judges.
- The district courts, courts of appeal and the Supreme Court of the Judiciary deal with Tax assessment disputes in special Tax Chambers.

- The Act on Administrative Justice concerning government decisions on trade and industry (*Wet bestuursrechtspraak bedrijfsorganisatie*) (1954) set up a Regulatory Industrial Organization Appeals Court (*College van Beroep voor het bedrijfsleven*). Here too, judgments are handed down by three judges.
- The judicial division of the Council of State (*Afdeling bestuursrechtspraak Raad van State*), set up in 1975, is based on the Council of State Act (*Wet op de Raad van State*). The judicial division works in Chambers. In principle, judgments are passed by three judges.
- Since 1994, the district courts of the Judiciary are not only criminal and civil courts, but also in most cases administrative courts in first instance.

314. As well as the institutions listed above, there are a few other administrative courts which are competent in very specific and narrowly defined areas.

315. Mention has already been made of the reference to disciplinary justice in the Constitution. If the government wishes to establish disciplinary proceedings, these must be regulated by or pursuant to an Act of Parliament. There are a number of disciplinary institutions which have been set up by the government, such as the Disciplinary Boards and the Disciplinary Court which are based on the Advocates Act (*Advocatenwet*). These institutions pass judgment on the professional conduct of lawyers.

316. Regarding the legal status of judicial officers, the following observations may be made. Members of the Judiciary are, as mentioned before, appointed for life by Royal Decree. Life tenure is further defined by Act of Parliament as meaning up to the age of 70. A judge can only be dismissed by his colleagues in the judiciary, and then only in circumstances laid down by Act of Parliament. Further aspects of the legal status (salary and so on) of the judiciary are also regulated by Act of Parliament. These rules aim to guarantee the independence of the judiciary. Safeguards concerning legal position do not by themselves create judicial independence. Such safeguards must be accompanied by an environment in which judges truly function independently. . Article 6.1 of the European Convention suggests such functional independence. This functional independence essentially means that the judge has decision-making freedom vis-à-vis the two other branches of government. In light of case law by the European Court on Human Rights (ECtHR) on Article 6.1 of the European Convention, judicial functional independence must be interpreted broadly. Normally, the ECtHR includes the following standard finding in its rulings: '(...) in order to establish whether a tribunal can be considered "independent" for the purpose of Article 6, par. 1, regard must be had, *inter alia*, to the manner of appointment of its members and their term of office, the existence of safeguards against outside pressures and the question whether it presents an appearance of independence' (ECtHR, 25 September 2001, *Yakis v. Turkey*). Two elements in this standard finding relate to functional independence, namely 'safeguards against outside pressures' and 'appearance of independence'. According to ECtHR case law, the first safeguard precludes administrative hierarchical relationships between the judiciary and the executive/legislative branch, in which judges receive guidelines/instructions and are held accountable. Advice or recommendations may not be given to judges, either.

The 'appearance of independence' requirement implies that a judicial body is not independent if there are legitimate doubts about this. In this connection, the ECtHR has ruled that judges must be trusted in democratic societies. 'Justice must not only be done, it must also be seen to be done.' It follows from this requirement that the judiciary needs to be able to maintain sufficient distance from government and parliament. Close ties with the administrative authorities are, in the eyes of the ECtHR, unacceptable. The ECtHR's case law demarcates the decision-making freedom of judges adequately. In this respect, Article 6.1 of the European Convention is of critical importance in shaping judicial independence in a constitutional manner. In the ECtHR's case law, judges have to be independent within their judicial organisation as well. According to the ECtHR, 'judicial independence demands that individual judges be free not only from undue influences outside the judiciary, but also from within. This internal judicial independence requires that they be free from directives or pressures from the fellow judges or those who have administrative responsibilities in the court such as the president of the court or the president of a division in the court' (EHRM 22 December 2009, (*Parlov-Tkalčić v. Croatia*)).

Since the partial revision of the Constitution of 2022, a provision similar to Article 6.1 of the European Convention has been included in the Constitution. Article 17.1 of the Constitution now states that in the determination of his civil rights and obligations or of any criminal charge against him, everyone is entitled to a fair trial within a reasonable time by an independent and impartial tribunal. This new provision in the Constitution aims to provide added value compared to Article 6 of the European Convention. Article 17 applies to all legal disputes, including certain categories of disputes that fall outside the scope of Article 6.

317. In 2002, Court-management has been subject to a far-reaching reorganization. The Courts used to be managed by the Court President (as '*primus inter pares*') and the assembly of judges. Financial management was allocated to the Ministry of Justice. The Minister of Justice divided the budgets between the Courts. The reorganization of 2002 introduced a new Court-management system. A Council for the Administration of Justice (*Raad voor de rechtspraak*) decides on the allocation of budgets and supervises financial management, personnel policy and accommodation in the courts.

Each court has its own management board, chaired by the Court President. The board is charged with day-to-day management of the court. The courts are accountable to the Council for Administration of Justice, which in turn reports to the Minister of Justice and Security for the way in which resources are utilized. It should be noted that the above-mentioned administrative institutions do not themselves administer justice. The Judiciary (Organization) Act expressly states that they may not assume this role. The Act provides that the court administrations, the Council for Administration of Justice and the Minister of Justice and Security may not, in fulfilling their duties pertaining to operations, get involved in the procedural handling and the decision regarding specific cases. Notably, this internal independence safeguard for judges pertains not only to the relationship between judge and Minister but also to that between judge and court management board and between judge and the Council for Administration of Justice. As the members of the court administration and the Council for Administration of Justice are not independent and fall under the responsibility of the Minister, it is logical that there are independence safeguards for judges with respect to all management organization institutions.

In performing their operational duties, however, these administrative institutions within the judiciary turn out in practice to be intensely involved in the way the courts handle cases. The funding system is particularly important in this respect. The Council for Administration of Justice and the court administrations have strongly emphasized production and cost control in recent years. In practice, these administrative directives can affect the internal judicial independence and restrict the freedom of judges to decide especially procedural matters in cases.

§2. COMPETENCE

318. The Constitution is brief on the subject of the competence of the Judiciary. This is largely determined in Acts of Parliament and in case law. Article 112, paragraph 1, of the Constitution, states that the judgment of disputes on civil rights and obligations shall be reserved for the Judiciary. In principle, this covers all disputes between citizens, between the government and citizens, and between different government bodies. Paragraph 2 of the same article states that the judgment of disputes which do not arise from relations under civil law (*burgerlijke rechtsbetrekkingen*) may be granted by Act of Parliament either to the Judiciary or to courts which do not form part of the Judiciary. As a result of this constitutional provision, the competence of the Judiciary is not fixed, since it may be extended or limited by the legislature, concerning administrative cases in which the government is involved.

319. In addition to Article 112, paragraph 1 of the Constitution, there are a number of other provisions concerning the competence of the judiciary in the Constitution, which the legislature must take into account. Article 113, paragraph 1 of the Constitution reserves the right to trie criminal cases to the Judiciary, and paragraph 3 of that article states that custodial sentences may only be imposed by the Judiciary. Finally, the Constitution assigns the judgment of certain types of offences in office of ministers and MPs to the responsibility of the Supreme Court (Article 119 of the Constitution).

320. Following this brief summary of the constitutional provisions on the powers of the Judiciary, we must now go on to consider how this relates to the competence of the administrative courts. As already indicated, Article 112, paragraph 1, of the Constitution allocates the power to adjudicate disputes involving civil rights and obligations to the Judiciary. In the case law, this article is interpreted in terms of what is known as *objectum litis* doctrine. If a plaintiff claims that his or her right under civil law has been infringed or that he or she has a claim for the recovery of a debt, the court of the Judiciary is competent to settle the matter. In principle, the ordinary Judiciary is always authorized to settle such cases, provided the plaintiff has formulated his or her claim properly.

However, on the basis of Article 112, paragraph 2, of the Constitution, the legislature has instituted administrative courts, which are not part of the Judiciary and which are competent to adjudicate appeal cases against various administrative decisions. These include, for example, decisions on social security benefits, civil servants cases and many other decisions made by central and decentralized government bodies. Given the existence of the above-mentioned administrative courts, one might think that the judiciary is not competent to adjudicate a dispute in connection with such a decision if there is a remedy in an administrative court. However, the Judiciary does not declare itself incompetent to adjudicate cases where there is, or has been, a remedy in administrative law. In such cases, although the court is competent, it declares the case inadmissible. To summarize, the system means that a citizen must first follow the special administrative law procedure, and the Judiciary acts as a safety net if there is no competent administrative court.

Thus in principle, in the Netherlands, for every case there is a competent court.

321. The same system applies in cases where citizens have a right to administrative appeal. Strictly speaking, this is not a form of independent administration of justice, but a method of dispute-settlement by an administrative body. It has developed from the old *recursus ad principem*. Article 115 of the Constitution provides the foundation for this form of legal protection, whereby not only the lawfulness but also the appropriateness of the disputed decision is judged. The administrative appeal procedure has been replaced for the most part by procedures in the courts of the Judiciary and in administrative courts, partly in response to a judgment of the ECtHR (ECtHR 23 October 1985 *Benthem* case).

322. The point was made earlier that the Judiciary alone is empowered to trie criminal offences and impose penalties. At first sight, this constitutional provision only seems to allow one interpretation, but closer examination reveals this is not to be the case. In particular, the demarcation between criminal offences on the one hand and administrative sanctions and disciplinary measures, on the other hand, is not simple.

323. The Constitution not only grants powers to the judiciary, it also lays down in general terms how the judiciary must exercise these powers. Thus, trials must be public and verdicts must be reasoned, except where an Act of Parliament provides otherwise. Further rules are laid down in Acts of Parliament. One characteristic feature of the Dutch judicial system as regulated by these Acts of Parliament is the absence of any system of dissenting or concurring opinions. The courts and chambers act as united bodies; no minority opinion comes out into the open.

Before proceeding to the subject of judicial review, a number of more specific points concerning the administration of justice should be made. The death penalty was abolished by the Dutch Constitution in 1983. The prohibition of capital punishment is moreover not included among those constitutional provisions which may be set aside in a state of emergency. These do include the possibility that in a state of emergency, justice may be administered by judges who are not members of the Judiciary and not appointed for life. This is also possible for the administration of justice outside the Netherlands.

§3. JUDICIAL REVIEW

324. In Part I, Chapter 6 a summary of the hierarchy of legal rules was given. This is important in connection with the question of judicial review. All Dutch courts are competent to test lower legal rules against higher ones and to declare the former to be incompatible with the latter. In addition, all courts are competent and obliged to test all national rules against the rules of EU law, which by virtue of their supranational character form part of the national system of law. In addition, Article 94 of the Constitution requires courts and other officials not to apply national laws where to do so would involve contravening treaty provisions or decisions of international organizations which are binding on all persons (*een ieder verbindend*).

This system, whereby courts must grant priority to higher law over lower law, has one notable exception. Under Article 120 of the Constitution, courts are not to decide on the constitutionality of Acts of Parliament. This provision, which dates back to 1848, aims to reserve the interpretation of the Constitution to the legislature. Even if a court considers an Act to be in conflict with the Constitution, that court is not authorized to declare it non-binding or to disapply it. The Supreme Court has given this prohibition against judicial review an even broader interpretation (Supreme Court 14 April 1989 *Harminisatiewet* case). The Supreme Court interpreted this Article to mean that not only may Acts of Parliament not be tested against the Constitution, but they may not be tested against the Charter for the Kingdom of the Netherlands or general legal principles either.

However, the existing system is shaky. Partly as a result of the possibility which does exist for judicial review against the EU law and provisions of international law which are binding on all persons, this prohibition and the interpretation of it in the case law have been subject to increasing criticism. There is regular discussion as to whether the prohibition should not be partly abolished, so as to allow judicial review of Acts of Parliament against all provisions of the Constitution which are binding on all persons. It is not clear, however, whether in that case, all judges would have the power of judicial review (the diffuse system), or whether this would be granted to a single judicial body, such as the Supreme Court or a special constitutional court appointed for the purpose (the concentrated system). Whatever option is chosen, the current constitutional system has to be regarded as an anomaly. An illustration of this is the fact that Dutch courts may test Acts of Parliament against the prohibition of discrimination contained in Article 26 of the International Convention on Civil and Political Rights (ICCPR), but may not do so against the comparable provision in Article 1 of the Dutch Constitution.

Chapter 6. The Council of State, the General Chamber of Audit and the Permanent Advisory Bodies

§1. THE COUNCIL OF STATE

325. Chapter 4 of the Constitution is mostly devoted to government institutions fulfilling an advisory role to the executive, and to a lesser extent also to parliament. Pre-eminent among these institutions is the Council of State (*Raad van State*). This institution has a rich history. It set up in 1531. During the period of the Republic of the United Netherlands, the Council of State was an executive and advisory body to the States General. It was partly responsible for the executive functions of the confederation of the seven provinces. When the Kingdom of the Netherlands was created, the Council of State became an advisory body to the King. In the early years of the Kingdom, that function was also fulfilled by the Council of Ministers and the cabinet council (a meeting of King and ministers). However, there was no clear division of responsibilities. The introduction of ministerial responsibility changed this. The Council of State remained as the major advisory body to the government, the latter comprising the King and ministers together.

326. The Constitution contains a few provisions concerning the composition, organization and powers of the Council of State. More detailed rules are to be found in the Council of State Act (*Wet op de Raad van State*). The King is chairman of the Council of State (Article 74, paragraph 1 of the Constitution). His role as chairman is now a ceremonial one. The King does not have a vote in the Council. The same applies to the heir presumptive to the throne, who automatically has a seat in the Council of State after attaining the age of 18.

The Council of State further comprises a vice-chairman, who in practice chairs the meetings, and a maximum of ten members of the Council of State (*leden van de Raad van State*). The Council of State has finally a not limited amount of 'other' members, called '*Staatsraden*'. All these members of the Council of State are appointed for life by Royal Decree. They retire at the age of 70. Their legal position is comparable to that of the members of the Judiciary, therefore, and this is also true with respect to other aspects of their legal position. Members of the Council of State can only be suspended or dismissed by the Council itself in circumstances laid down in an Act of Parliament.

On the occasion of the 1983 constitutional reform, consideration was given as to whether the government's right to appoint members of the Council of State should not be limited by a binding recommendation from the Second Chamber, as is the case in the appointment of members of the Supreme Court and the General Chamber of Audit which will be discussed next. The government resisted this because the Council of State mainly serves as advisory body to the government.

Other members of the royal family may be granted a seat in the Council by Act of Parliament. Again, they do not have the right to vote.

327. The Constitution and the Council of State Act attribute first and foremost advisory powers to the Council of State. A distinction can be made between its advisory role on behalf of the government and that on behalf of parliament. The government is required to hear the views of the Council of State on government bills, draft Orders in Council and proposals to approve treaties. Departures from this requirement may be made by Act of Parliament, and the Council of State Act does make provision for two such exceptions. The Council of State tenders its advice on a bill before the bill is submitted to the Second Chamber.

328. The Council of State is also in charge of presenting draft decisions for Royal Decrees settling disputes between public bodies (Article 136 of the Constitution).

Finally, the Council may, upon its own initiative, make general recommendations to the government on legislative and executive matters, and make its views known to the government on matters of particular concern.

329. There is one circumstance where the Council of State advises parliament rather than the government. If a member of the Second Chamber introduces a bill, the Council of State will advise the Chamber before the bill is debated.

330. The advice of the Council of State is public. In principle, the Council's advice on government bills will be handed over to the States General. In practice, especially in the Second Chamber, this advice is sometimes used to give the government a hard time.

331. The Constitution assumes that the Council of State may have separate departments for the exercise of its powers. The previous chapter showed that the Council of State does not only have an advisory role, it also has a judicial function in the area of administrative law. The Council of State Act institutes one separate department for this: the Judicial Division (*Afdeling Bestuursrechtspraak*). Since the 2010 revision of the Council of State Act, a second separate department has been established for advising on legislation. Most members of the Council of State are appointed in one of these two departments. Some members (maximum ten) can be appointed in both departments.

332. Finally, it should be recalled that under Dutch constitutional law it is possible for the Council of State to exercise the role of the executive. Under Article 38 of the Constitution, the Council of State may assume the powers of the King under certain circumstances.

§2. THE GENERAL CHAMBER OF AUDIT

333. In order to maximize the power of the purse of the States General, it is necessary for an accurate check to be kept upon the regularity and efficiency of income and expenditure. The States General are not really equipped to do this for themselves. A specialized organization is necessary. The Constitution assigns this task to

the General Chamber of Audit (*Algemene Rekenkamer*). Article 76 of the Constitution states that the General Chamber of Audit is responsible for examining the revenues and expenditures of the State.

334. The Chamber of Audit as an institution, like the Council of State, existed
long before the creation of the Kingdom of the Netherlands. As far back as the
middle ages, the Chamber of Audit was in the service of the monarch. During the
time of the Republic of the United Netherlands, there was a Confederal Chamber of
Audit, consisting of fourteen members, two from each province, which was responsible for keeping a check on the financial management of the confederation. The
General Chamber of Audit came into being in 1814, at first operating on behalf of
the King. Its position was strengthened by the constitutional reform of 1840, in
response to the financial mismanagement of King William I in the years following
the break with Belgium.

Since then, the Chamber has worked on behalf of both government and parliament. The current Constitution contains three provisions on the General Chamber
of Audit (Articles 76–78). More detailed rules are found in Chapter 7 of the Government Accounts Act (*Comptabiliteitswet*).

The Constitution provides that members of the General Chamber of Audit are
appointed for life by Royal Decree from a shortlist of three, drawn up by the Second Chamber. The shortlist of recommendations from the Second Chamber is
intended to guarantee that the General Chamber of Audit is independent of the government. Before the shortlist is made up the General Chamber of Audit submits its
own list of six recommendations, but the Second Chamber does not have to, and
does not always, follow these.

The rules governing dismissal and the legal position of members of the General
Chamber of Audit are the same as those for members of the Judiciary. The Government Accounts Act sets the number of members at three, from which the government appoints a chairperson. A deputy is appointed for each member. Like the
Council of State, the General Chamber of Audit has a large staff of about 330, without whose work, it would not be possible to achieve an effective financial audit.

335. Nowhere does the Constitution explicitly attribute an advisory role to the
General Chamber of Audit. Article 76 merely speaks of examining the revenues and
expenditures of the State. The Government Accounts Act contains a number of provisions which refer to an advisory role. The General Chamber of Audit can advise
on the efficiency of national administration and the organization and functioning of
government departments. In addition, it provides the ministers concerned, the Minister of Finance and the Chambers of the States General with any information which
it deems necessary in the interests of the State. The recommendations of the General Chamber of Audit are made public (Article 80 of the Constitution).

336. The General Chamber of Audit has three other functions: First, it conducts
a cash audit of the civil service departments which manage national finances and
are therefore responsible for them. Second, it supervises State revenue and expenditure. Its investigation into the lawfulness of the accounts must, among other
things, answer the question as to whether the expenditure conforms to the relevant

budget item. The ministers send statements to the Chamber of Audit. If the Chamber objects to a particular item of expenditure, the minister must accommodate the objections or must ensure that an Act of Parliament is passed – known as an Indemnity Act – to justify the expenditure concerned. Third, the Chamber of Audit directs its attention to the efficiency of central government financial management.

The Chamber of Audit presents the government and parliament with an annual report on its activities over the preceding year. During the 1980s, two parliamentary enquiries were held in the Netherlands which concluded, among other things, that the financial management of national expenditure and the supervision of that management displayed serious shortcomings on a number of important points. Some of the criticism was directed at poor supervision of government finances by the States General and the General Chamber of Audit. Both parliament and the Chamber of Audit have learned a lesson from this. The Chamber of Audit has made efforts in recent years to carry out its responsibilities more effectively. This has resulted in an impressive number of reports identifying numerous alleged financial abuses in government departments.

§3. THE PERMANENT ADVISORY BODIES

337. As well as the Council of State, which is a general advisory body to the government, there are several other advisory bodies which are concerned with specific areas of policy. The Constitution contains one provision on the so-called permanent advisory bodies in matters of legislation and administration of the State (Article 79). These bodies have to be instituted by or pursuant to an Act of Parliament. The requirement for a statutory base is intended to prevent the government from furnishing itself with all kinds of permanent advisory bodies without the consent of parliament, which could de facto have undermined the authority of parliament. The organization, composition and powers of these advisory bodies must also be regulated by Act of Parliament, and they may also be assigned functions other than advisory ones by or pursuant to an Act of Parliament. The Constitution further states that the advice of the permanent advisory bodies shall be made public.

338. To define the concept of permanent advisory body more closely, it is important that they fulfil a permanent advisory role to central government on matters of policy and general regulations. They are also external organizations, which means that at least half of their ordinary members must be persons who are not State civil servants whose main function involves advising their minister on the same problem area as that for which the advisory body has been set up.

It would not be appropriate in a work of this kind to list all the permanent advisory bodies in existence now. Moreover, there are many differences between them, which may or may not be linked with the purpose for which they were set up. Advisory bodies may be set up with a view to representing and obtaining advice from interest groups, obtaining advice from experts, or a combination of these purposes.

There are a number of important advisory bodies which nevertheless deserve mention: the Social Economic Council (*Sociaal-Economische Raad*), the Advisory

Council on Government Policy (*Wetenschappelijke Raad voor het Regerings-beleid*), the Advisory Council for Education (*Onderwijsraad*), the Electoral Council (*Kiesraad*) and the Municipal Finance Board (*Raad voor de Gemeentefinanciën*). Some of these advisory bodies also have functions other than giving advice. The Electoral Council, for example, also functions as the central polling office for elections to the Chambers of the States General. The Social Economic Council also has rule-making and administrative functions.

339. In the Constitution, permanent advisory bodies are mentioned. In addition to these, temporary advisory bodies frequently have been set up. Their institution, organization, composition and powers do not have to be founded on an Act of Parliament. Where this kind of committee is set up by Royal Decree, it is usually referred to as a state commission (*staatscommissie*).

Part IV. Citizenship, Fundamental Rights and Judicial Review

Chapter 1. Rules Concerning Nationality and the Relevance of Nationality

340. Article 2 of the Constitution deals with Dutch nationality, the admission and expulsion of aliens, extradition and the right to leave the country. Dutch nationality is regulated in the Act of the Kingdom on Dutch Nationality. This Act lays down rules for the acquisition and loss of Dutch nationality. Its main points are as follows: One of the main rules is that someone whose father or mother was Dutch at the time of his or her birth, is Dutch. This rule easily leads to cases of dual nationality if other States operate the same principle, and this is often the case. This effect is strengthened by a second basic rule under which married persons retain their own nationality. A child born of such a marriage would therefore have dual nationality. The acknowledgement of a child by a Dutch national and the legitimation of a child and his or her children results in the acquisition of Dutch nationality in the same way as through birth. There is a comparable rule governing cases of adoption.

341. As well as these cases, where Dutch nationality is automatic, some persons have the option of choosing Dutch nationality and some may have it granted by naturalization. The option of Dutch nationality is available to adult foreigners who were born in the Netherlands, Curaçao, Sint Maarten or Aruba and who have lived there since their birth. The option of Dutch nationality may also be available to persons who were born in the Netherlands, Curaçao, Sint Maarten or Aruba, have lived there for at least three years and have been stateless since birth.

The naturalization procedure is as follows: Dutch nationality is granted by Royal Decree upon request. With respect to adults who wish to be considered for naturalization, there must be no objection to their residing for an indefinite period in the Netherlands, Curaçao, Sint Maarten or Aruba; they must have lived in the Netherlands, Curaçao, Sint Maarten or Aruba for five years prior to their request for naturalization, and be deemed to be integrated in one of these countries. In some cases, shorter periods apply. Children under the age of majority are granted citizenship at the same time if the decree thus expressly states.

Loss of Dutch nationality can occur first, through the loss of certain relationships in family law which are listed in the Act of the Kingdom. An adult may moreover lose his or her Dutch nationality by voluntarily assuming another nationality, by declaring that he or she has renounced his or her Dutch nationality, and when he or she has lived for an uninterrupted period of ten years outside the Netherlands, Curaçao, Sint Maarten or Aruba, in the country of his or her birth and whose nationality he or she also possesses, unless his or her residence there was connected with employment or service connected with the Netherlands, Curaçao, Sint Maarten or Aruba, or with employment with an international organization in which the Netherlands is represented. Dutch nationality acquired by naturalization can also be withdrawn in certain other circumstances.

342. Minors lose their Dutch nationality if they are acknowledged, legitimized or adopted by a foreigner if thereby the minor acquires or already possessed the parent's nationality. Subject to the same conditions, minors also lose their Dutch nationality if their father or mother voluntarily assumes another nationality; if their father or mother loses their Dutch nationality as a consequence of renouncement, ten years residence abroad or withdrawal; and finally if they independently acquire the nationality of the father or mother. Two comments need to be added to this. A minor never loses Dutch nationality as long as one of his or her parents possesses it and in other special cases. Furthermore, no one loses his or her Dutch nationality if, as a result, he or she would become stateless.

343. There are a number of important legal consequences attached to the possession of Dutch nationality. We shall do with mentioning just a few of them. The right to vote and to stand for election to the Chambers of the States General and the provincial states is only available to Dutch nationals; the Constitution only grants the right to national assistance (welfare) to Dutch nationals; Dutch nationality is a prerequisite for appointment to certain governmental posts; Dutch nationals have the right of entry to their own country; Dutch nationals cannot, in principle, be extradited.

Chapter 2. Legal Position of Aliens

344. Article 2 of the Constitution states that the rules governing the admission and expulsion of aliens must be set by Act of Parliament. As far as the territory in Europe is concerned, the rules are laid down in the Aliens Act (*Vreemdelingenwet*). Since it came into operation, this Act has been buried under a mass of implementing rules and administrative circulars. The whole field is occupied by specialists, especially in view of the large number of treaties which govern the status of various categories of aliens, for example, EU nationals and refugees. We shall here provide an outline of the main points.

345. A number of requirements must be met for a person to be admitted to the Netherlands. He or she must be in possession of personal identification and a visa or temporary residence permit. In principle, foreigners are admitted for three months. Anyone who wants to stay longer will be admitted for eight days only, during which time he or she can apply for a temporary residence permit. Conditions may be attached to the granting of a temporary residence permit.

A residence permit, which is usually granted after a person has been a temporary resident for five years, offers the holder more legal security and can only be refused for a limited number of reasons. As far as expulsion is concerned, the Aliens Act lays down stricter rules for those possessing a residence permit than for those with only a temporary residence permit.

The statutory regulations governing refugees are quite different from the usual rules. Persons with refugee status are admitted to the territory, and admission can only be refused for strong reasons of public interest if by doing so the refugee would immediately be returned to a country where he or she is threatened with persecution.

346. The Aliens Act contains a number of rules concerning supervision of foreigners. In general, they may be required to carry identity papers and to inform the authorities if they change their place of abode. Those who do not have permission to stay indefinitely may be required to report within a specified period after they come into the country and periodically thereafter. Under certain circumstances, their freedom of movement may be curtailed. Finally, the minister may declare an alien to be undesirable on grounds laid down by the Aliens Act.

347. Aliens who have not been granted permission to stay in the Netherlands, or whose permit has been withdrawn, can be expelled immediately. However, in principle, a reasonable period is allowed for the person to arrange his or her departure. In certain circumstances, aliens may be detained in custody.

348. The Aliens Act makes provision for a special system of legal remedies tailored to the aliens' situation. There are several legal remedies: objection, reconsideration and judicial review. The reconsideration procedure is conducted by the Minister of Security and Justice, who, in cases where a residence permit has been refused, is sometimes obliged to hear the views of the Advisory Committee for Matters concerning Aliens. Where an objection or reconsideration is refused, the person has recourse to a district court. In a number of cases, appeal to the judicial division of the Council of State is possible.

349. Finally we need to mention the special position enjoyed by nationals of other EU countries. EU nationals who come to the Netherlands to work have unimpeded entrance, may seek employment, and as soon as they have found permanent employment they are granted a residence permit valid, in principle, for five years.

Chapter 3. Fundamental Rights and Liberties

§1. GENERAL

350. In Dutch constitutional law and in the doctrine, the fundamental rights and liberties are usually referred to as fundamental rights (*grondrechten*, comparable with the German *Grundrechte*). A distinction is made between the classic fundamental rights on the one hand and social and economic rights on the other. The term political rights is seldom used.

The classic fundamental rights can be invoked before the courts and in most cases establish a duty on the government to abstain. The majority of the social fundamental rights cannot be invoked in court. They are to be considered as instructions addressed to the public authorities to take certain actions to promote the economic, social and cultural well-being of subjects. Since the partial revision of 2022, a general provision is included in the Constitution. It states that the Constitution safeguards fundamental rights and democracy based on the rule of law. Fundamental rights are considered one of the three foundations of the Dutch constitutional system.

351. A number of sources of fundamental rights can be indicated in Dutch constitutional law. In the first place Chapter 1 of the Constitution, entitled Fundamental Rights, comprises twenty-three articles containing the classic and social rights. Elsewhere in the Constitution, one comes across occasional provisions which can be classified as fundamental rights. For example, Article 114 prohibits the imposition of the death penalty, and Article 99 states that the conditions under which exemption from military service is to be granted on account of serious conscientious objection are to be specified by Act of Parliament.

A second source of fundamental rights is primary and secondary EU law and rulings of the European Court of Justice. By virtue of its supranational character, EU law is automatically part of the Dutch national system of law. Because of this, fundamental rights which have been drawn up or recognized at Community level are at the same time national rights. The EU Charter of Fundamental Rights forms an important source of fundamental rights as well. The third source of fundamental rights is provided by various international treaties. The Netherlands adheres to a monist system for the relationship between international law and national law. Under this system, international law is incorporated into national law without transformation and without any national order. Insofar as international law contains provisions which 'can be binding on all persons', it can be invoked in court.

352. The most important treaties for the Netherlands in the sphere of fundamental rights are the ECHR and its protocols, the European Social Charter, the ICCPR with its optional protocol and the International Covenant on Economic, Social and Cultural Rights.

353. Finally, it should be pointed out that under certain circumstances, case law may formulate fundamental rights itself and may apply general legal principles such as the principles of legal certainty and equality.

354. Insofar as supra- or international law offers subjects greater protection than national law, the former prevails over the latter. However, situations sometimes arise where national law offers the subjects more guarantees, in which case the national law, in principle, takes precedence.

§2. CLASSIC FUNDAMENTAL RIGHTS

355. Our analysis of the classic fundamental rights contained in the Constitution is organized around a number of themes. These are:

(a) Who enjoys these fundamental rights?
(b) In what relationships do the fundamental rights apply?
(c) Fundamental rights in vertical relationships.
(d) The system of restrictions.
(e) Fundamental rights as social rights.

After this analysis, we shall proceed to discuss social and international fundamental rights, followed by an analysis of the relevant articles one-by-one.

I. Who Enjoys Fundamental Rights?

356. Classic fundamental rights are, in principle, personal rights enjoyed by individuals without further qualification. Age, nationality and residence are in principle irrelevant. However, certain fundamental rights only apply to Dutch nationals, and residence plays a part in electoral suffrage as does age. As well as individuals, corporate legal persons and groups lacking corporate legal personality may also enjoy fundamental rights, depending on the nature of the right in question. It is reasonable to say that, in general, the government cannot invoke fundamental rights, since their purpose is to protect subjects vis-à-vis the government. Moreover, many fundamental rights could not by their very nature apply to the government. The government cannot have religious faith, cannot be deported and cannot be deprived of its liberty.

II. In What Relationships Do Fundamental Rights Apply?

357. According to the classic view of fundamental rights, namely as a limit on government power, they only apply to the relationship between the government and the subject. This so-called vertical effect (*verticale werking*) does not only apply to the government as such, that is to say in its fulfilment of typical government functions, but it also applies in principle where the government is operating on an equal footing with the subject. This refers to activities carried out by the government which could be or could have been, carried out by an ordinary citizen. The constitutional principle is hence that fundamental rights are valid in whatever capacity the government acts.

358. A second question in this context concerns the validity of fundamental rights for persons who have a special legal position with respect to the government. This may be because they are in a subordinate relationship to the government, as are military personnel and civil servants, or because they have been entrusted to the care of the government, as are prisoners. The parliamentary debate on the 1983 constitutional reform revealed that fundamental rights are fully valid for persons in a special legal position. This means that the constitutional system of restrictions (*see* below) is also applicable to them. One cannot conclude from this that persons in a special legal position have the same freedom to exercise their fundamental rights as ordinary subjects, since the legislature may, on the basis of the constitutional limitation clauses, subject them to more stringent limitations than ordinary subjects.

359. Up to now we have been speaking of the vertical effect of fundamental rights. The so-called horizontal effect (*horizontale werking*) of fundamental rights is one of the themes of constitutional law on which a great deal of confusion exists. This can partly be blamed on the statements of the government during the constitutional reform of 1983. The government asserted that fundamental rights could also operate between one citizen and another, but it did not make clear to what extent and when. Nevertheless, fundamental rights are sometimes applied in case law concerning the relationship between one citizen and another. Fundamental rights were not designed for this, and their wording is not geared to this relationship. Fundamental rights in most cases only enter into the relationships between citizens indirectly, in interpreting open legal concepts such as the civil law concept of good faith (*goede trouw*) or as general legal principles. The courts balance an interest expressed in a fundamental right against other interests protected by civil law. In some cases, fundamental rights are applied as legal principles. The system of limitations which applies in the vertical relationship has no place in the horizontal relationship.

III. Fundamental Rights in Vertical Relationships

360. It will be clear by now that fundamental rights primarily concern the relationship between the government and the subject. The next question is what kind of demands fundamental rights place upon the government. The classic fundamental rights involve a duty on the government to abstain, which can be invoked in court. These fundamental rights can be invoked against the government in all its capacities: as legislature, executive or judge as well as when it is acting on an equal footing with the subject.

While the Constitution grants a number of fundamental rights which can be invoked in court, the precise protection they offer is not clear. Two factors are important in this context: the interpretation of the fundamental rights and the restrictions or limitations which may be imposed upon them. Like all legal concepts, fundamental rights also need to be interpreted. This interpretation leads to a delimitation of the right, that is, a determination of its scope. Thus it is for a court to decide which of a person's activities are protected by his or her right to profess his or her religion or belief. The court does not have to accept everything that the individual experiences or claims as a profession of his or her religion or belief. The Court will apply certain 'objective standards' to the situation.

361. Only when the scope of a fundamental right has been established through interpretation, does the question of restrictions arise. It will be clear that the interpretation of the scope of fundamental rights and restrictions upon the rights can be seen as communicating vessels. If a particular right is narrowly interpreted, then a government Act will be less likely to impose limitations than where the right is interpreted very broadly. It is only possible to speak of limits, therefore, after the range of a particular fundamental right has been established.

362. When does the exercise of public authority constitute a limitation of fundamental rights? The traditional view, which still prevails, is that there is a limitation of a fundamental right if the government exercises its authority to impose limitations in an area where it would not be authorized to do so without a constitutionally recognized competence. We shall now proceed to look at these limitations further.

363. According to their nature and purpose, government activities can be divided into those which aim to limit the exercise of a fundamental right, and those which have unintended consequences for fundamental rights as a consequence of taking care of other interests, such as road safety, public health and so on. These activities have other motives than the limitation of fundamental rights.

The first type of limitations is called particular limitations (*bijzondere beperkingen*), and the second type is called general limitations (*algemene beperkingen*). During the constitutional reform of 1983, the government adopted the view that both types of limitations, to be admissible, must be able to be traced back to a constitutional limitation clause. If this standpoint were to be realized in its pure form it would result in an enormous quantity of legislation, given that the constitutional limitation system requires almost all limitations of fundamental rights to be laid down in an Act of Parliament or to have an explicit basis in such an Act (delegation). In practice, the government's standpoint is not usually followed, either by the legislature or the courts. A way out is found through a reasonable interpretation of the scope of a fundamental right, or through an acceptance (explicit or otherwise) of general limitations.

IV. The System of Limitations

364. When are limitations of fundamental rights admissible? When are they lawful? In general, the answer is that a limitation of a fundamental right is lawful if it conforms to a constitutional limitation clause or, sometimes, criteria developed by the courts. In the constitutional system, three systems of limitation can be distinguished, which may occur separately or in combination. These are competence clauses, clauses specifying legitimate aims and procedural rules. These will be discussed in turn.

365. In the first place there are fundamental rights which, taken literally, cannot be limited, such as the prohibition against the imposition of the death penalty and the prohibition against censorship. In other cases, only the legislature is competent to impose limitations. In still other cases the legislature may impose limitations, but an Act of Parliament may also delegate the power to do so to other central or decentralized offices. Whether delegation is possible or not can be determined on the basis of the delegation terminology in the Constitution, which was discussed earlier.

There are also occasions where authorities other than the legislature are authorized to restrict fundamental rights through their general regulatory powers, that is: without explicit delegation by the legislature. This is true, for example, in the case of the right to distribute printed material. However, the courts have set certain limits to restrictions imposed by these authorities. Absolute prohibitions against the distribution of printed material are not acceptable.

366. As far as the clauses specifying legitimate aims are concerned we can be brief. In the case of some fundamental rights, the legislature or other authorities must take into account the legitimate aims specified in the constitutional provisions, if they wish to limit lawfully the exercise of those rights. It is not possible to state exactly what these criteria require. They are liable to multifarious interpretations by the authority that is imposing the restrictions. The courts tend to show judicial restraint in adjudicating this matter.

367. The procedural requirements which are sometimes set by fundamental rights only need a cursory glance. The rules contained in Article 12 of the Constitution relating to entry into a home without the consent of the occupant is a typical example of such procedural rules. They require in principle that prior identification and notice of purpose must be given, and a written report of the entry issued to the occupant.

V. Classic Fundamental Rights as Social Rights

368. We have shown that classic fundamental rights must be seen primarily as requirements upon the government to abstain from acting. They aim to guarantee a certain area of personal liberty for the individual. Whether this liberty exists in fact or can be realized by the individual is not the main issue. Nevertheless, there has been a tendency in the last years to interpret fundamental rights in such a way that they do not merely bestow rights of non-interference, but give also a right to help from the government. In this way, the classic rights are acquiring some of the traits of social and economic fundamental rights. This interpretation can be found in both national and international spheres. Seen from a social point of view, there is something to be said for such an interpretation. However, the legal problems which it entails are not insignificant. In the first place, there is the question of how far the government's duty to act extends. Second, the limitation clauses of the fundamental rights are not tailored to such an interpretation. Finally, there is the risk that such an interpretation would do precisely what the classic rights aim to resist: government interference, which is already prevalent in most areas of life nowadays.

§3. Social Fundamental Rights

369. The social, economic and cultural rights (referred to in the Dutch context as 'social rights') have an entirely different structure and significance from the classic fundamental rights, even though the Constitution lumps them all together in Chapter 1. Broadly speaking, the following differences between social and classic rights can be indicated: In the first place social rights rarely involve rights which can be enforced in law by a court. During the 1983 constitutional reform, repeated reference was made to claims which are not judicially enforceable. Some care is needed here though, since Articles 18–23 of the Constitution, which were contained in the 1983 constitutional reform proposal on social rights, do contain a couple of provisions which are enforceable in law. Furthermore, courts are not prohibited from interpreting a provision which is formulated as a social fundamental right, as a guaranteed standard.

370. A second difference is that it is difficult to conceive of social fundamental rights having horizontal effect. The citizen is not required to bear the responsibility for sufficient employment, public health and so on, neither under the Constitution nor under international treaties. A third difference is that the question of limitations does not affect social fundamental rights either. A fourth difference can be seen in the constitutional structure of social fundamental rights, which is different from that of classic fundamental rights. While classic rights bestow a right upon every person or every Dutch person, social rights are generally addressed to the government or the legislature. Finally, attention must be given to the relationship between classic and social rights. The Constitution does not recognize any hierarchy of constitutional provisions in general, nor of fundamental rights in particular. Nevertheless, constitutional history has shown that there is a form of subordination between classic and social rights because measures to implement social rights must take the classic fundamental rights into consideration.

§4. International Fundamental Rights

371. In the section on the sources of fundamental rights, we noted that certain treaties form a part of Dutch constitutional law. The two most important treaties for fundamental rights in the Netherlands are the ECHR and the ICCPR with its optional protocol. In addition, the Netherlands has from the beginning recognized the competence of the ECtHR and the Human Rights Committee.

Almost all of the fundamental rights contained in the ECHR and ICCPR are provisions which may be 'binding on all persons' in the sense of Article 93 of the Constitution. Citizens can therefore invoke these rights in court. This is not the case with the social rights laid down in the treaties. They are usually not binding on all persons. Due to the extensive case law and the binding rulings from the ECtHR, the fundamental rights of the European Convention nowadays are most important in Dutch constitutional law.

372. The ECHR and the ICCPR contain a large number of fundamental rights which, with a few exceptions, follow the same broad structure. In general, a treaty provision is structured as follows: the first paragraph describes the right and the second and any subsequent paragraphs give the possible limitations. The limitations in turn usually comprise the following elements: they must be provided by law (*wet, loi*) and they must be necessary in a democratic society in the interests of … (here follows a number of legitimate aims). These criteria specifying the legitimate aims which a restriction may serve do not give rise to any particular questions. They are comparable to the Dutch constitutional criteria. The courts show judicial restraint in reviewing these criteria.

373. The question of what is intended by the word 'law' in the treaties is not so simple to answer. Dutch Courts do not only take this to mean Acts of Parliament but also include in it other legislation, by-laws, policy rules and unwritten law provided they comprise rules or law that is 'accessible' and 'foreseeable'. In this way, national case law aims to conform to that of the ECtHR.

§5. The Specific Classic Fundamental Rights

374. The Constitution opens the catalogue of classic fundamental rights with the principle of equality and the prohibition against discrimination (Article 1 of the Constitution). It is evident from legislation and case law that this is one of the most difficult rights to define, especially where the right is asserted against a legislative authority. What criteria should be used to decide which cases are alike and what discrimination is? Frequently the legislature and the court have to resort to stating that 'under current public opinion' something does or does not amount to unlawful unequal treatment or discrimination.

According to both the legislature and the courts, this article does not rule out certain forms of affirmative action, provided they are of a temporary nature. One of the problems in this context is how long this temporary situation is allowed to continue. It is also difficult to decide which individuals or groups are in a position to be able to claim preferential treatment.

375. One question of particular relevance to Article 1 of the Constitution is that of horizontal effect. In the Netherlands, the prohibition against discrimination tends to be applied not only in the relationship between the government and citizens but also in the relationship between one citizen and another. It ought to be clear that such a development can result in the significance of civil liberties being undermined since one of their aims is precisely to defend differentiation and plurality in the civil society. The Equal Treatment Act (*Algemene wet gelijke behandeling* 1994) contains general rules to provide protection against discrimination on the grounds of religion, belief, political opinion, race, sex, nationality, sexual orientation or civil status.

376. Article 2 of the Constitution, dealing with Dutch nationality and the admission and expulsion of aliens, has already been dealt with above. Both these matters have to be regulated by Act of Parliament. This article also lays down that extradition can only take place pursuant to a treaty, and that everyone has the right to leave the country, except in circumstances laid down by Act of Parliament. A Passport Act (*Paspoortwet*) has been enacted to regulate the issue and withdrawal of passports.

377. Article 3 of the Constitution contains a specification of the principle of equality. It states that all Dutch nationals shall be equally eligible for appointment to public office. However, this provision needs to be interpreted with caution. It does not prevent demands being made concerning suitability for the appointment. These demands may include matters related to a person's political persuasion or, his or her beliefs, notwithstanding the second sentence of Article 1. Furthermore, persons who are not Dutch may be eligible for appointment to many public posts. This is the case for other EU nationals under EU law. The grounds for excluding foreigners from appointment to public office are laid down by Act of Parliament.

378. Article 4 of the Constitution guarantees to all Dutch nationals the right to elect members of the general representative bodies directly and the right to be elected as a member of those bodies (active and passive voting right). Limitations and exceptions to this right may be laid down by Act of Parliament. The text of the Constitution does not make clear which are the general representative bodies. They are currently taken to be only the Second Chamber and First Chamber of the States General, the provincial states and the municipal councils. For that matter, the Constitution itself contains an exception to Article 4, since the members of the First Chamber are not elected directly but indirectly by the members of the provincial states.

379. Article 5 of the Constitution contains an age-old right, the right of petition, which is applicable to all without exception. In practice, petitions directed to the Chambers of the States General are the most important. Both Chambers have petitions committees to deal with petitions. These committees each produce an annual report of their activities.

380. Article 6 of the Constitution contains a right which also has a long history, namely the freedom of religion, which was recognized by the Union of Utrecht as early as 1579. Since the reform of 1983, this protection has been extended to cover freedom of (non-religious) belief. The provision distinguishes between the exercise of this right inside buildings and enclosed places on the one hand, and outside buildings and enclosed places on the other hand. Only the legislature is competent to impose limitations upon the former. In the second situation, the legislature is empowered to delegate in order to protect certain interests. The Act on Public Demonstrations (*Wet openbare manifestaties*) regulates, among other matters, the right to exercise this fundamental right outside buildings and enclosed places. This Act grants specific powers of limitation to municipal councils and mayors.

381. The freedom of expression is protected by Article 7 of the Constitution. The Article distinguishes between the different forms which this freedom can take. Freedom of the press enjoys the strongest protection: censorship is prohibited and the content of published material may only be restricted by Act of Parliament. The distribution of printed matter, however, can also be restricted by decentralized authorities. However, any restrictions applied may not result in a general prohibition or a general licensing system relating to a single specific method of distribution. The case law concerning the right of distribution is extensive and has recognized various separate methods of distribution, such as the distribution of leaflets, posters and the book trade.

382. Paragraph 2 of Article 7 covers radio and television. Censorship is prohibited in these media too, but limitations may be imposed by or pursuant to Acts of Parliament. The most important Act based on this paragraph is the Media Act (*Mediawet*). It regulates both public and commercial broadcasting.

383. Paragraph 3 of Article 7 concerns the expression of opinions by other means than the press, radio and television and demonstrations. Censorship is prohibited here too, and the legislature alone is authorized to impose restrictions upon the content of such expressions. The form, place and time for such expressions may be subjected to restrictions by any authority that has rule-making powers. However, according to the courts, they may not render the exercise of this right completely impossible.

384. Finally, paragraph 4 states that this system does not apply to commercial advertising, which does not enjoy any formal constitutional protection.

385. Article 8 of the Constitution guarantees freedom of association. This may be restricted by Act of Parliament in the interests of public order. Further rules on freedom of association are given in the Civil Code and the Penal Code. Under Article 20 of the second book of the Civil Code, a court must, on the demand of the Public Prosecution Service, ban and disband a legal person (including an association) if its activities are deemed to be in conflict with public order. If it is only the aims of the legal person which conflict with public order, it will be disbanded but not banned. The judge may grant the legal person the opportunity to change their aims within a specified period of time. This system does probably not apply to churches. Article 140 of the Penal Code states that participation in the continued activities of a legal person which has been banned by an irrevocable judicial verdict and thus disbanded is a criminal offence.

386. Article 9 of the Constitution regulates the freedom to hold meetings and demonstrations. Under the first paragraph, the legislature is empowered to set any limitations deemed desirable. However, delegation of the power to impose limitations is bound by the criteria on objectives laid down in paragraph 2. The Act on Public Demonstrations, mentioned in connection with Article 6, regulates the exercise of the right of assembly and demonstration. The Act makes a distinction between public and private places. More restrictions can be imposed in the case of public places.

387. Articles 10–13 inclusive cover the protection of rights in the sphere of privacy (*persoonlijke levenssfeer*).

388. Paragraph 1 of Article 10 states that restrictions to privacy may only be imposed by or pursuant to an Act of Parliament. Therefore, delegation is admissible. Paragraph 2 of Article 10 charges the legislature to lay down rules to protect privacy in connection with the recording and dissemination of personal data. Paragraph 3 charges the legislature to lay down rules in connection with the right of individuals to have access to information recorded concerning them, the use that may be made of such information and to have that information corrected. Paragraphs 2 and 3 have been implemented by a number of Acts of Parliament, among others the Act on Information and the Security Services (*Wet op de inlichtingen- en veiligheidsdiensten*), the Data Protection Act (*Wet basisregistratie personen*), the Data Protection Police Files Act (*Wet politieregisters*), and the EU General Data Protection Regulation and its Implementation Act General Data Protection Regulation.

389. Article 11 of the Constitution states that everyone has the right to inviolability of his or her physical person subject to limitations laid down by or pursuant to an Act of Parliament. This article is actually superfluous in view of paragraph 1 of Article 10, which contains the same possibilities for limitation as Article 11. The most that can be said about Article 11 is that it removes possible uncertainty about the scope of privacy.

Both Article 10, paragraph 1, and Article 11 lend themselves to horizontal application in certain circumstances. In the medical sphere especially, situations might arise where this would be the case.

390. Article 12 of the Constitution contains a provision aimed at protecting privacy within the home against government interference. Paragraph 1 prohibits entry without the consent of the occupant except in circumstances laid down by or pursuant to an Act of Parliament and then only by such persons as are authorized by or pursuant to an Act of Parliament. Paragraph 2 gives a number of procedural rules which must be followed when a dwelling is entered against the occupant's will unless an exception laid down in an Act of Parliament applies. Identification must be produced before the property is entered and a reason for entry given. Afterwards, a written report must in principle be given to the occupant. The General Act on Entry of Private Homes (*Algemene wet op het binnentreden*) contains more detailed rules concerning this fundamental right.

391. Article 13 of the Constitution guarantees everyone's right to respect the privacy of his correspondence and telecommunications. This right cannot be violated except in cases laid down by or pursuant to an Act of Parliament, by order of a court or, in the interests of state security, by or with the authorisation of those designated for the purpose by Act of Parliament

392. The first two paragraphs of Article 14 deal with expropriation. Expropriation may only take place in the general interest and under prior guarantee of compensation, in accordance with rules laid down by or pursuant to an Act of Parliament. In an emergency, prior assurance of compensation is not necessary. Narrowly interpreted, this article offers few real guarantees against expropriation. The concept of general interest is open to multiple interpretations. The court, though, tests expropriation orders against the prohibition of arbitrariness. The requirement that compensation be paid is the most important guarantee to the citizen. Up to now, compensation has always been calculated according to the market value of the expropriated goods. However, the legislature and the court may opt to calculate compensation based on user value, for example, if they wish. Further rules governing expropriation are laid down in the Expropriation Act (*Onteigeningswet*).

393. Paragraph 3 of Article 14 regulates the situation where there is no transfer of ownership, but property is nevertheless lost or the exercise of the owner's rights to it are restricted. The Constitution does not guarantee full or partial compensation in these circumstances. The legislature has the duty to lay down rules on whether compensation is paid or not.

394. A better protected fundamental right is to be found in Article 15 of the Constitution, referred to as the habeas corpus provision. Paragraph 1 requires that there be a ground laid down in an Act of Parliament before anyone may be deprived of his or her liberty. Paragraph 2 states that anyone who has been deprived of his or her liberty other than by an order of a court can request a court to order his or her release. Where such a request is made, the case must be heard by a court within a period of time specified by Act of Parliament. The court must order the person's immediate release if he or she is found to have been detained unlawfully. Thus anyone deprived of his or her liberty without the involvement of a court has a right to a speedy judicial hearing of his or her case.

Paragraph 3 offers a guarantee against unreasonably long remand detention by providing that anyone who is remanded in custody pending trial must have his or her case heard within a reasonable period of time. Finally, paragraph 4 gives a general regulation with regard to the exercise of fundamental rights by those who have been lawfully deprived of their liberty. They may be restricted in the exercise of their fundamental rights insofar as the exercise thereof is incompatible with the deprivation of liberty. Thus a completely different system of limitations upon fundamental rights applies to prisoners than that which applies to ordinary citizens.

395. Article 16 contains the classic prohibition against retrospective legislation in the area of substantive criminal law. As far as other types of legislation are concerned, constitutional law does not rule out retrospective force. Nevertheless, it is generally accepted that laws which are onerous for citizens should not work retrospectively, except in very special circumstances.

396. As mentioned before, Article 17, paragraph 1 includes a right for everyone to access independent and impartial tribunals to settle legal disputes and criminal cases. Since the partial revision of 2022, it states: Everyone shall have the right, in the determination of his rights and obligations or of any criminal charge against him, to a fair trial within a reasonable time before an independent and impartial tribunal. Article 17, paragraph 2, of the Constitution grew out of the former *ius de non evocando*, but it no longer has this meaning. Since 1814, class-based jurisdiction has no longer been recognized in the Netherlands. The current meaning of Article 17 is that subjects may not be deprived by the government of their right to appeal to a judicial procedure to which they are entitled under the law. Constitutional history has shown that this provision does not rule out the establishment of special courts, provided the establishment of such courts is founded upon an Act of Parliament.

397. The fundamental rights discussed above were classified as classic fundamental rights at the time of the reform of the Constitution. Articles 18–23 also contain some provisions which can be invoked in court, but most of them are social and economic rights which, as was noted earlier, only involve instructions. The following fundamental rights which can be invoked in court still deserve mention.

398. Article 18, paragraph 1 states that everyone is entitled to legal representation in judicial and administrative proceedings. The government may not prevent a citizen from obtaining legal representation.

399. Article 19, paragraph 3 guarantees the right to a free choice of work, though this right may be limited by or pursuant to an Act of Parliament. In practice, many limitations exist as a result of demands with regard to qualifications, place of residence, rules regarding shop closing hours, driving time, and so on.

400. Article 20, paragraph 3 guarantees to all Dutch nationals living in the Netherlands the right to a minimum income, and national assistance (welfare), to be regulated by Act of Parliament.

401. Finally, we point to Article 23 of the Constitution which guarantees the freedom to provide education. As with almost all fundamental rights this is also subject to limitations. The government has the right to supervise the provision of education in accordance with rules laid down by or pursuant to an Act of Parliament and to set standards of competence and moral integrity for teachers for forms of education designated by Act of Parliament. A special feature of Article 23 is that it assumes as a matter of principle that State and denominational education will be financed by the government on an equal footing. The latter have to demonstrate the same standards as the State schools. Requirements regarding educational standards are regulated by Act of Parliament, having due regard to the so-called freedom of orientation according to religious or other beliefs. Thus, in setting standards for the denominational schools the legislature must leave their particular character, based on religion or other beliefs, unaffected.

§6. Social, Economic and Cultural Rights

402. As has been noted Articles 18–23 of the Constitution contain what are called in the Dutch situation social fundamental rights. There is little point in dwelling on these provisions for very long. In principle, they are not enforceable in law. They should be considered as government tasks, and resemble parts of party political programmes. The extent to which they can be realized is very dependent upon socioeconomic developments and the financial priorities set by those in power. This is clear from the following items referred to in the social fundamental rights: legal aid to people on a low income, sufficient employment, employee participation at the workplace, the right of the population to secure the means of subsistence, the distribution of wealth, the right to social security, the duty of the authorities to keep the country habitable, the improvement of the environment, the promotion of public health and provision of sufficient housing, the creation of opportunities for social and cultural development and recreation, and the continuing responsibility for education. These all amount to government tasks rather than citizens' rights. We shall therefore give no further consideration to the social fundamental rights.

Chapter 4. Constitutional Protection of Minorities

403. The question of the protection of minorities within a State can be viewed on two levels. The first is the level of constitutional organization and the constitutional offices themselves. At this level, Dutch constitutional law contains a number of provisions which protect minorities vis-à-vis majorities. In the first place, there is the procedure for constitutional reform itself. At the second reading of a bill to revise the Constitution, a majority of two-thirds of the votes is required in both Chambers of the States General. Also, a bill approving a treaty which departs from the Constitution requires a two-thirds majority.

There are other occasions when a qualified majority is required. This is the case when a person is to be excluded from succession by Act of Parliament, when a person is appointed as successor to a King who is still alive when a person is appointed King, and when rules are drawn up regarding the salary and pension arrangements for members and former members of the States General.

There are other instances of minority protection at parliamentary level. The procedure whereby treaties are tacitly approved can be halted if one-fifth of the constitutional number of members of one of the Chambers of the States General object, and a session can be held behind closed doors if one-tenth of the members present demand it. Furthermore, every MP has the right to demand information from a minister state secretary.

404. The second level on which it is possible to speak of the protection of minorities is in the relationship between the government and society. First of all, of course, there are fundamental rights to which individuals and groups are entitled. These rights enable minorities to practice their religion or belief, express their opinions, have their own organizations, hold meetings, and so on. In connection with fundamental rights, there are various statutory rules which release individuals from statutory obligations on the grounds of conscientious objection.

405. The second type of protection at this level is referred to as positive discrimination or affirmative action. Temporary preferential treatment of minority groups based on criteria such as race and sex has been judged acceptable by both the legislature and the courts, where normally speaking a difference in treatment would not be admissible. Thus, in applications to government posts, women are quite often preferred over men, and not only when the candidates are equally qualified. When subsidies are granted, minority groups sometimes get extra support, as with the education of immigrants, for example.

406. In the third place, there is the phenomenon of group actions. In a number of cases, group actions to protect interests of the group, or even in areas of general interest such as environmental protection, have been judged admissible by the courts, even though the members of the group had no immediate interest in the action.

407. In conclusion, we need to mention a form of indirect protection of minorities. Since 1985 residents of a municipality who are not Dutch have had the right to elect and to be elected as members of the municipal council. This also opens up the opportunity for them to become members of the municipal executive, since any member of the town council may be appointed to the municipal executive.

Chapter 5. Judicial Review of Administrative Action

§1. Prior Legal Protection

408. Under the rule of law, citizens have many means at their disposal to assist them to contest decisions or actions by the public authorities which infringe on their rights or interests. In the first place, protection of citizens against the administration is offered by the Judiciary and by special administrative courts. In addition, this protection can be given through appeal to a higher administrative body, which is known as administrative appeal. These three forms of legal protection against administrative activities are dealt with in the next section.

409. Before the citizen gets to the stage of appealing to a judicial body or an administrative appeals body, there are other means available to him or her to protest against the administration. These are the avenues referred to as prior legal protection.

410. First of all, there is the right of petition laid down in Article 5 of the Constitution. This right enables a citizen to submit a request to the competent authority asking it to abandon, undo, or amend a decision by which he or she feels himself to be disadvantaged.

Second, there are opportunities for citizens to participate in the decision-making procedures of public authorities. A number of Acts, especially in the area of town and country planning, contain detailed provisions on consultation procedures.

A third form of prior legal protection is the opportunity to submit a written objection to an administrative authority requesting it to reconsider a decision it has taken. This is not a case of administrative appeal, since the same administrative authority which took the decision is being asked to reconsider it. An objection in writing can, in principle, be effective in all cases where the administrative authority is free to reverse its decision. There is a legal duty upon the authority to reconsider, if new arguments are presented, or if there is an objection procedure laid down in statutory rules.

411. This type of legal protection has gained importance over the last decades. The objection procedure (*bezwaarschriftenprocedure*) was set up initially to try to avoid too many court appeals. Now, the general view is that this procedure is a separate and important form of legal protection. It has the following advantages. It creates an opportunity to reconsider aspects that were given insufficient consideration when the decision was originally taken. Often people other than those who prepared the original decision are involved in the reassessment. This is the case when the decision in response to the written objection is in fact taken at a 'higher level'. Frequently a more or less independent advisory committee is called in to give the matter serious reconsideration. Practice has shown that solutions are often found to the dispute.

In addition, the objection procedure plays a role in identifying and solving shortcomings in administrative organization. These positive aspects have prompted the legislature to expand considerably the written objection procedures. The General

Administrative Law Act (*Algemene Wet Bestuursrecht*) now prescribes that the written objection procedure must in principle always be followed before an appeal is made to an administrative court.

§2. *EX POST* LEGAL PROTECTION: JUDICIAL REVIEW

412. Up to the present day, the system of legal protection for citizens against the administration in the Netherlands has been clearly pluriform. In general terms, three elements of this system can be distinguished. First, the ordinary Judiciary has a role, on the basis of Article 112, paragraph 1 of the Constitution. Second, under Article 112, paragraph 2, of the Constitution and the laws based on that article, a number of administrative courts have been set up which offer legal protection to citizens in specific areas of administrative activity. Third, there are the administrative appeal bodies which are based on Article 115 of the Constitution.

413. The current system of legal protection is the culmination of a long historical development. We have already seen in Part III, Chapter 1 that upon the creation of the Dutch Constitution in 1814, the principle of the separation of powers (*trias politica*) was initially predominant. Judicial supervision of government operations on behalf of the citizens did not fit into this conception very well. That is why until 1844 the King, pursuant to the so-called Conflict Order (*Conflictenbesluit*), which was borrowed from French law, had the competence to take the settlement of disputes between the administration and citizens out of the hands of the Judiciary and settle them himself. The idea of the rule of law, in which judicial control over government activities is an important basic principle, was a fairly late development in Dutch constitutional law. The constitutional reform of 1887 opened the way for disputes involving institutions of the administration to be settled either by the Judiciary or by administrative courts. However, the Dutch legislature proved unable to create a uniform system of legal protection against administrative action. Consequently, in the early years of the twentieth century, the ordinary Judiciary took the lead and developed extensive case law in this area. Nevertheless, as the century progressed, after a great deal of procrastination, the legislature set up a number of administrative courts to deal with specific areas, so that the role of the ordinary Judiciary became more and more a supplementary one.

414. Against this background, it is advisable in the first place to pay some attention to the development of civil case law in the sphere of legal protection against administrative action. We noted in Part III, Chapter 5 that under Article 112 of the Constitution, the Judiciary is always competent, as long as a plaintiff claims that a civil right has been infringed or that he or she has a claim under private or public law. Thus, in principle, all disputes between the citizen and the government fall within the competence of the ordinary civil courts. Nevertheless, from way back in time, ordinary (civil law) courts have always approached disputes involving a public authority differently from disputes between citizens.

The separation of powers principle has continued to play a certain role in case law. In the nineteenth century, courts still exercised great restraint as far as the settlement of disputes between citizens and public authorities was concerned. Where a dispute concerned the lawfulness of a typical official act, the court adopted the position that it could not test such an act against rules of private law. The court only accepted that it had a role in settling the dispute when the administration entertained legal relations on an equal footing with citizens.

415. The turning point came in 1901. The Supreme Court (Supreme Court 10 May 1901 *Rotterdamse huizen*) decided that civil law was in principle also applicable to the administration when it was acting as a public authority. The Supreme Court considered that both natural persons and legal persons could be legal subjects of civil law. Government bodies like the State, province and municipality could be considered as legal persons who are to comply with civil law standards. The activities of public offices must, according to the judgment of the Supreme Court, be attributed to the legal person of which these offices are part. With this judgment, the Supreme Court gave a decisive thrust to civil case law on acts of public authorities which contravene the law. In the following, a number of elements of this case law receive further explanation.

416. After 1901 the Supreme Court concluded, that the public authorities acted unlawfully vis-à-vis the citizen not only if they broke a private law rule, but also if they broke a rule of public law. In later cases, the Supreme Court refined this standpoint. The decisive question is whether the rule of public law which has been broken imposes a duty in law upon the public authority with respect to the citizen. Only if the citizen appeals to a rule intended to provide guarantees to citizens is his or her claim sustainable in the civil law court.

The classic fundamental rights contained in Chapter 1 of the Constitution are examples of this. Moreover, it should be noted that it is not just written law which provides standards for judicial review. Both unwritten standards of civil law developed in case law and administrative case law, such as the general principles of proper administration, have been increasingly used as the years have gone by as criteria by which to judge the lawfulness of government action.

417. It is important to realize that powers under administrative law are often laid down in very broad terms. Government authorities possess a measure of discretion in how they carry out their powers. In such cases, courts take into account the statutory definition of the government task, the nature of the task, and the circumstances under which it is being carried out.

Using these factors as a guide, a court defines the boundaries within which the administration is free to use its discretion. Thus, the courts have limited powers of judicial review, that is to say, they must also take into account the administration's discretionary powers. In this context, a court investigates the question of whether the government body, after balancing the interests of the parties involved, could have arrived at the decision which it did in all reasonableness. Limited judicial review of government decisions where the authority possesses discretionary powers, reveals a certain restraint on the part of the court with respect to official decisions. This attitude can be explained in terms of the *trias politica* principle. The courts must not usurp the role of the legislature or the administration.

418. The administration occupies a special position in the rulings of the civil law courts in other areas of civil law, apart from the question of unlawful acts. Where the administration exercises the right of ownership and in connection with obligations flowing from contracts to which the government is a party, the public interest – which at least in law is always a characteristic of government action – may mean that specific civil law rules must not be applied. This can affect a citizen disadvantageously. At the present time, however, courts are more inclined to make a compensation order against the administration in such cases.

419. In carrying out an official task, the government authorities often have the option of employing either civil law rights or administrative law powers based on statutory regulations. The question that arises here is whether they are free in their choice of either the administrative law or civil law means. According to the case law of the Supreme Court, the government authorities are free to use the private law route in dealing with matters of public interest, even if an administrative law route is available unless this is specifically prohibited in an Act of Parliament or if it would involve misuse of powers or authority. In the Supreme Court's view, the law prohibits the use of the civil law route if, for example, this would lead to the law being obstructed in an unacceptable way. This would be the case, for example, if use of the civil law route resulted in the inapplicability of a system of legal protection for citizens founded on the relevant rules of administrative law. In such a case, the court would decide that in view of the special legal protection offered to the citizen by the rules of administrative law, the authorities are bound to follow the administrative law route.

420. With respect to the official exercise of public law powers vis-à-vis citizens, it should also be noted that in principle all government Acts are subject to adjudication by courts. In other words, courts may adjudicate the lawfulness of legislation as well as administration, and the administration of justice too. It is obvious that the majority of cases before the courts concern the lawfulness of administrative action regarding citizens. Nevertheless, there are also occasions when courts are asked to rule on the lawfulness of legislation. In 1969, the Supreme Court (Supreme Court 24 January 1969 *Pocketbooks II*) judged that the State had acted unlawfully in issuing a ministerial regulation concerning the establishment of bookshops because the regulation was found to be in conflict with the freedom of the press (Article 7 of the Constitution).

In 1986, the Supreme Court (Supreme Court 16 May 1986 *Landbouwvliegers*) ruled that courts are competent to declare an Order in Council not binding and its implementation unlawful, if arbitrariness was involved to the extent that the government could not in all reasonableness have enacted the rule in question. The Supreme Court did make an exception in this judgment as far as Acts of Parliament are concerned, consistent with the interpretation by the Supreme Court of the prohibition of judicial review laid down in Article 120 of the Constitution.

421. We have mentioned above that the courts are competent to adjudicate the lawfulness of judicial decisions. This does not mean judicial review to a higher instance or cassation, but the question of unlawful action by the courts in judgments which are res judicata. This question has not been developed very much in Dutch constitutional law to date. The Supreme Court has taken the position that the State can only be held responsible in exceptional circumstances for unlawful court decisions. Only if, during the preparation of a judicial decision, fundamental legal principles are disregarded to such an extent that the case cannot be regarded as having been dealt with properly and impartially, and if there is, or was, no legal remedy available, then the State can be held liable for contravening Article 6 of the ECHR and Fundamental Freedoms (Supreme Court 3 December 1971 *Onrechtmatige rechtspraak*).

422. Finally, we come to the question of what sanctions the civil court can use against a government authority which has acted unlawfully towards a citizen. In principle, the court can award compensation, order the government authority to take a particular action or prohibit a particular action. In practice, courts tend to be fairly conservative in the action they take, usually providing a compensation award. The Supreme Court (Supreme Court 21 March 2003 *Waterpakt*) decided in 2003 that it is impossible for a court to make an order or prohibition against the State which would have the effect of requiring new legislation because such an order would raise objections in the light of the traditional place of the judiciary in the Dutch Constitution. As we have seen before the Supreme Court reversed the *Waterpakt* Case in part in *the Urgenda Climate* Case (Supreme Court 20 December 2019).

423. We have been discussing judicial review of the civil law courts of the Judiciary. However, within the Judiciary, this function is not exercised exclusively by these courts. In Part III, Chapter 5 we said that the Supreme Court, the courts of appeal and a number of district courts have tax chambers. The General Tax Act gives citizens the opportunity to appeal to the tax chamber of the district court against tax assessments. Thereafter, appeal and in last instance cassation to the Supreme Court is also available against the decision of the district court. Furthermore, all the district courts are administrative courts in first instance. In addition, all courts fulfil a special judicial review function, seen from a constitutional perspective, because they all test lower legal rules against higher ones. Consider, for example, the decisions of the courts in criminal cases on the compatibility of lower rules, such as municipal penal regulations, with fundamental rights laid down in the Constitution and with treaties.

424. As far as the judicial review function of administrative courts is concerned, the first thing to be said is that the developments here have been shaped not so much by case law (as in the case of the civil courts) as by legislation. For a long time, as was explained above, the Dutch legislature was not in favour of setting up general administrative courts. As time went by, the legislature gradually established special courts in specific areas (social security, civil servants, industrial organizations), which adjudicate certain limited categories of administrative disputes. Through narrowly defined competence clauses on access to the court and its decision-making powers, the legislature aimed to keep a firm grip on the scope of judicial supervision of the executive.

The enactment of the Administrative Decisions Appeals Act in 1975 did considerably extend this judicial supervision, though. As of 1 January 1976, citizens had the opportunity under this Act of a supplementary general appeal, in principle against all administrative decisions of an individual character, to an independent administrative court, the Judicial Division of the Council of State. On 1 January 1994, the General Administrative Law Act (*Algemene Wet Bestuursrecht*) entered into force. Since then, citizens have had the possibility of a general appeal against nearly all administrative decisions to the district courts, against whose decisions appeal can be brought before the Judicial Division of the Council of State or the administrative Central Court of Appeal.

425. It would not be appropriate in this work to give a detailed description of the different aspects of the judicial process in these and other administrative courts. We shall confine ourselves to a brief outline of some general features which are characteristic of judicial review by administrative courts.

The first characteristic of judicial review in administrative courts is that, unlike the situation with regard to civil courts, the legal personality of the government organization is irrelevant. The citizen directs his or her appeal against the decision itself, which is taken by a public authority, such as the government, a minister or the municipal executive. Next, it should be noted that not all administrative decisions are subject to appeal in this way. Thus, the General Administrative Law Act excludes 'generally binding provisions' (*algemeen verbindende voorschriften*) and policy rules from review by an administrative court. It must be remembered, however, that citizens do have the possibility to appeal to a civil law court against generally binding provisions and other generally applicable decisions, as has been explained above.

426. As far as procedures in administrative courts are concerned, interested parties only have a short period, usually six weeks, after the contested decision has been taken within which to appeal. There are not many formal requirements that the written appeal has to comply with. In other respects, too, administrative procedural law is characterized by a minimum of formal requirements. The court has a great deal of freedom in how to conduct the case. The court may, for example, supplement the grounds for appeal ex officio. The administrative court procedure is inquisitorial. Legal representation is usually not compulsory.

427. Like the civil law courts, the administrative courts test the decision or action of the executive against statutes and unwritten law. This is known as appeal on the grounds of lawfulness. Globally, the following grounds for appeal can be invoked:

(1) the decision contravenes a generally binding provision;
(2) in issuing an order, the executive has clearly used its powers for purposes other than those for which the powers were granted, so-called *détournement de pouvoir*;
(3) in considering the various interests involved, the executive could not reasonably have arrived at the decision that it did (arbitrariness);

(4) the executive has in some other way contravened a generally accepted principle of proper administration.

These other principles of proper administration can be subdivided into formal principles, such as the requirement that the contested decision be carefully prepared and comprehensibly reasoned, and substantive principles such as the principle of equality and the principle of legal certainty.

Administrative courts are generally competent to annul executive decisions. They also have powers of suspension and are able to take interim measures in summary proceedings. They are authorized to impose damages or award compensation. Depending on the situation, the administrative court may settle the case itself.

428. To conclude this section a few observations remain to be made on the system of administrative appeals. Administrative appeal refers to a situation where a decision by one government authority can be submitted to another government authority for review, the latter usually being part of a different sector of government or at a different level of administration than the former. We have seen already that administrative appeal is not a form of appeal to an independent court, but a way of settling disputes by the executive. Nevertheless, in Chapter 6 on the administration of justice, the Constitution does devote a special provision (Article 115) to the legal protective function of administrative appeal. The administrative appeal authority, like the civil and administrative courts, investigates the lawfulness of government decisions. In addition, it examines the 'appropriateness' of government decisions. Aspects of policy of a political or financial nature, for example, may be brought into consideration. This is a clear difference between the administrative appeal and judicial review of administrative action. Furthermore, the administrative appeal authority takes account of all the facts and circumstances in arriving at its decision, including those which came into being after the contested decision. In legal doctrine this is known as an *ex-nunc* review, to be distinguished from the usual judicial *ex tunc* review, where only the facts and circumstances which were applicable when the decision was taken are used as a measure for review. The administrative appeal authority also has other powers which extend beyond those of a judge. It was pointed out earlier that the administrative court may in some situations be competent to settle a case by substituting its own judgment for the original decision. While in the case of the judiciary this is rather an exception, it is the rule in the case of administrative appeal.

429. Article 115 of the Constitution states that administrative appeal is available for certain disputes – administrative disputes. It does not prescribe a statutory foundation. In principle, therefore, any government institution may open up a route to administrative appeal. There are no general statutory rules guaranteeing the institution of such an appeals procedure. In practice, an administrative appeal is usually made to the municipal council, the provincial executive or a minister. Since the introduction of the supplementary general appeal to the judicial division of the Council of State (1975), followed by the General Administrative Law Act (1994), the citizen also has the possibility of appeal to an administrative court after an administrative appeal.

430. It should be noted that for nearly a century the so-called Crown Appeal was the most authoritative form of administrative appeal. Due to a judgment of the ECtHR against the Netherlands in 1985 (ECtHR 23 October 1985 *Benthem*) the legislature decided in 1987 to suppress most cases of Crown Appeals. In 1994, the Crown Appeal was completely abandoned and replaced by a review by administrative courts.

431. Finally, it should be noted that the Crown's general power of annulment over the decisions of lower authorities is not regarded as a form of administrative appeal in Dutch constitutional law. In Part II, Chapter 2 we saw that the annulment of the orders of the decentralized authorities is a form of 'repressive' supervision in decentralized government. This power of annulment can also fulfil a legal protective function, since the citizen may use his or her right of petition to request the competent authority to overturn a decision taken by a lower authority to which he or she objects.

§3. OPEN GOVERNMENT AND THE OMBUDSMAN

432. The openness of government functioning is now considered to be an important principle of democracy. The Constitution gives expression to this principle in a number of places. As we have seen, the meetings of the States General are in principle open to the public (Article 66), as are the recommendations of the Council of State, the General Chamber of Audit and the permanent advisory bodies on legislation and administration (Article 80). One can also point to Article 121 of the Constitution which states that in principle, court hearings shall be held in public and that judgments shall be pronounced in public.

433. In addition, Article 110 of the Constitution states that as a general rule government bodies should practice openness in the exercise of their duties, in accordance with rules laid down by Act of Parliament. The Open Government Act (*Wet Open Overheid*) gives further rules on this. This Act gives citizens the right to information from government bodies insofar as that information is recorded in document form. It covers ministers, the executive bodies of the provinces, municipalities, the water boards and public industrial organizations, and nearly all other administrative offices. As an extension to Article 110 of the Constitution, this Act also imposes a duty upon government bodies to publish information about their policies where this is in the interests of good and democratic administration, on their own initiative.

Information may be withheld in certain circumstances, for example, if the information could threaten the unity of the Crown or could damage the security of the State. The Act also assumes that information will not be divulged if the benefit from doing so is outweighed by other interests named in the Act.

If an official body decides not to comply with a request for information, then the citizen may, after an objection procedure, appeal against this decision to the district court. The Open Government Act not only enables the citizen to monitor government policy to a certain extent, but it is also important from the point of legal protection. As a result of access to government information, the citizen is sometimes able to take court action at an early stage if he or she feels his or her interests are damaged through government activities.

434. The National Ombudsman supplements the legal protection available through the civil and administrative courts and the administrative appeals procedure. The office of Ombudsman, which is held by a single person, was established by the National Ombudsman Act (*Wet Nationale Ombudsman*). Later on, the Constitution devoted an article to the Ombudsman (currently Article 78a). The Ombudsman is appointed by the Second Chamber for a six-year term. The role of the Ombudsman is not strictly to pronounce judgment or to advise. It resembles the judicial function insofar as he or she expresses an independent judgment on concrete actions of government authorities. It resembles the advisory function in that the Ombudsman's judgment is not binding on the government body concerned.

The powers of the Ombudsman are enumerated in the National Ombudsman Act. They relate, in general, to the ministers, to the institutions of provinces, municipalities and water boards, insofar as these have been designated by ministerial decree, and to other administrative authorities unless they have been excluded by Order in Council.

435. The Ombudsman may initiate investigations in response to a complaint or upon his or her own initiative, though the latter situation rarely presents itself in practice. The Ombudsman reports on whether the authority concerned has or has not acted properly in the situation under investigation. This entails more than just investigating the legality of the official action.

The National Ombudsman Act contains certain provisions which limit the Ombudsman's powers. He or she may not investigate matters of general government policy or the general policy of a specific authority. If the matter concerns generally binding provisions, or there is an appeals procedure open via an administrative court, or if there is a procedure pending in a court of law, the Ombudsman is not authorized to investigate.

When the Ombudsman has concluded his or her investigations, he or she makes a report on his or her findings and his or her recommendations. These have no force in law. The Ombudsman reports annually to the Chambers of the States General and the ministers.

Part V. Specific Items

Chapter 1. War Powers, Treaties and Foreign Affairs

436. Articles 96–100 of the Constitution contain a number of provisions relating to war powers.

437. Article 96 of the Constitution opens with the declaration-of-war statement. The government is authorized to declare the Kingdom to be in a state of war. Except in practical situations where this is impossible, the exercise of this power requires prior approval by the States General, which consider and decide the issue in a joint session. Traditionally, the intent of the declaration of war is that the government may not declare a war of aggression but only that the Kingdom is at war due to actions by third parties. The declaration of war traditionally has significance only in international legal matters. In the course of the twentieth century, the declaration of war has become altogether obsolete in international law. Wars are nowadays no longer declared officially. They are in fact conducted without any form of prior declaration. In that sense Article 96 of the Constitution has no practical significance anymore. For the deployment of the Dutch armed forces, such as in recent decades in Afghanistan or Iraq, Article 96 of the Constitution is not applied.

Article 97 of the Constitution contains several provisions regarding the Dutch armed forces. This article describes, as task of the armed forces, the defence and protection of the interests of the Kingdom as well as the enforcement and enhancement of the international rule of law (Article 97, paragraph 1). This article also sets out that the government has supreme authority over the armed forces (Article 97, paragraph 2). In other words, the government has political authority over the armed forces. This does not, however, imply that this authority is exclusive in the sense that other offices, such as the States General, may not exercise authority. For example, Article 97 of the Constitution does not prevent parliament from setting rules about the structure and organization of the armed forces.

Article 98 of the Constitution determines that the armed forces consist of volunteers and that it can also have conscripts. The army, therefore, does not by definition have to consist of conscripts. The legislature has an obligation to establish detailed rules for military service. Exemption from military service due to grave conscientious objections must also be regulated in the law (Article 99 of the Constitution).

438. In principle, all Dutch males aged 17 and over, and since 2018, also all females aged 17 and over, may be called up for military service. Serious conscientious objection to military service is acknowledged, in which case the objector has to carry out a different form of service which is one-third longer than the time spent in military service. Since 1997, however, military service has been suspended. At present, the Netherlands only has a regular army.

Since its revision in 2000, the Constitution contains, in Article 100, a separate provision with regard to the deployment of the armed forces. The new constitutional article regulates the involvement of parliament regarding the deployment or making available of the armed forces for the enforcement or advancement of the international rule of law. The article states that the government is obliged to inform the States General in advance. Information in advance is intended to mean notification to the Chambers of the States General of the government's decision to deploy armed forces at such early moment that the Chambers have the possibility in principle to exchange ideas with the government before the actual deployment of troops. In light of this possibility that the Chambers have for consultation before the decision is effectively made, the position has been defended that Article 100 of the Constitution establishes a 'substantive right of consent' for the States General for the deployment of armed forces. After all, the Chambers have the opportunity to express their opinion regarding the decision of the government to deploy armed forces. However, this position is not convincing. The Chamber can only express an opinion regarding a government decision through a resolution. Such a resolution only binds the Chamber itself but not the government.

Under the Standing Orders, resolutions generally give the Chambers only the possibility of expressing an opinion or wish. For the government, requesting and obtaining permission from the Chambers to deploy the armed forces is not a constitutional requirement. The government autonomously decides on this and is only required to inform the Chambers. It needs neither formal nor substantive parliamentary consent. As such, it is misleading to speak of a parliamentary right of consent in the context of Article 100 of the Constitution.

439. Articles 90–94 inclusive of the Constitution deal with international relations. The most important points here concern the power to enter into treaties, the procedures involved and the effect of treaties within the national legal order. Before going into this any further, it must be noted that EU (EC) law does not come under these provisions. Since the judgments of the European Court of Justice of 1963 and 1964 (European Court of Justice 5 February 1963 *Van Gend &Loos* and European Court of Justice 15 July 1964 *Costa/Enel*), it has been accepted that the EU system of law is a supranational system and that it is therefore not subject to national law regulating the effect of classic international law within the national legal order. The observations which follow therefore only relate to classic international law.

440. The Constitution does not actually state which national authority is competent to enter into treaties. However, it can be inferred from constitutional history that this power rests with the government. However, the government may not commit the Kingdom to binding provisions under international law without the approval of the States General. There are a number of circumstances, specified in the

Approval and Publication of Treaties Act *(Rijkswet goedkeuring en bekendmaking van verdragen)*, where this prior approval is not required. The Constitution does not prescribe the form that this approval has to take. That is regulated in the same Act.

441. A distinction must be made between explicit and tacit approval. Explicit approval is effected by Act of Parliament. The procedure for tacit approval is as follows: The government places the treaty before both Chambers of the States General for tacit approval. Approval is granted unless, within thirty days, one of the Chambers, or the Speaker acting on behalf of one of the Chambers, or at least one-fifth of the constitutional number of members of the Chambers indicates that they wish to have the treaty approved explicitly. In that case, a bill to approve the treaty has to be submitted.

442. Article 91, paragraph 3, of the Constitution, contains a construction that one seldom meets in the constitutional law of western States. Under Dutch constitutional law, treaties which conflict with the Constitution, or may lead to conflicts with it, may nevertheless be entered into. Most other western States do not allow treaties to be concluded that conflict with their national Constitutions, without the Constitution first being revised. This is not necessary in the Netherlands, but a treaty which departs from provisions of the Constitution has to be approved by Act of Parliament voted by both Chambers with at least a two-thirds majority. However, the question of whether a treaty conflicts with the Constitution or not is decided by a simple majority. Moreover, the Judiciary may not judge whether a treaty which conflicts with the Constitution has been concluded in accordance with constitutional requirements. Article 120 of the Constitution rules this out where it states that the courts may not review the constitutionality of treaties.

443. Treaties produce a bond under international law between States or other subjects of international law. International law has nothing to say about the manner in which a State realizes its obligations under international law in its internal system of law. The State may choose a monist or dualist system. The Netherlands has had a monist system for a long time. Provisions of treaties are automatically applicable within the national system of law with no need for transformation into national law.

There are different types of treaty provisions just as there are different types of national statutory provisions. A provision may be directed at the legislature or another rule-making authority that will have to implement the provision. In this case, it would be proper to speak of an indirectly applicable treaty provision. If the treaty provision is addressed to a public authority which can apply the provision directly without the intervention of a rule-making authority, then one can speak of a directly applicable treaty provision.

This distinction is not the same as the one made in the Constitution between 'provisions which may be binding on all persons' and provisions not binding on everyone. It is true that a directly applicable treaty provision is often at the same time binding on everyone, but an indirectly applicable treaty provision may also be binding on everyone as well. For a treaty provision to be binding on all persons, it is not relevant whether an implementation procedure is necessary or not, but whether citizens have the right to invoke the treaty provision or not before the courts.

444. The Constitution only uses the term 'provisions of treaties and of decisions by international organizations, which may be binding on all persons'. These must be applied as soon as they have been published. Neither the Constitution nor any other Act of Parliament specifies who is competent to decide whether a treaty provision is binding on all persons or not. Usually, it is assumed that the courts have the power to make this decision. Nevertheless, it could be argued that the court is not exclusively competent in this. In our view, the legislature may classify a treaty provision as being not binding on all persons, or it may claim the right to judge on the matter itself. However this may be, in practice, it is the court that decides whether a treaty provision is binding on all persons or not, on the basis of the wording, nature, scope and historical background of the provision. The debate in parliament on the bill leading to the Act of Parliament approving the treaty may also play a part in this. However, such considerations are not binding on the court.

445. The question of whether a treaty provision is binding on all persons does not only affect whether the citizen can invoke it before a court or not. Article 94 of the Constitution lays down a rule for situations where the application of a national statutory provision (including provisions of the Constitution) conflicts with a treaty provision which is binding on all persons. In that case, the court must disapply the national provision. This article imposes upon the court both an injunction to review and an order not to review. The court does not review the application of national statutory provisions against anything other than those treaty provisions which are binding on all persons. Nor does it review them against unwritten international law.

446. In fact, the order not to apply national provisions is not always taken literally. Sometimes when a court has identified a conflict with a treaty provision which is binding on everyone, the court may not want or be able to find a solution that conforms to the treaty. In that case, the court will refer back to the legislature, generally observing that the solution lies outside the competence of the court. In case the legislature appears to be not capable to address the issue and find a solution for it, the court can step in and find a solution for the issue (Supreme Court 12 May 1999 *Arbeidskostenforfait* case).

447. The last few years have witnessed an increase in the number of occasions where national provisions have been subject to review on the grounds of their incompatibility with treaty provisions which are binding on everyone, especially those of the ECHR and the ICCPR. While at first it was mainly lower rules which were invalidated, even Acts of Parliament have not remained untouched. It is remarkable in this context that in a number of cases, national courts have not hesitated to apply stricter criteria than the ECtHR requires.

448. To conclude our observations in the field of international relations, reference should be made to Article 92 of the Constitution. This provision authorizes the transfer of legislative, executive and judicial powers to international organizations by or pursuant to a treaty, and if so desired departing from the Constitution. As was mentioned above, the decisions of these organizations may contain provisions which are binding on all persons, as understood in the Constitution, just like treaty provisions.

Chapter 2. Taxing and Spending Powers

449. In the Dutch constitutional system, a distinction can be made between national, that is, central, taxes and levies, and those of the decentralized bodies. Article 104 of the Constitution states that taxes imposed by the State are to be levied pursuant to an Act of Parliament. Through the use of the phrase 'pursuant to an Act of Parliament' (*uitkracht van een wet*), the Constitution aims to indicate that legislative authority in this field may be delegated, but only to a limited extent. The essential features of the tax system, such as who and what is liable to be taxed and the tax rate, must be laid down in Acts of Parliament.

As far as levies by the State are concerned, the Constitution employs the usual delegation terminology. Thus, the legislature is competent to decide how much is delegated. One problem inherent to this provision is that the concepts of a tax and a levy are difficult to distinguish from each other. There are no clear points of departure in legislation, case law or the literature. This means that the limits on possibilities for delegation in respect of certain levies can be evaded by classifying them not as taxes but as 'other levies'.

450. Tax can be divided into direct taxation (income tax, tax on unearned income, company tax) and indirect taxation (VAT, excise duty). By European standards, the Netherlands places a greater emphasis on direct taxation. Levies (fees) can, in principle, be considered as charges in return for actual services and facilities provided by or on behalf of the government: tolls, administrative charges, entry fees, harbour dues, pollution levies, and so on. The original intention behind these levies was that the money raised would be spent on maintaining and improving specific services and facilities. Nowadays, though, the income from these levies disappears for the most part into the general coffers, which is another reason for regarding these levies as ordinary taxes.

451. Apart from the income from taxes and levies, the State receives other monies from the social security and pension contributions which are paid by employers and employees. These are not credited to the general funds of the state, and they do not appear in the national budget; they are managed by separate bodies such as the General Pension Fund for Public Employees.

452. A third source of income is the income from State assets held in private law: income from State property, State shares in companies and the national lottery.

453. Finally, there is the government borrowing policy. The government takes out loans on a regular basis. In the last few decades, this has led to high interest payments which hang like a millstone around the neck of the government and, indirectly, the citizens.

454. Article 132, paragraph 6 of the Constitution states that the taxes that may be levied by the administrative organs of provinces and municipalities are to be regulated by Act of Parliament. There is no mention of levies, though they do exist too. Provincial and municipal authorities are empowered to levy taxes, but the greater part of their financing comes from the central government which makes payments out of the Provinces Fund and the Municipalities Fund. Thus both the provincial and municipal authorities are financially highly dependent upon the State.

The Constitution does not mention water taxes but these exist as well. They are paid by, among others, the owners and the users of property situated in a water board district.

455. At central level, spending power rests with the ministers as heads of ministries. Ministers may only spend funds authorized in the budget for his or her ministry, which is fixed by Act of Parliament. A Budget Act is a special kind of Act. It does not contain any general rules but is a concrete authorization for a minister to make payments. A Budget Act does not impose any duty to make the agreed payments. The Netherlands operates a system of annual Budget Acts. Estimates extending over more than one year do exist, but these are not binding as far as the annual budget Acts are concerned.

456. Article 105 of the Constitution does not require a budget to be drawn up for each ministry. However, the Government Accounts Act (*Comptabiliteitswet 2016*) does do so. That Act lays down what budgets are part of the State budget (Rijksbegroting). The most important are: a budget for each ministry, a special budget for the King, a budget for specific institutions of the State, a budget for the national debt, and budgets for a number of funds. . Under Article 2.1 of this Act, each minister has to draft the bills for his or her own areas of responsibility and send them to the Finance Minister before a date fixed by him or her. The Finance Minister may object, and if a difference of opinion arises the Council of Ministers decides.

457. As we have seen, the budget is put before parliament on the day of the Speech from the Throne that is on the third Tuesday in September. Often the parliamentary discussions on the budget are not completed before the following 1 January, in which case, as we have said above, ministers may nevertheless carry out expenditure.

458. The Government Accounts Act charges ministers with managing the different chapters of the budget. The Minister of Finance has the power to decide that no payments may be made without his or her consent in certain areas. In addition to this control within the administration, external control is exercised by the General Chamber of Audit, which was discussed in Part III, Chapter 6 above.

459. It must be added that the annual power of the purse in practice amounts to less than one might think. The economic and financial position of the Netherlands is strongly interwoven with that of other countries. A very large proportion of the income and expenditure is fixed in advance by statutory rules. National income cannot easily be increased because the tax burden is already very high and because of the high level of the national debt. And, since the Netherlands participates in the Economic and Monetary Union of the EU, it is bound under the relevant rules at that level too. In short, the financial course can only be shifted minimally in any direction.

Chapter 3. Emergency Laws

460. Article 103 of the Constitution contains provisions for dealing with a state of emergency. The Constitution has not opted for a system which makes no mention at all of states of emergency, nor for one like that in Article 16 of the French Constitution which grants the president almost unfettered powers in a state of emergency. In the Dutch system, fairly minor departures from constitutional law are admissible in the case of a duly promulgated state of emergency.

461. What kind of law is concerned here? The term emergency law (*staatsnoodrecht*) is often used in this context. Depending on the point of view one takes, emergency law can be said to comprise:

(a) the rules based on Article 103 of the Constitution which are enacted before a state of emergency is actually declared;
(b) orders which are issued during a state of emergency founded on the rules based on Article 103 of the Constitution;
(c) orders issued during a state of emergency which cannot be traced back to any constitutional or statutory rules.

462. These distinctions can be further clarified. The rules mentioned under (a) are rules based on Article 103 of the Constitution passed before a state of emergency is in fact declared. It is law formulated in advance to deal with circumstances which may arise at a later date.

The orders mentioned under (b), based on the rules *ex*-Article 103 of the Constitution, are of a different nature. They are issued during emergency situations. Such orders can properly be called emergency laws.

The orders mentioned under (c) are also referred to as emergency laws. They are orders which are based on a so-called subjective emergency law. Such orders can however only be classified as law if they have a legal foundation. This is not to be found in written constitutional law and must therefore be based on unwritten (possibly retrospectively recognized) powers. It is evident from case law that it is indeed possible for orders to be legally valid which nevertheless do not have any foundation in written constitutional law.

463. Be that as it may, the Constitution does not give any general ground upon which the government can base its actions in a state of emergency. It merely charges the legislature to draw up rules to deal with emergency situations and gives the possibility, if necessary, of departing from some constitutional provisions in so doing. Any action taken during a state of emergency which is not based on statutory law can only be justified *ex post* on the basis of unwritten law. This question will not be given any further consideration here, even though it played an important role during and after the Second World War in the form, for example, of the statutory orders issued by the Dutch government in exile in London.

464. The government's authority to declare a state of emergency is based on Article 103 of the Constitution. In such a situation, a number of constitutional provisions (which are listed in paragraph 2 of that article) may be departed from. The Constitution does not rule out the declaration of states of emergency under other circumstances, but in such cases, there is no possibility to deviate from the Constitution. Under Article 103 of the Constitution, the legislature is not limited in the number of situations a state of emergency is declared, provided that in each case, it is 'to maintain internal or external security'. Furthermore, the state of emergency must be defined as such by Act of Parliament. This means that the legislature has to state explicitly that the situation the Act covers is a state of emergency, and that it allows the enactment of emergency rules as intended under Article 103.

465. As has been indicated, the power to declare a state of emergency as defined by Act of Parliament rests with the government. A state of emergency has to be declared by Royal Decree. The government is not free, however, to decide how long the state of emergency will continue. Paragraph 3 of Article 103 states that, immediately after the declaration of a state of emergency, and thereafter as long as they consider it necessary, and as long as the state of emergency is not terminated by Royal Decree, the States General in joint session shall decide on the duration of the state of emergency. If the States General decides not to allow a state of emergency to continue, this ends the state of emergency.

466. Paragraph 2 of Article 103 of the Constitution allows the statutory rules under paragraph 1 to authorize departures from constitutional powers of the executive bodies of the provinces, municipalities and water boards.

467. Certain constitutional provisions relating to the fundamental rights – listed in Article 103, paragraph 2 – may also be set aside in a state of emergency, as may the provisions of Article 113, paragraphs 1 and 3, of the Constitution. The latter rule is based on the assumption that mobile courts-martial within the country, which do not form part of the judiciary, must be able to try criminals and impose prison sentences during a state of emergency.

468. In 1996, the legislation relating to the implementation of Article 103 was completely revised. The main implementing Acts of Parliament are the Coordination Act Emergency Situations (*Coördinatiewet uitzonderingstoestanden*), the War Act for the Netherlands (*Oorlogswet voor Nederland*, hereafter: *OWN*) and the Extraordinary Civil Powers Act (*Wet buitengewone bevoegdheden burgerlijk gezag*, hereafter: *Wet BBBG*).

469. The Coordination Act regulates the declaration, the repeal and the end of an emergency situation, plus the transition from one emergency situation to another. The Coordination Act refers to two states of emergency: a limited and a general one. They cannot coexist. They can be declared in case of emergencies, to maintain the external or internal security of the country.

470. According to the Coordination Act, the declaration of a state of emergency has to be made by Royal Decree which is immediately communicated to the States General. Article 103 of the Constitution then applies. The States General decide whether the state of emergency may continue. Apart from that decision, the government is competent to repeal the state of emergency by Royal Decree.

471. The declaration of a state of emergency, as such, does not imply the possibility to use emergency powers. For that purpose, a separate Royal Decree is required. Under the limited state of emergency, the Royal Decree can put into force provisions of a list A which is annexed to the Coordination Act. These provisions do not allow any departure from the Constitution. Under the general state of emergency, the Royal Decree may put into force provisions of a list B annexed to the Coordination Act. In this case, departure from the Constitution is allowed.

472. The most important substantive emergency provisions are contained in the *OWN* and the *Wet BBBG*. Under the *OWN*, the emergency powers can be exercised by the Minister of Defence or military authorities. Under the *OWN*, it is possible to limit the exercise of a number of fundamental rights. Moreover, the minister and the military authorities are granted a number of powers which normally belong to the (civil) decentralized authorities.

473. Under the *Wet BBBG*, emergency powers continue to be vested in the civil authorities. The most characteristic feature of this Act of Parliament is the strong centralization of powers. The Minister of Home Affairs becomes a real commander of the Royal Commissioners and of the Mayors. As to the limitations of fundamental rights, the *Wet BBBG* is very similar to the *OWN*.

474. The *OWN* and the *Wet BBBG* may be put into force according to the procedure in the Coordination Act, described above. Both Acts also contain a so-called separate application system. According to this, a Royal Decree may put provisions of only one of these Acts into force, after which a bill to prolong the use of emergency powers has to be put before Parliament immediately. Under the separate application, system deviation from the Constitution is excluded.

475. Apart from the regulations based on the Constitution discussed here, there are provisions relating to abnormal and emergency situations in many other Acts of Parliament. Some of these may be applied if the government has declared that there is a threat of war. Others come into play in disaster situations such as floods, epidemics, riots and other threats to the population. Under these rules, however, deviations from the provisions of the Constitution are not permitted. During the COVID 19 (Corona) Pandemic (2020–2022), the previously mentioned general Emergency Acts were not applied, apart from one provision in the Extraordinary Civil Powers Act (to establish a curfew). During the first months of the pandemic public authorities more or less improvised with emergency orders. It took government and parliament more than six months to establish new temporary provisions in an Act of Parliament (Public Health Act) to impose the necessary measures (restrictions) to fight the Corona virus.

Chapter 4. The Constitutional Relationship Between the Church and the State

476. We have already seen that Article 6 of the Constitution guarantees religious freedom. This freedom extends to the establishment and organization of churches and other organizations based on religion or belief. Article 2 of Book 2 of the Civil Code grants churches and their separate component parts the status of legal persons. They are autonomous bodies, following their own internal rules as long as these do not conflict with the law. It is probably not possible for a church to be judicially disbanded or banned.

477. The Constitution does not actually proclaim the separation of church and State. Nevertheless from the provisions just mentioned, it can be assumed that this separation exists in principle. The government does not interfere with church organization, and activities and the churches do not have any special powers within the government. Nevertheless, certain special legal connections between the government and the churches do exist. They are mainly of a financial nature. Thus in the armed forces, the prison system and government institutions are for the care of young persons; there are pastoral workers from various denominations whose work is financed by the government. Subsidies may be granted to build places for prayer. Church buildings may be granted the status of religious monuments, which enables them to claim relatively high subsidies for maintenance and restoration. Churches may also receive public funds for broadcasting activities. They are exempt from municipal property tax on buildings whose principal use is for religious services. In the fiscal sphere, gifts to churches are deductible for income tax purposes. The Inheritance Act (*Successiewet*) also has special rules for churches. It must also be remembered that the government finances special (usually denominational) education on the same terms as State education and that numerous social facilities, such as hospitals, are based on religiously inspired private initiatives and yet are partly or wholly financed by government.

Selected Bibliography

De Lange R., Loeffen S.C., Efthymiou N.S., Julicher M.M., Munneke S.A.J., *Beginselen van Nederlands Staatsrecht*, 19th ed., Deventer: Wolters Kluwer 2020.

Berg, van den J.Th.J. & Vis J.J., *De eerste honderdvijftig jaar parlementaire geschiedenis van Nederland 1796–1946*, Amsterdam: Bert Bakker 2013.

Besselink Leonard, Bovend'Eert Paul, Broeksteeg Hansko, Voermans Wim, *Constitutional Law of the EU Member States*, Deventer: Kluwer 2014.

Bosmans, Jac en Kessel van Alexander, *Parlementaire geschiedenis van Nederland*, Amsterdam: Boom 2011.

Borman C., *Het Statuut voor het koninkrijk*, 2e ed, Deventer: Kluwer 2012.

Bovend'Eert P.P.T. *Inleiding Constitutioneel recht*, 7th ed. Deventer: Wolters Kluwer 2018.

Bovend'Eert P.P.T., *Rechterlijke Organisatie, rechters en rechtspraak in de democratische rechtsstaat*, Deventer: Wolters Kluwer 2022.

Bovend'Eert P.P.T. et al., *Grondwet en Statuut, tekst & commentaar*, 4th ed., Deventer: Wolters Kluwer 2018.

Bovend'Eert P.P.T. & Kummeling H.R.B.M., *Het Nederlandse parlement*, 12th ed., Deventer: Wolters Kluwer 2017.

Burkens M.C., *Algemene leerstukken van grondrechten naar Nederlands constitutioneel recht*, Zwolle: Tjeenk Willink 1989.

Burkens M.C., et al. *Beginselen van de democratische rechtsstaat*, 7th ed., Deventer: Wolters Kluwer 2022.

Van Dijk Pieter, Van Hoof Fried, Vanb Rijn Arjen, Zwaak Leo (eds), *Theory and Practice of the European Convention on Human Rights*, Antwerpen/Oxford: Intersentia 2018.

Broeksteeg J.L.W, Gemeenterecht, Deventer: Wolters Kluwer 2021.

Elzinga D.J., H.R.B.M. Kummeling & Schipper-Spanninga J., *Het Nederlandse kiesrecht*, 3d ed., Deventer: Kluwer 2012.

Van Emmerik M.L. e.a., Grondrechten. *De nationale, Europese en internationale dimensie*, Nijmegen: Ars Aequi Libri 2013.

Gerards Janneke, *EVRM- Algemene beginselen*, Den Haag: Sdu Uitgevers 2011.

Van Rijn, Arjen, Handboek Caribisch Staatsrecht, Den Haag: Boom juridisch 2019.

Hoogers H.G., *De normenhiërarchie van het Koninkrijk der Nederlanden*, Nijmegen: Wolf Legal Publishers 2009.

Kortmann C.A.J.M., *Constitutioneel recht*, 8th ed., Deventer: Wolters Kluwer 2021.

Kortmann C.A.J.M., *De Grondwetsherzieningen*, 2d ed., Deventer: Kluwer 1987.

Kuijer M., *The Blindfold of Lady Justice*, Leiden, E.M. Meijers Institute 2004.

Selected Bibliography

Nap M., *Wetgeving van het Koninkrijk der Nederlanden*, Zutphen: Walburg Pers 2003.

Nehmelman R. & Noorlander C.W., *Horizontale werking van grondrechten. Over een leerstuk in ontwikkeling*, Deventer: Kluwer 2013.

Oud P.J., *Het constitutioneel recht van het Koninkrijk der Nederlanden deel I en deel II*, 2d ed., Zwolle: W.E.J. Tjeenk Willink 1967 en 1970.

Pot, van der, *Handboek van het Nederlandse staatsrecht*, 16th ed., Deventer: Kluwer 2014.

Schlössels R.J.N. & Zijlstra S.E., *Bestuursrecht in de sociale rechtsstaat*, 7th ed., Deventer: Wolters Kluwer 2017.

Van der Tang G.F.M., *Grondwetsbegrip en grondwetsidee*, Rotterdam: Gouda Quint 1998.

Zijlstra S.E., *Bestuurlijk organisatierecht, 2nd ed.*, Deventer: Wolters Kluwer 2019.

Index

Index

Index

political groups, 115, 136, 220, 231, 259, 264, 281, 285
Presidium
  quorum, 229
  Second Chamber, 173–235
  Speaker, 198, 206, 228, 230, 233, 234, 257, 273, 441
  speech from the throne, 179
  swearing-in, 192
  temporary committee, 214, 232
  year of sitting, 196
Parliamentary system, 3, 7, 11, 34, 64, 110, 112, 116, 119, 120, 127, 139, 141, 170, 173, 175, 178, 197, 266, 279–281, 286, 289, 291
Party charters, 135
Passport Act, 376
Pillarization, 132
Plaintiff, 320, 412
Policy rules, 300, 373, 425
Political parties, 3, 27, 62, 115, 128–138, 142, 184–186, 204, 207, 231, 260, 268, 281
Political practices, 28
Proportional representation, 3, 26, 58, 130, 184, 185, 189, 254, 290
Provinces
  clerk, 69, 203
Provinces Act, 26, 50, 57, 64, 65, 67–69, 73, 81, 82, 85, 86, 91
Provincial bye-laws
  provincial executive, 61, 73, 78, 85, 87, 100, 429
  provincial states, 58–65, 67, 72, 78, 80, 81, 92, 94, 115, 118, 173, 182, 189, 191, 293, 343, 378

Referendum, 36, 142, 144
Representative monarchy, 112, 120, 127, 139–144
Right of parliamentary enquiry, 175, 218
Right of interpellation, 3, 118, 273
Right of questioning, 175, 217, 273, 274
Royal decree, 6, 39, 44, 65, 86, 95, 109,

116, 156, 168–170, 237, 238, 250, 252, 263, 271, 287, 294, 305, 311, 312, 316, 326, 328, 334, 339, 341, 465, 470, 471, 474
Royal Commissioner, 59, 61, 65, 66, 73, 78, 79, 135, 190, 191, 473
Rule of law, 5, 12, 13, 16, 21, 27, 112, 121, 123, 125, 127, 350, 408, 413, 437, 438
Rule-giving/making powers, 1, 3, 7, 56, 106, 296–301, 383

Separation of Powers, 13, 27, 61, 71, 107–109, 112, 193, 202, 265, 413, 414
Social Economic Council, 30, 56, 338
Sovereign, 5, 49, 50, 84, 169, 173, 211
Standing Orders, 60, 92, 94–97, 133, 198, 205–207, 213, 227–232, 241, 246–248, 257, 273, 302, 438
State secretary, 59, 119, 160, 201, 202, 220, 250, 253, 262, 265, 279, 403
States General, 172–192
  meetings of the States General, 229, 432
  Proceedings of the Dutch States General, 229
State of emergency
  emergency law, 460–475

Taxes, 81, 82, 449–459, 477
Territory and population, 14–15
Treaties
  approval of treaties, 441
  directly applicable provisions, 32, 111, 443
  international law, 439
  monist system, 443
  treaty conflicts with the Constitution, 442
Trias politica, 13, 109, 193, 413

War Act for the Netherlands, 468
Water boards, 88–100
Water board bye-laws, 97

The Netherlands

Text of the Constitution

2023

Wolters Kluwer

Introductory Note

Constitution

The Constitution dates from 1814, when a constitutional monarchy and a unitary state were established in the Netherlands. A drastic revision of the Constitution took place in 1815 in consequence of the unification with Belgium. With the constitutional revision of 1840 the Constitution was amended in light of the secession of Belgium. This revision also involved a first major political reform regarding the relationship between the King and the cabinet ministers. The revision of the Constitution in 1848 was the most drastic in Dutch political history. This revision involved laying the foundations for the development of the parliamentary democracy and of the modern decentralized unitary state. Since that year the Constitution has not drastically changed in substance. Still, there have been many minor changes to the Constitution over the years, such as in 1884, 1887, 1917, 1922, 1938, 1946, 1948, 1953, 1956, 1963, 1972, 1987, 1995, 1999, 2000, 2005, 2006, 2008, 2018 and 2022. The cumbersome procedure to revise the Constitution was not an obstacle for these frequent revisions.

In 1983 a general revision of the Constitution took place, which mainly involved modernization of the design and the text, without drastic political reforms taking place. For example, the persistent mention of the King in the old text of the Constitution of 1814 largely disappeared in the new text of 1983. The Constitution starts since 1983 with a first chapter concerning fundamental rights.

The way the current 'modern' Constitution is set up is comparable to that of other present-day constitutions of European nations. The Constitution consists of eight chapters and 142 articles. It does not have a preamble.

Charter for the Kingdom of the Netherlands

Since 1814, the Kingdom of the Netherlands has encompassed not only the territory in Europe, but also colonies in other parts of the world. The Netherlands – the Country in Europe – as the 'motherland', formed the heart of the Kingdom. The other countries, the Dutch East Indies, Surinam and the Netherlands Antilles, were more or less considered as appendages.

The Netherlands – Text of the Constitution

For a long time, governmental authority in the overseas territories lay entirely in the hands of Dutch constitutional institutions. The 1815 Constitution stated that the King had supreme authority over the colonies.

In the Netherlands, it gradually came to be realized that the principal task of the motherland was to assist in the political, social and economic development of the colonies instead of treating them as conquered territories. Thus a process of decolonization was started which was eventually supposed to lead to the overseas territories gaining autonomy and equivalent status with the motherland.

The decolonization process accelerated after the Second World War. Following an armed struggle, and under pressure from the United Nations and the United States, the motherland was forced to grant Indonesia its independence through a transfer of sovereignty in 1949.

In the meantime, in the Netherlands Antilles and Surinam it proved possible to reach a negotiated solution, whereby a new structure was determined for the Kingdom, which guaranteed the autonomy and equivalent status of these overseas territories *vis-à-vis* the Netherlands. This new legal system came into operation in 1954. The Charter for the Kingdom of the Netherlands, which was democratically adopted in the three countries that made up the Kingdom, laid down the fundamental principles of the new legal system. The Charter functioned unchanged for about twenty years. Then, at the end of the 1960s, dissatisfaction with the political relationships within the Kingdom manifested itself among large sections of the population, especially in Surinam, but also in the Antilles. The struggle for complete independence gained more and more support. Against this background the Dutch government felt compelled to draw up a policy to revise the Charter to give priority to the realization of autonomy.

In 1975, Surinam left the federation of the Kingdom and became an independent State. In 1985, the Charter was changed again, when the island of Aruba split away from the Netherlands Antilles. Since then, Aruba formed the third country in the Kingdom alongside the Netherlands and the Netherlands Antilles, which now comprise five islands. The concept of the Netherlands Antilles as a separate country within the Kingdom of the Netherlands never enjoyed full support of all the five islands involved. Following referendums on all five islands, the Netherlands Antilles were finally dissolved on 10 October 2010. Curaçao and Sint Maarten became two new countries within the Kingdom of the Netherlands. These two countries nowadays form together with Aruba and the Netherlands, the territory in Europe, a federation of four separate countries.

The Charter contains the Constitution for the Kingdom. It is also the highest constitutional document of the four countries of the Kingdom. The form of State which it lays down resembles at first sight a federation or federal State.

The Editors

Paul Bovend'Eert (born 26 June 1957) is a professor of Constitutional Law at the Radboud University of Nijmegen, Netherlands. In 1988, the University of Nijmegen awarded him a doctorate degree in Law for a thesis on coalition agreements in the Dutch parliamentary democracy. He teaches Constitutional Law and Comparative Constitutional Law. He has been dean of the Faculty of Law at the Radboud University (2010-2014). He is joint editor and co-author of a handbook on *Constitutional Law of the EU Member States* (2014). He is the author of *Introduction to Dutch Constitutional Law* (2019), co-author of *Manual on the Dutch Parliament* (2023), co-author of a handbook on Dutch Constitutional Law (2021) and author of *Treatise on the Judiciary and the Administration of Justice* (2022).

Constantijn Kortmann (born 14 March 1944, deceased 24 January 2016) was professor of constitutional law and general theory of state at the Radboud University of Nijmegen, Netherlands (1981-2009). He received his doctorate degree in 1971. He was professor of Dutch and comparative constitutional law at the University of Amsterdam (1976-1981). His publications include a manual on the constitutional reforms of 1983 and 1987, A handbook on Constitutional Law (2008). He was joint editor of a handbook on the Constitutional Law of the 15 EU Member States (2004). He was dean of the faculty of law of the Radboud University and of the faculty of Law of the University of Amsterdam. He was doctor honoris causa of the University of Poitiers, France.

5

The Editors

Constitution for the Kingdom of the Netherlands

Text of the Constitution (2017)
Content

1. Constitution for the Kingdom of the Netherlands

CHAPTER 1 FUNDAMENTAL RIGHTS

General Provision

**The Constitution guarantees fundamental rights and democracy based on
the rule of law**

Article 1.

All persons in the Netherlands shall be treated equally in equal circumstances. Discrimination on the grounds of religion, belief, political opinion, race, sex or on any other grounds whatsoever shall not be permitted.

The Netherlands – Text of the Constitution

Article 2.
  (1) Dutch nationality shall be regulated by Act of Parliament.
  (2) The admission and expulsion of aliens shall be regulated by Act of Parliament.
  (3) Extradition may take place only pursuant to a treaty. Further regulations concerning extradition shall be laid down in an Act of Parliament.
  (4) Everyone shall have the right to leave the country, except in the cases laid down in an Act of Parliament.

Article 3.

All Dutch nationals shall be equally eligible for appointment to public service.

Article 4.

Every Dutch national shall have an equal right to elect the members of the general representative bodies and to stand for election as a member of those bodies, except for the limitations and exceptions laid down in an Act of Parliament.

Article 5.

Everyone shall have the right to submit petitions in writing to the competent authorities.

Article 6.
  (1) Everyone shall have the right to manifest freely his religion or belief, either individually or in community with others, without prejudice to his responsibility established by Act of Parliament.
  (2) Rules concerning the exercise of this right other than in buildings and enclosed places may be laid down by Act of Parliament for the protection of health, in the interest of traffic and to combat or prevent disorders.

Article 7.
  (1) No one shall require prior permission to reveal thoughts or opinions through the press, without prejudice to everyone's responsibility established by Act of Parliament.
  (2) Rules concerning radio and television shall be laid down by Act of Parliament. There shall be no prior supervision of the content of a radio or television broadcast.
  (3) No one shall be required to submit thoughts or opinions for prior approval in order to reveal them by means other than those mentioned in the preceding paragraphs, without prejudice to everyone's responsibility established by Act of Parliament. The holding of performances open to persons younger than sixteen years of age may be regulated by Act of Parliament in order to protect good morals.
  (4) The preceding paragraphs do not apply to commercial advertising.

Article 8.

The right of association shall be recognized. This right may be restricted by Act of Parliament in the interest of public order.

Article 9.
(1) The right of assembly and demonstration shall be recognized, without prejudice to everyone's responsibility established by Act of Parliament.
(2) Rules to protect health, in the interest of traffic and to combat or prevent disorders may be laid down by Act of Parliament.

Article 10.
(1) Everyone shall have the right to respect of his privacy, without prejudice to restrictions laid down by or pursuant to an Act of Parliament.
(2) Rules to protect privacy shall be laid down by Act of Parliament in connection with the recording and dissemination of personal data.
(3) Rules concerning the rights of persons to be informed of recorded data concerning them and of the use that is made thereof, and to have such data corrected shall be laid down by Act of Parliament.

Article 11.

Everyone shall have the right to inviolability of his physical person, without prejudice to restrictions laid down by or pursuant to an Act of Parliament.

Article 12.
(1) Entry into a dwelling without the consent of the occupant shall be permitted only in the cases laid down by or pursuant to an Act of Parliament, by those designated for the purpose by or pursuant to an Act of Parliament.
(2) Prior identification and notice of purpose shall be required in order to enter a dwelling under the preceding paragraph, except for the exceptions laid down in an Act of Parliament. A written report of the entry shall be issued to the occupant.
(3) A written report of the entry shall be issued to the occupant as soon as possible. If the entry was made in the interests of state security or criminal proceedings, the issue of the report may be postponed under rules to be laid down by act of parliament, where such issue would never be in the interests of state security.

Article 13.
(1) Everyone shall have the right to respect for the privacy of his correspondence and telecommunications.
(2) This right may be restricted in the cases laid down by Act of Parliament with the authorisation of the courts or, in the interests of state security, by or with the authorisation of those designated for the purpose by Act of Parliament.

Article 14.

(1) Expropriation may take place only in the public interest and on prior assurance of full compensation, in accordance with regulations laid down by or pursuant to an Act of Parliament.

(2) Prior assurance of full compensation shall not be required if in an emergency immediate expropriation is called for.

(3) In the cases laid down by or pursuant to an Act of Parliament there shall be a right to full or partial compensation if in the public interest the competent authority destroys property or renders it unusable or restricts the exercise of the owner's rights to it.

Article 15.

(1) Except for the cases laid down by or pursuant to an Act of Parliament, no one may be deprived of his liberty.

(2) Anyone who has been deprived of his liberty otherwise than by order of a court may request a court to order his release. In such a case he shall be heard by the court within a period to be laid down in an Act of Parliament. The court shall order his immediate release if it considers the deprivation of liberty to be unlawful.

(3) The trial of a person who has been deprived of his liberty pending trial shall take place within a reasonable time.

(4) A person who has been lawfully deprived of his liberty may be restricted in the exercise of fundamental rights in so far as this exercise is incompatible with the deprivation of liberty.

Article 16.

No offence shall be punishable except by virtue of a prior law.

Article 17.

1. Everyone shall have the right, in the determination of his rights and obligations or of any criminal charge against him, to a fair trial within a reasonable time before an independent and impartial court.

2. No one can be prevented against his will from being heard by the courts to which he is entitled to apply under the law.

Article 18.

(1) Everyone may be legally represented in legal and administrative proceedings.

(2) Rules concerning the granting of legal aid to persons of limited means shall be laid down by Act of Parliament.

Article 19.

(1) It shall be the concern of the authorities to promote sufficient employment.

(2) Rules concerning the legal status and protection of working persons and concerning co-determination shall be laid down by Act of Parliament.

The Netherlands – Text of the Constitution

(3) The right of every Dutch national to a free choice of work shall be recognized, without prejudice to the restrictions laid down by or pursuant to an Act of Parliament.

Article 20.
(1) It shall be the concern of the authorities to secure the means of subsistence of the population and to achieve the distribution of wealth.
(2) Rules concerning entitlement to social security shall be laid down by Act of Parliament.
(3) Dutch nationals resident in the Netherlands who are unable to provide for themselves shall have a right, to be regulated by Act of Parliament, to aid from the authorities.

Article 21.
It shall be the concern of the authorities to keep the country habitable and to protect and improve the environment.

Article 22.
(1) The authorities shall take steps to promote the health of the population.
(2) It shall be the concern of the authorities to provide sufficient living accommodation.
(3) The authorities shall promote social and development and leisure activities.

Article 23.
(1) Education shall be the constant concern of the Government.
(2) All persons shall be free to provide education, without prejudice to the authorities' right of supervision and, with regard to forms of education designated by Act of Parliament, its right to examine the competence and moral integrity of teachers, to be regulated by Act of Parliament.
(3) Education provided by public authorities shall be regulated by Act of Parliament, paying due respect to everyone's religion or belief.
(4) The authorities shall ensure that public primary education is provided in a sufficient number of public-authority schools in every municipality and in each of the public bodies, referred to in Article 132a. Deviations from this provision may be permitted under rules to be established by Act of Parliament on condition that there is opportunity to receive the said form of education, whether or not in a public-authority school.
(5) The standards required of schools financed either in part or in full from public funds shall be regulated by Act of Parliament, with due regard, in the case of denominational schools, to the freedom to provide education according to religious or other belief.
(6) The requirements for primary education shall be such that the standards both of denominational schools fully financed from public funds and of public-authority schools are fully guaranteed. The relevant provisions shall respect in particular the freedom of denominational schools to choose their teaching aids and to appoint teachers as they see fit.

11

(7) Denominational primary schools that satisfy the conditions laid down in an Act of Parliament shall be financed from public funds according to the same standards as public-authority schools. The conditions under which denominational secondary education and pre-university education shall receive contributions from public funds shall be laid down by Act of Parliament.

(8) The Government shall submit annual reports on the state of education to the States General.

CHAPTER 2. GOVERNMENT

Section 1. The King

Article 24.

The Throne shall be hereditary and shall vest in the legitimate descendants of King William I, Prince of Orange-Nassau.

Article 25.

On the death of the King, the Throne shall pass by hereditary succession to the King's legitimate descendants in order of seniority, the same rule governing succession by issue of descendants who predecease the King. If the King has no descendants, the title to the Throne shall pass in the same way to the legitimate descendants of the King's parent and then of his grandparent who are in the line of succession but are not further removed from the deceased King than the third degree of consanguinity.

Article 26.

For the purposes of hereditary succession, the child of a woman pregnant at the moment of the death of the King shall be deemed already born. If it is stillborn it shall be deemed never to have existed.

Article 27.

Hereditary succession to the Throne in the event of abdication shall take place according to the rules set out in the above articles. Children born after an abdication and their descendants shall be excluded from the hereditary succession.

Article 28.

(1) The King shall be deemed to have abdicated if he contracts a marriage without having obtained approval by Act of Parliament.

(2) Anyone in line of succession to the Throne who contracts such a marriage shall be excluded from the hereditary succession, together with any children born of the marriage and their issue.

(3) The two Chambers of the States General shall meet to consider and decide upon a bill for granting such approval in joint session.

Article 29.

(1) One or more persons may be excluded from the hereditary succession by Act of Parliament if exceptional circumstances necessitate it.

(2) The bill for this purpose shall be presented by or on behalf of the King. The two Chambers of the States General shall consider and decide upon the matter in joint session. Such a bill can be passed only if at least two-thirds of the votes cast are in favour.

Article 30.

(1) A successor to the Throne may be appointed by Act of Parliament if it appears that there will otherwise be no successor. The bill shall be presented by or on behalf of the King, upon which the Chambers shall be dissolved. The newly convened Chambers shall discuss and decide upon the matter in joint session. Such a bill can be passed only if at least two-thirds of the votes cast are in favour.

(2) The Chambers shall be dissolved if there is no successor on the death or abdication of the King. The newly convened Chambers shall meet in joint session within four months of the decease or abdication in order to decide on the appointment of a King. They may appoint a successor only if at least two-thirds of the votes cast are in favour.

Article 31.

(1) An appointed King may be succeeded only by his legitimate descendants by virtue of hereditary succession.

(2) The provisions on hereditary succession and the first paragraph of this article shall apply by analogy to an appointed successor who has not yet become King.

Article 32.

Upon assuming the royal authority the King shall be sworn in and inaugurated as soon as possible in the capital, Amsterdam, at a public and joint session of the two Chambers of the States General. The King shall swear or promise allegiance to the Constitution and that he will faithfully discharge his duties. Further rules shall be laid down by Act of Parliament.

Article 33.

The King shall not exercise the royal authority before having attained the age of eighteen.

Article 34.

The parental authority and the guardianship of a King who is a minor and the supervision thereon shall be regulated by Act of Parliament. The two Chambers of the States General shall meet in joint session to consider and decide upon the matter.

Article 35.

(1) When the Council of Ministers is of the opinion that the King is incapable to exercise the royal authority, it shall inform the two Chambers of the States General accordingly and shall also present to them the advice it has requested from the Council of State. The two Chambers of the States General shall then meet in joint session.

(2) When the two Chambers of the States General share this opinion, they shall then resolve that the King is incapable to exercise the royal authority. This resolution shall be made public on the instructions of the Speaker of the joint session and shall enter into force immediately.

(3) As soon as the King regains the ability to exercise the royal authority, this shall be declared by Act of Parliament. The two Chambers of the States General shall consider and decide upon the matter in joint session. The King shall resume the exercise of the royal authority as soon as the act has been made public.

(4) If it has been resolved that the King is incapable to exercise the royal authority, guardianship over his person shall, if necessary, be regulated by Act of Parliament. The two Chambers of the States General shall consider and decide upon the matter in joint session.

Article 36.

The King may temporarily relinquish the exercise of the royal authority and resume the exercise thereof pursuant to an Act of Parliament. The relevant bill shall be presented by or on behalf of the King. The two Chambers of the States General shall consider and decide upon the matter in joint session.

Article 37.

(1) The royal authority shall be exercised by a Regent:
  (a) until the King has attained the age of eighteen;
  (b) if the title to the Throne may vest in an unborn child;
  (c) if it has been resolved that the King is incapable to exercise the royal authority;
  (d) if the King has temporarily relinquished the exercise of the royal authority;
  (e) in the absence of a successor following the death or abdication of the King.

(2) The Regent shall be appointed by Act of Parliament. The two Chambers of the States General shall consider and decide upon the matter in joint session.

(3) In the cases specified in paragraph 1. c) and d) above, the descendant of the King who is the heir presumptive shall become Regent by right if he has attained the age of eighteen.

(4) The Regent shall swear or promise allegiance to the Constitution and that he will faithfully discharge his duties before the two Chambers of Parliament meeting in joint session. Rules regarding the office of Regent shall be made by Act of Parliament, which may contain provisions for succession and

replacement. The two Chambers of the States General shall consider and decide upon the matter in joint session.

(5) Articles 35 and 36 shall apply by analogy to the Regent.

Article 38.

The royal authority shall be exercised by the Council of State as long as its exercise is not provided for.

Article 39.

Membership of the Royal House shall be regulated by Act of Parliament.

Article 40.

(1) The King shall receive annual payments from the State according to rules to be laid down by Act of Parliament. The act shall also specify which other members of the Royal House shall receive payments from the State and shall regulate these payments.

(2) The payments received by them from the State, together with such assets as are of assistance to them in the exercise of their duties, shall be exempt from personal taxation. In addition, anything received by the King or his heir presumptive from a member of the Royal House by inheritance or as a gift shall be exempt from inheritance tax, transfer tax or gifts tax. Additional exemption from taxation may be granted by Act of Parliament.

(3) Bills containing legislation as referred to in the previous paragraphs can be passed by the States General only if at least two-thirds of the votes cast are in favour.

Article 41.

The King shall organize his Royal Court, taking due account of the public interest.

Section 2. The King and the Ministers

Article 42.

(1) The Government shall comprise the King and the Ministers.

(2) The King is inviolable; the Ministers shall be responsible.

Article 43.

The Prime Minister and the other Ministers shall be appointed and dismissed by royal decree.

Article 44.

(1) Ministries shall be established by royal decree. They shall be headed by a Minister.

(2) Ministers without portfolio may also be appointed.

Article 45.
  (1) The Ministers shall together constitute the Council of Ministers.
  (2) The Prime Minister shall be the chairman of the Council of Ministers.
  (3) The Council of Ministers shall consider and decide upon general government policy and promote its coherence.

Article 46.
  (1) State Secretaries may be appointed and dismissed by royal decree.
  (2) A State Secretary shall act with ministerial authority instead of the Minister in cases in which the Minister considers it necessary; the State Secretary shall observe the Minister's instructions in such cases. Responsibility shall rest with the State Secretary without prejudice to the responsibility of the Minister.

Article 47.

All Acts of Parliament and royal decrees shall be signed by the King and by one or more Ministers or State Secretaries.

Article 48.

The royal decree appointing the Prime Minister shall be countersigned by himself. Royal decrees appointing or dismissing Ministers and State Secretaries shall be countersigned by the Prime Minister.

Article 49.

Upon accepting office, Ministers and State Secretaries shall swear an oath or make an affirmation and promise in the presence of the King, in the manner described by Act of Parliament, that they have not done anything which may legally debar them from holding office, and shall also swear or promise allegiance to the Constitution and that they will faithfully discharge their duties.

CHAPTER 3. THE STATES GENERAL

Section 1. Organization and Composition

Article 50.

The States General shall represent the entire people of the Netherlands.

Article 51.
  (1) The States General shall consist of a Second Chamber and a First Chamber.
  (2) The Second Chamber shall consist of one hundred and fifty members.
  (3) The First Chamber shall consist of seventy-five members.
  (4) The two Chambers shall be deemed a single entity when they meet in joint session.

Article 52.
(1) The duration of both Chambers shall be four years.
(2) The duration of the First Chamber shall be amended accordingly if the duration of the provincial states is altered by Act of Parliament to a term other than four years.

Article 53.
(1) The members of both Chambers shall be elected by proportional representation within the limits to be laid down by Act of Parliament.
(2) Elections shall be by secret ballot.

Article 54.
(1) The members of the Second Chamber shall be elected directly by the Dutch nationals who have attained the age of eighteen. Exceptions may be made by Act of Parliament concerning nationals who are not resident in the Netherlands.
(2) Anyone who has committed an offence designated by Act of Parliament and has been sentenced as a result by irrevocable judgment of a court of law to a custodial sentence of not less than one year and simultaneously disqualified from voting shall not be entitled to vote;

Article 55.
1. The members of the Upper House shall be chosen by the members of the provincial councils and the members of the electoral colleges as referred to in paragraph 2 and in Article 132a, paragraph 3. The election shall take place not more than three months after the election of the members of the provincial councils except in the event of the dissolution of the House.
2. For Dutch nationals who are not resident in the Netherlands and who satisfy the requirements laid down for elections to the Lower House of the States General, elections shall be held for an electoral college for the Upper House. The members of this electoral college shall be directly elected by these Dutch nationals. The same conditions apply to membership. Article 129, paragraphs 2 to 6 shall apply mutatis mutandis.'

The members of the First Chamber shall be elected by the members of the provincial states and the members of an electoral college, referred to in Article 132a, paragraph 3. The election shall take place not more than three months after the election of the members of the provincial states, except in the event of the dissolution of the Chamber.

Article 56.

To be eligible for membership of the States General, a person must be a Dutch national, must have attained the age of eighteen years, and must not have been disqualified from voting.

Article 57.

(1) No one may be a member of both Chambers.
(2) A member of the States General may not be a Minister, State Secretary, member of the Council of State, member of the General Chamber of Audit, member of the Supreme Court, or Attorney General or Advocate General at the Supreme Court.
(3) Notwithstanding the above, a Minister or State Secretary who has offered to tender his resignation may combine the said office with membership of the States General until such time as a decision is taken on such resignation.
(4) Other public functions which may not be held simultaneously by a person who is a member of the States General or of one of the Chambers may be designated by Act of Parliament.

Article 57a.

The temporary replacement of a member of the States General for reasons of pregnancy and childbearing, as well as for reasons of illness, is regulated by act of parliament.

Article 58.

Each Chamber shall examine the credentials of its newly appointed members and shall decide with due reference to rules to be established by Act of Parliament any disputes arising in connection with the credentials or the election.

Article 59.

All other matters pertaining to the right to vote and to elections shall be regulated by Act of Parliament.

Article 60.

Upon accepting office members of the Chambers shall swear an oath or make an affirmation and promise before the Chamber in the manner prescribed by Act of Parliament that they have not done anything which may legally debar them from holding office, and shall also swear or promise allegiance to the Constitution and that they will faithfully discharge their duties.

Article 61.

(1) Each Chamber shall appoint a Speaker from among its members.
(2) Each Chamber shall appoint a Clerk who, like the other officials of the two Chambers, may not be a member of the States General.

Article 62.

The Speaker of the First Chamber shall preside when the two Chambers meet in joint session.

Article 63.

Financial remuneration for members and former members of the States General and their dependents shall be regulated by Act of Parliament. The Chambers can pass a bill on the matter only if at least two-thirds of the votes cast are in favour.

Article 64.
(1) Each of the Chambers may be dissolved by royal decree.
(2) A decree for dissolution shall also require new elections to be held for the Chamber which has been dissolved and the newly elected Chamber to meet within three months.
(3) The dissolution shall take effect on the day on which the newly elected Chamber meets.
(4) The duration of a Second Chamber that meets following a dissolution shall be determined by Act of Parliament; the term may not exceed five years. The duration of a First Chamber that meets following a dissolution shall end at the time at which the duration of the dissolved Chamber would have ended.

Section 2. Procedure

Article 65.

A statement of the policy to be pursued by the Government shall be given by or on behalf of the King before a joint session of the two Chambers of the States General that shall be held every year on the third Tuesday in September or on such earlier date as may be fixed by Act of Parliament.

Article 66.
(1) The meetings of the States General shall be held in public.
(2) The meetings shall be held in camera if one tenth of the members present so require or if the Speaker considers it necessary.
(3) The Chamber, or the two Chambers meeting in joint session, shall then decide whether the deliberations are to continue and the decisions to be taken in camera.

Article 67.
(1) The two Chambers may deliberate or make decisions, either separately or in joint session, only if more than half of the members are present.
(2) Decisions shall be made by majority of the votes cast.
(3) The members shall not be bound by a mandate or instructions when casting their votes.
(4) Voting on items of business not related to individuals shall be oral and by roll call if requested by one member.

Article 68.

Ministers and State Secretaries shall provide orally or in writing the Chambers either separately or in joint session, with any information requested by one or more members, provided that the provision of such information does not conflict with the interests of the State.

Article 69.
(1) Ministers and State Secretaries shall have the right to attend meetings of the States General and to participate in the deliberations.
(2) They may be invited to be present at meetings of the Chambers of the States General meeting either separately or in joint session.
(3) They may be assisted at the meetings by persons nominated by them.

Article 70.

The two Chambers shall jointly and separately have the right of enquiry to be regulated by Act of Parliament.

Article 71.

Members of the States General, Ministers, State Secretaries and other persons taking part in deliberations may not be prosecuted or otherwise held liable in law for anything they say during the meetings of the States General or of its committees or for anything they submit to them in writing.

Article 72.

Each Chamber of the States General and the two Chambers in joint session shall draw up Standing Orders.

CHAPTER 4. COUNCIL OF STATE, GENERAL CHAMBER OF AUDIT, NATIONAL OMBUDSMAN AND PERMANENT ADVISORY BODIES

Article 73.
(1) The Council of State or a section of the Council shall be consulted on bills and bills for Orders in Council as well as proposals for the approval of treaties by the States General. Such consultation may be dispensed with in cases to be laid down by Act of Parliament.
(2) The Council or a section of the Council shall be responsible for investigating administrative disputes where the decision has to be given by royal decree, and for advising on the ruling to be given in the said dispute.
(3) The Council or a section of the Council may be required by Act of Parliament to settle administrative disputes.

Article 74.

(1) The King shall be Chairman of the Council of State. The heir presumptive shall be legally entitled to have a seat on the Council on attaining the age of eighteen. Other members of the Royal House may be granted a seat on the Council by or pursuant to an Act of Parliament.

(2) The members of the Council shall be appointed for life by royal decree.

(3) They shall cease to be members of the Council on resignation or on attaining an age to be determined by Act of Parliament.

(4) They may be suspended or dismissed from membership by the Council in instances specified by Act of Parliament.

(5) Their legal status shall in other respects be regulated by Act of Parliament.

Article 75.

(1) The organization, composition and powers of the Council of State shall be regulated by Act of Parliament.

(2) Additional duties may be assigned to the Council or a section of the Council by Act of Parliament.

Article 76.

The General Chamber of Audit shall be responsible for examining the State's revenues and expenditures.

Article 77.

(1) The members of the General Chamber of Audit shall be appointed for life by royal decree from a list of three persons per vacancy drafted by the Second Chamber of the States General.

(2) They shall cease to be members on resignation or on attaining an age to be determined by Act of Parliament.

(3) They may be suspended or dismissed from membership by the Supreme Court in cases to be laid down by Act of Parliament.

(4) Their legal status shall in other respects be regulated by Act of Parliament.

Article 78.

(1) The organization, composition and powers of the General Chamber of Audit shall be regulated by Act of Parliament.

(2) Additional duties may be assigned to the General Chamber of Audit by Act of Parliament.

Article 78a.

(1) On request or on his own initiative the National Ombudsman investigates actions of public authorities of the State and of other public authorities designated by or pursuant to an Act of Parliament.

(2) The National Ombudsman and a substitute-ombudsman are appointed by the Second Chamber of the States General for a period to be determined by Act of Parliament. On their own request or on attaining an age to be determined

by Act of Parliament they are dismissed. In cases laid down by Act of Parliament they can be suspended or dismissed by the Second Chamber of the States General. Their legal status shall in other aspects be regulated by Acts of Parliament.

(3) The powers and procedures are regulated by Act of Parliament.

(4) Additional duties may be assigned to the National Ombudsman by or pursuant to an Act of Parliament

Article 79.

(1) Permanent bodies to advise on matters relating to legislation and administration of the State shall be established by or pursuant to an Act of Parliament.

(2) The organization, composition and powers of such bodies shall be regulated by Act of Parliament.

(3) Duties in addition to advisory ones may be assigned to such bodies by or pursuant to an Act of Parliament.

Article 80.

(1) The advices of the bodies referred to in the present chapter shall be made public according to rules to be laid down by Act of Parliament.

(2) Other than in cases to be laid down by Act of Parliament, advices concerning bills presented by or on behalf of the King shall be submitted to the States General.

CHAPTER 5. LEGISLATION AND ADMINISTRATION

Section 1. Acts of Parliament and Other Regulations

Article 81.

Acts of Parliament shall be passed jointly by the Government and the States General.

Article 82.

(1) Bills may be presented by or on behalf of the King or by the Second Chamber of the States General.

(2) Bills which require consideration by a joint session of the States General may be presented by or on behalf of the King or by a joint session of the States General insofar as this is consistent with the relevant articles of Chapter 2.

(3) Bills to be presented by the Second Chamber or by a joint session of the States General shall be introduced in the Chamber or the joint session as the case may be by one or more members.

Article 83.

Bills presented by or on behalf of the King shall be sent to the Second Chamber or to the joint session if consideration by a joint session of the States General is required.

Article 84.
(1) A bill presented by or on behalf of the King that has not yet been passed by the Second Chamber or by a joint session of the States General may be amended by the Chamber or the joint session as the case may be on the proposal of one or more members or by the Government.
(2) Any bill being presented by the Second Chamber or a joint session of the States General that has not yet been passed may be amended by the Chamber or joint session as the case may be on the proposal of one or more members or by the member or members introducing the bill.

Article 85.

As soon as the Second Chamber passes a bill or resolves to present a bill, it shall send it to the First Chamber which shall consider the bill as sent to it by the Second Chamber. The Second Chamber may instruct one or more members to defend a bill presented by it in the First Chamber.

Article 86.
(1) A bill may be withdrawn by or on behalf of the proposer until such time as it is passed by the States General.
(2) A bill which is to be presented by the Second Chamber or by a joint session of the States General may be withdrawn by the member or members introducing it until such time as it is passed.

Article 87.
(1) A bill shall become an Act of Parliament once it has been passed by the States General and ratified by the King.
(2) The King and the States General shall inform each other of their decision on any bill.

Article 88.

The publication and entry into force of Acts of Parliament shall be regulated by Act of Parliament. They shall not enter into force before they have been published.

Article 89.
(1) Orders in Council shall be established by royal decree.
(2) Any regulations to which penalties are attached shall be embodied in such orders only pursuant to an Act of Parliament. The penalties to be imposed shall be determined by Act of Parliament.
(3) Publication and entry into force of Orders in Council shall be regulated by Act of Parliament. They shall not enter into force before they have been published.
(4) The second and third paragraphs shall apply by analogy to other generally binding regulations established on behalf of the State.

The Netherlands – Text of the Constitution

Section 2. Miscellaneous Provisions

Article 90.

The Government shall promote the development of the international rule of law.

Article 91.
(1) The Kingdom shall not be bound by treaties, nor shall such treaties be denounced without the prior approval of the States General. The cases in which approval is not required shall be specified by Act of Parliament.
(2) The manner in which approval shall be granted shall be laid down in an Act of Parliament, which may provide for tacit approval.
(3) Any provisions of a treaty that conflict with the Constitution or which lead to conflicts with it can be approved by the Chambers of the States General only if at least two-thirds of the votes cast are in favour.

Article 92.

Legislative, executive and judicial powers may be conferred on international organizations by or pursuant to a treaty, subject, where necessary, to the provisions of Article 91, paragraph 3.

Article 93.

Provisions of treaties and of decisions by international organizations, which may be binding on all persons by virtue of their contents shall become binding after they have been published.

Article 94.

Statutory regulations in force within the Kingdom shall not be applicable if such application is in conflict with provisions of treaties or of decisions by international organizations that are binding on all persons.

Article 95.

Rules concerning the publication of treaties and decisions by international organizations shall be laid down by Act of Parliament.

Article 96.
(1) A declaration that the Kingdom is in a state of war shall not be made without the prior approval of the States General.
(2) Such approval shall not be required in cases where consultation with parliament proves to be impossible as a consequence of the actual existence of a state of war.
(3) The two Chambers of the States General shall consider and decide upon the matter in joint session.
(4) The provisions of the first and third paragraphs shall apply by analogy to a declaration that a state of war has ceased.

Article 97.
(1) There shall be armed forces for the defence and protection of the interests of the Kingdom, and in order to maintain and promote the international legal order.
(2) The Government shall have supreme authority over the armed forces.

Article 98.
(1) The armed forces shall consist of volunteers and may also include conscripts.
(2) Compulsory military service and the power to defer the call-up to active service shall be regulated by Act of Parliament.

Article 99.

The conditions on which exemption is granted from military service because of serious conscientious objections shall be specified by Act of Parliament.

Article 99a.

In accordance with rules laid down by Act of Parliament obligations may be imposed with a view to civil defence.

Article 100.
(1) The government shall provide prior information to the States General concerning the deployment of or making available armed forces for the maintenance or promotion of the international legal order. This includes information concerning the deployment of or making available armed forces for humanitarian assistance in cases of armed conflict.
(2) The first paragraph shall not apply if peremptory considerations prevent the provisions of prior information. In this case, the information shall be provided as soon as possible.

Article 101.

Lapsed.

Article 102.

Lapsed.

Article 103.
(1) The cases in which a state of emergency, as defined by Act of Parliament, may be declared by royal decree in order to maintain internal or external security, shall be specified by Act of Parliament. It regulates the consequences of such a declaration.
(2) In such cases may be departed from the provisions of the Constitution relating to the powers of the executive bodies of the provinces, municipalities, public bodies, referred to in Article 132a, and water boards, the fundamental

rights laid down in Article 6, insofar as the exercise of the right contained in this Article other than in buildings and enclosed places is concerned, Articles, 7, 8, 9 and 12, paragraph 2, Article 13 and Article 113, paragraphs 1 and 3.

(3) Immediately after the declaration of a state of emergency and whenever it considers it necessary, until such time as the state of emergency is terminated by royal decree, the States General shall decide on the duration of the state of emergency. The two Chambers of the States General shall consider and decide upon the matter in joint session.

Article 104.

Taxes imposed by the State shall be levied pursuant to an Act of Parliament. Other levies imposed by the State shall be regulated by Act of Parliament.

Article 105.

(1) The estimates of the State's revenues and expenditures shall be laid down by Act of Parliament.
(2) Bills containing general estimates shall be presented by or on behalf of the King every year on the date specified in Article 65.
(3) A statement of the State's revenues and expenditures shall be presented to the States General in accordance with the provisions of an Act of Parliament. The balance sheet approved by the General Chamber of Audit shall be presented to the States General.
(4) Rules relating to the management of the State's finances shall be laid down in an Act of Parliament.

Article 106.

The monetary system shall be regulated by Act of Parliament.

Article 107.

(1) Civil law, criminal law and civil and criminal procedure shall be regulated by Act of Parliament in general legal codes without prejudice to the power to regulate certain matters in separate Acts of Parliament.
(2) The general rules of administrative law shall be laid down in an Act of Parliament.

Article 108.

lapsed

Article 109.

The legal status of public servants shall be regulated by Act of Parliament. Rules regarding employment protection and co-determination for public servants shall also be laid down by Act of Parliament.

Article 110.

In the exercise of their duties government bodies shall observe the right of public access to information in accordance with rules to be established by Act of Parliament.

Article 111.

Honours shall be established by Act of Parliament.

CHAPTER 6. THE ADMINISTRATION OF JUSTICE

Article 112.
(1) The judgment of disputes on civil rights and obligations shall be the responsibility of the judiciary.
(2) Responsibility for the judgment of disputes which do not arise from relations under civil law may be granted by Act of Parliament either to the judiciary or to courts which do not form part of the judiciary. The method of dealing with such cases and the consequences of the decisions shall be regulated by Act of Parliament.

Article 113.
(1) The judgment of offences shall also be the responsibility of the judiciary.
(2) Disciplinary proceedings established by government bodies shall be regulated by Act of Parliament.
(3) A sentence entailing deprivation of liberty may be imposed only by the judiciary.
(4) Different rules may be established by Act of Parliament for the trial of cases outside the Netherlands and for martial law.

Article 114.

Capital punishment may not be imposed.

Article 115.

Administrative appeal shall be admissible in the case of the disputes referred to in Article 112, paragraph 2.

Article 116.
(1) The courts which form part of the judiciary shall be specified by Act of Parliament.
(2) The organization, composition and powers of the judiciary shall be regulated by Act of Parliament.

(3) In cases provided for by Act of Parliament, persons who are not members of the judiciary may take part in the administration of justice by the judiciary.

(4) The supervision by members of the judiciary responsible for the administration of justice of the manner in which such members and persons referred to in the previous paragraph fulfil their duties shall be regulated by Act of Parliament.

Article 117.

(1) Members of the judiciary responsible for the administration of justice and the Attorney General at the Supreme Court shall be appointed for life by royal decree.

(2) Such persons shall cease to hold office on resignation or on attaining an age to be determined by Act of Parliament.

(3) In cases laid down by Act of Parliament such persons may be suspended or dismissed by a court that is part of the judiciary and designated by Act of Parliament.

(4) Their legal status shall in other respects be regulated by Act of Parliament.

Article 118.

(1) The members of the Supreme Court of the Netherlands shall be appointed from a list of three persons drawn up by the Second Chamber of the States General.

(2) In the cases and within the limits laid down by Act of Parliament, the Supreme Court shall be responsible for annulling court judgments which violate the law.

(3) Additional duties may be assigned to the Supreme Court by Act of Parliament.

Article 119.

Present and former members of the States General, Ministers and State Secretaries shall be tried by the Supreme Court for malfeasance in office. The order to prosecute shall be given by royal decree or by a resolution of the Second Chamber.

Article 120.

The constitutionality of Acts of Parliament and treaties shall not be reviewed by the courts.

Article 121.

Except in cases laid down by Act of Parliament, trials shall be held in public and judgments shall specify the grounds on which they are based. Judgments shall be pronounced in public.

Article 122.

(1) Pardon shall be granted by royal decree upon the advice of a court designated by Act of Parliament and with due regard to regulations to be laid down by or pursuant to an Act of Parliament.

(2) Amnesty shall be granted by or pursuant to an Act of Parliament.

CHAPTER 7. PROVINCES, MUNICIPALITIES, CARIBBEAN PUBLIC BODIES, WATER BOARDS AND OTHER PUBLIC BODIES

Article 123.

(1) Provinces and municipalities may be suppressed and new ones established by Act of Parliament.

(2) Revisions to provincial and municipal boundaries shall be regulated by Act of Parliament.

Article 124.

(1) The powers of provinces and municipalities to regulate and administer their own affairs shall be left to their administrative organs.

(2) Provincial and municipal administrative organs may be required by or pursuant to an Act of Parliament to provide regulation and administration.

Article 125.

(1) The provinces and municipalities shall be headed by the provincial states and the municipal council respectively. Their meetings shall be public except in cases provided for by or pursuant to an Act of Parliament.

(2) In addition, the administration of a province shall comprise the provincial executive; the administration of a municipality shall comprise the municipal executive.

Article 126.

An Act of Parliament may prescribe that the Royal Commissioner also be charged with the execution of official instructions to be given by the Government.

Article 127.

Provincial and municipal bye-laws shall be enacted by the provincial states or municipal council respectively, except in cases specified by Act of Parliament or by them pursuant to an Act of Parliament.

Article 128.

Except in cases laid down in Article 123, the powers referred to in Article 124, paragraph 1, may be assigned to organs other than those specified in Article 125 only by the provincial states or municipal council respectively.

Article 129.
(1) The members of the provincial states and the municipal council shall be directly elected by Dutch nationals resident in the province or municipality as the case may be who satisfy the requirements laid down for elections to the Second Chamber of the States General. The same conditions apply to membership.
(2) The members shall be elected by proportional representation within the boundaries to be laid down by Act of Parliament.
(3) Articles 53, paragraph 2, and 59 shall apply. Article 57a applies accordingly.
(4) The duration of provincial states and the municipal council shall be four years unless otherwise provided for by Act of Parliament.
(5) The positions which may not be held simultaneously with membership shall be specified by Act of Parliament. An act may also provide that obstacles to membership will arise from kinship or marriage and that the commission of certain acts designated by Act of Parliament may result in loss of membership.
(6) The members shall not be bound by a mandate or instructions when casting their votes.

Article 130.

The right to elect members of a municipal council and the right to be a member of a municipal council may be granted by Act of Parliament to residents who are not Dutch nationals, provided they fulfil at least the requirements applicable to residents who are Dutch nationals.

Article 131.

The Royal Commissioner and the mayor shall be appointed, suspended and dismissed in a manner to be determined by Act of Parliament. Pursuant to Act of Parliament, further rules may be laid down on the procedures to be followed.

Article 132.
(1) Both the organization of provinces and municipalities and the composition and powers of their administrative organs shall be regulated by Act of Parliament.
(2) Supervision of the administrative organs shall be regulated by Act of Parliament.
(3) Decisions by the administrative organs shall be subject to prior supervision only in cases specified by or pursuant to an Act of Parliament.

(4) Decisions by the administrative organs may be reversed only by royal decree and on the ground that they conflict with the law or the public interest.

(5) Provisions in the event of non-compliance in matters of regulation and administration required under Article 124, paragraph 2, shall be regulated by Act of Parliament. In cases of gross neglect of duty by the administrative organs of a province or municipality provisions may be made by Act of Parliament as a departure from Articles 125 and 127.

(6) The taxes which may be levied by the administrative organs of provinces and municipalities and their financial relationships with the central Government shall be regulated by Act of Parliament.

Article 132a.

(1) By Act of Parliament, in the Caribbean part of the Netherlands other territorial public bodies than provinces and municipalities may be established and suppressed.

(2) Articles 124, 125 and 127 to 132 shall apply by analogy in respect of these public bodies.

(3) Elections are held in these public bodies for the sake of an electoral college for the First Chamber. Article 129 shall apply by analogy.

(4) Rules may be laid down for these public bodies and other specific measures are being taken with a view to special circumstances that make these public bodies significantly different from the European part of the Netherlands.

Article 133.

(1) Insofar as it is not otherwise provided by or pursuant to an Act of Parliament, the establishment or suppression of water boards, the regulation of their duties and organization together with the composition of their administrative organs shall be effected by provincial bye-law according to rules laid down by Act of Parliament.

(2) The rule-making and other powers of the administrative organs of water boards and public access to their meetings shall be regulated by Act of Parliament.

(3) Supervision of these administrative organs by provincial and other bodies shall be regulated by Act of Parliament. Decisions by these administrative organs may be reversed only if they conflict with the law or the public interest.

Article 134.

(1) Public bodies for the professions and trades and other public bodies may be established and suppressed by or pursuant to an Act of Parliament.

(2) The duties and organization of such bodies, the composition and powers of their administrative organs and public access to their meetings shall be regulated by Act of Parliament. Rule-making powers may be granted to their administrative organs by or pursuant to an Act of Parliament.

(3) Supervision of these administrative organs shall be regulated by Act of Parliament. Decisions by the administrative organs may be reversed only if they are in conflict with the law or the public interest.

Article 135.

Rules pertaining to matters in which two or more public bodies are involved shall be laid down by Act of Parliament. These may provide for the establishment of a new public body, in which case Article 134, paragraphs 2 and 3, shall apply.

Article 136.

Disputes between public bodies shall be settled by royal decree unless they fall within the competence of the judiciary or their settlement is assigned to others by Act of Parliament.

CHAPTER 8. REVISION OF THE CONSTITUTION

Article 137.
1. An Act of Parliament shall be passed stating that an amendment to the Constitution in the form proposed shall be considered.
2. The Lower House may divide a Bill presented for this purpose into a number of separate Bills, either upon a proposal presented by or on behalf of the King or otherwise.
3. The Lower House elected after the Act of Parliament referred to in the first paragraph has been published shall consider, at second reading, the Bill for the amendment of the Constitution as referred to in the first paragraph. If this Lower House does not decide on the Bill, the Bill lapses. As soon as this Lower House has passed the Bill, the Upper House shall consider it at second reading. The Bill shall be passed by both Houses only if at least two-thirds of the votes cast are in favour.
4. The Lower House may divide a Bill for the amendment of the Constitution into a number of separate Bills, either upon a proposal presented by or on behalf of the King or otherwise, if at least two-thirds of the votes cast are in favour.

Article 138.
(1) Before bills to amend the Constitution which have been given a second reading have been ratified by the King, provisions may be introduced by Act of Parliament whereby:
    (a) the bills adopted and the unamended provisions of the Constitution are adjusted to each other as required;
    (b) the division into chapters, sections and articles and the headings and numbering thereof are modified.
(2) A bill containing provisions as referred to under paragraph 1(a) can be passed by the two Chambers only if at least two-thirds of the votes cast are in favour.

Article 139.

Amendments to the Constitution passed by the States General and ratified by the King shall enter into force immediately after they have been published.

Article 140.

Existing Acts of Parliament and other regulations and decisions which are in conflict with an amendment to the Constitution shall remain in force until provisions are made in accordance with the Constitution.

Article 141.

The text of the revised Constitution shall be published by royal decree in which the chapters, sections and articles may be renumbered and references to them altered accordingly.

Article 142.

The Constitution may be brought into conformity with the Charter for the Kingdom of the Netherlands by Act of Parliament. Articles 139, 140 and 141 shall apply by analogy.

2. THE CHARTER FOR THE KINGDOM OF THE NETHERLANDS

Text of the Charter (2017)

PREAMBLE

The Netherlands, Aruba, Curaçao and Sint Maarten, noting that in 1954 the Netherlands, Suriname and the Netherlands Antilles expressed freely their will to establish a new constitutional order in the Kingdom of the Netherlands, in which they will conduct their internal interests autonomously and their common interests on a basis of equivalence and will accord each other assistance, and resolved in consultation to adopt the Charter for the Kingdom; noting that the ties with Suriname under the Charter were terminated as of 25 November 1975 by means of an amendment to the Charter by Kingdom Act of 22 November 1975, Bulletin of Acts and Decrees no. 617, Official Bulletin of the Netherlands Antilles no. 233; considering that Aruba has expressed freely its will to accept the aforesaid constitutional order as a Country for a period of ten years as of 1 January 1986 and for an indefinite period as of 1 January 1996; considering that Curaçao and Sint Maarten each have expressed freely their will to accept the aforesaid constitutional order as a Country; have resolved in consultation to adopt the Charter for the Kingdom as follows.

§ 1. GENERAL PROVISIONS

Article 1

The Kingdom shall consist of the Countries of the Netherlands, Aruba, Curaçao and Sint Maarten.

Article 1a

The Crown of the Kingdom shall devolve by inheritance upon Her Majesty Queen Juliana, Princess of Orange-Nassau, and upon her lawful successors.

Article 2
1. The King shall reign over the Kingdom and over each of the Countries. He shall be inviolable. The Ministers shall be responsible.
2. The King shall be represented by the Governor in Aruba, Curaçao and Sint Maarten. The powers, duties and responsibility of the Governor as representative of the Government of the Kingdom shall be determined by Kingdom Act or, as the case may be, by order in council for the Kingdom.
3. Matters related to the appointment and removal of the Governor shall be determined by Kingdom Act. The appointment or removal of the Governor shall be effected by the King as Head of the Kingdom.

Article 3
1. Without prejudice to provisions elsewhere in the Charter, Kingdom affairs shall include:

a.   enforcement of independence and defence of the Kingdom;
b.   foreign relations;
c.   Netherlands nationality;
d.   regulation of the orders of chivalry, the flag and the coat of arms of the Kingdom;
e.   regulation of the nationality of vessels and the standards required for the safety and navigation of seagoing vessels flying the flag of the Kingdom, with the exception of sailing ships;
f.   supervision of the general rules governing the admission and expulsion of Netherlands nationals;
g.   general conditions for the admission and expulsion of aliens;h. extradition.

2.   Other matters may be declared to be Kingdom affairs in consultation. Article 55 shall apply by analogy.

Article 4

1.   The Royal power in Kingdom affairs shall be exercised by the King as Head of the Kingdom.
2.   The Legislative power in Kingdom affairs shall be exercised by the legislature of the Kingdom. Kingdom Bills shall be considered according to the provisions of Articles 15 to 21 inclusive.

Article 5

1.   The Monarchy and the succession to the Throne, the Organs of the Kingdom referred to in the Charter, and the exercise of Royal and legislative power in Kingdom affairs shall be governed, if not provided for by the Charter, by the Constitution of the Kingdom.
2.   The Constitution shall observe the provisions Charter.
3.   Articles 15 to 20 inclusive shall apply to any proposal for amendment of the Constitution containing provisions concerning Kingdom affairs, as well as to the Bill stating the grounds for considering such a proposal.

§ 2. THE CONDUCT OF KINGDOM AFFAIRS

Article 6

1.   Kingdom affairs shall be conducted in cooperation by the Netherlands, Aruba, Curaçao and Sint Maarten, in accordance with the following provisions.
2.   Wherever possible the Organs of the Countries shall participate in the conduct of these affairs.

Article 7

The Council of Ministers of the Kingdom shall be composed of the Ministers appointed by the King and the Ministers Plenipotentiary appointed by the Governments of Aruba, Curaçao and Sint Maarten.

Article 8

1. The Ministers Plenipotentiary shall act on behalf of the governments of their Countries, which shall appoint and remove them. They must be of Netherlands nationality.
2. The Government of the relevant Country shall provide for a deputy for the Minister Plenipotentiary in the event of absence. The provisions of the Charter with regard to the Minister Plenipotentiary shall apply by analogy to his deputy.

Article 9

1. Before assuming office the Minister Plenipotentiary shall, in the presence of the Governor, take an oath or make a promise of allegiance to the King and to the Charter. The form of the oath or promise shall be prescribed by order in council for the Kingdom.
2. A Minister Plenipotentiary who is in the Netherlands shall take the oath or make the promise in the presence of the King.

Article 10

1. The Minister Plenipotentiary shall participate in the deliberations of the Council of Ministers and of the permanent boards and special committees of the Council whenever Kingdom affairs are discussed which affect the Country in question.
2. The Governments of Aruba, Curaçao and Sint Maarten each shall be entitled to appoint - if they see reason to do so in relation to a particular matter - a Minister, in addition to the Minister Plenipotentiary, to participate with an advisory vote in the deliberations referred to in the preceding paragraph.

Article 11

1. Proposals for the amendment of the Constitution containing provisions relating to Kingdom affairs shall affect Aruba, Curaçao and Sint Maarten.
2. The defence of the territory of Aruba, Curaçao or Sint Maarten, and agreements or arrangements relating to any territory within their sphere of interest, shall be deemed to affect Aruba, Curaçao and Sint Maarten respectively.
3. Foreign relations shall be deemed to affect Aruba, Curaçao or Sint Maarten whenever the particular interests of Aruba, Curaçao or Sint Maarten are involved, or whenever arrangements are contemplated which may have significant consequences for such interests.
4. Establishing the contribution to the expenses referred to in Article 35 shall be deemed to affect Aruba, Curaçao and Sint Maarten respectively.
5. Proposals for naturalization shall be deemed to affect Aruba, Curaçao and Sint Maarten only if they relate to persons resident in the Country concerned.
6. The governments of Aruba, Curaçao and Sint Maarten may determine which Kingdom affairs affect their respective Countries other than those mentioned in paragraphs 1 to 4.

Article 12

1. If the Minister Plenipotentiary of Aruba, Curaçao or Sint Maarten, indicating his reasons for expecting that a proposed instrument containing generally binding rules would be seriously detrimental to his Country, has declared that his Country could not be bound by such an instrument, the instrument may not be adopted in such a way as to apply to the Country concerned, unless such a course would be inconsistent with the Country's ties with the Kingdom.

2. If the Minister Plenipotentiary of Aruba, Curaçao or Sint Maarten has serious objections to the initial opinion of the Council of Ministers on the binding nature of the provision referred to in paragraph 1, or on any other matter in the consideration of which he has participated, deliberations thereon shall continue at his request, if necessary having regard to a time-limit to be determined by the Council of Ministers.

3. The deliberations referred to above shall be conducted by the Prime Minister, two Ministers, the Minister Plenipotentiary and a Minister or special representative to be designated by the Government concerned.

4. If several Ministers Plenipotentiary desire to participate in the continued deliberations, these deliberations shall be conducted by these Ministers Plenipotentiary, an equal number of Ministers and the Prime Minister. Article 10, paragraph 2 shall apply by analogy.

5. The Council of Ministers shall take a decision in accordance with the result of the continued deliberations. If the opportunity for continued deliberations has not been utilized within the time-limit specified, the Council of Ministers shall decide.

Article 12a

By Kingdom Act, provisions shall be made for reviewing/settling disputes, designated by Kingdom Act, between the Kingdom and the Countries.

Article 13

1. There shall be a Council of State of the Kingdom.

2. If the Government of Aruba, Curaçao or Sint Maarten so desires, the King shall appoint, in agreement with the relevant government, a member to represent Aruba, Curaçao or Sint Maarten respectively in the Council of State. The said member shall not be removed without prior consultation with his Government.

3. The members of the Council of State for Aruba, Curaçao and Sint Maarten shall participate in the Council of State's proceedings whenever the Council or a division thereof is being heard on bills for Kingdom Acts or orders in council for the Kingdom which are to apply in Aruba, Curaçao or Sint Maarten, or on other matters which, pursuant to Article 11, affect Aruba, Curaçao or Sint Maarten.

4. Regulations concerning the said members of the Council of State which depart from the Council of State Act may be laid down by order in council for the Kingdom.

The Netherlands – Text of the Constitution

Article 14
1. Provisions regarding Kingdom affairs shall be laid down - if the matter in question is not regulated by the Netherlands Constitution and subject to international agreements and the provisions of paragraph 3 - by Kingdom Act or, if appropriate, by order in council for the Kingdom. Such an Act or order in council may instruct or allow other organs to lay down further rules. In the case of the countries, the appropriate organs shall be the legislature or the government of the countries.
2. If the regulation of a matter is not reserved for a Kingdom Act, it may be reserved for an order in council for the Kingdom.
3. Provisions concerning Kingdom affairs which do not apply in Aruba, Curaçao or Sint Maarten shall be established by Act of Parliament or order in council.
4. Persons resident in Aruba, Curaçao or Sint Maarten shall be naturalized by or pursuant to a Kingdom Act.

Article 15
1. The King shall forward bills for Kingdom Acts, at the same time as they are introduced in the States- General, to the representative assemblies of Aruba, Curaçao and Sint Maarten.
2. If a Bill for a Kingdom Act was initiated by the States-General, the bill shall be forwarded by the Second Chamber immediately following its introduction in the Second Chamber.
3. The Minister Plenipotentiary of Aruba, Curaçao or Sint Maarten shall have the power to propose that the Second Chamber introduce a Kingdom bill.

Article 16

The representative assembly of the Country in which the legislation is to apply shall be empowered, before the bill is publicly debated in the Second Chamber, to examine the bill and to issue a written report thereon, if necessary within a fixed time-limit.

Article 17
1. The Minister Plenipotentiary of the Country in which the legislation is to apply shall be afforded the opportunity to attend the debates on the bill in the Chambers of the States-General and to furnish such information to the Chambers of the Sates General as he considers desirable.
2. The representative assembly of the Country in which the legislation is to apply may decide to designate, for the purposes of the debate on a particular bill in the States-General, one or more special delegates who shall likewise be empowered to attend the debates and furnish information.
3. The Ministers Plenipotentiary and the special delegates shall be immune from any legal proceedings in respect of anything they say in or submit in writing to the meetings of the Chambers of the Sates General.

4. The Ministers Plenipotentiary and the special delegates shall be empowered to propose amendments to a bill during the proceedings in the Second Chamber.

Article 18

1. Before a final vote is taken on any Kingdom bill in the Chambers of the States General, the Minister Plenipotentiary of the Country in which the legislation is to apply shall have the opportunity to express his opinion on the bill. If the Minister Plenipotentiary states his opposition to the proposal, he may request the Chamber at the same time to postpone the vote till the following meeting. If, after the Minister Plenipotentiary has stated his opposition to the bill, the Second Chamber adopts it with a majority of less than three-fifths of the number of votes cast, the proceedings shall be suspended and the Council of Ministers shall consider the bill further.
2. If the meetings of the Chambers of the States General are being attended by special delegates, the power referred to in paragraph 1 shall devolve upon the delegate designated for the purpose by the representative assembly.

Article 19

Articles 17 and 18 shall apply by analogy to proceedings in joint session of the States General.

Article 20

Further rules relating to the provisions of articles 15 to 19 may be laid down by Kingdom Act.

Article 21

If, in the event of war or in other exceptional circumstances in which immediate action is required, the King is of the opinion, after consultation with the Ministers Plenipotentiary of Aruba, Curaçao and Sint Maarten, that it is impossible to await the result of the examination referred to in Article 16, a departure may be made from the provisions of that Article.

Article 22

1. The government of the Kingdom shall ensure the publication of Kingdom Acts and orders in council for the Kingdom, which shall appear in the official bulletin of the Country where the legislation is to apply. The governments of the Countries shall lend all the assistance necessary to that end.
2. Kingdom Acts and orders in council for the Kingdom shall enter into force on the date determined therein or pursuant thereto.
3. The terms of the publication of Kingdom Acts and orders in council for the Kingdom shall state that the provisions of the Charter for the Kingdom have been observed.

The Netherlands – Text of the Constitution

Article 23

1. The jurisdiction of the Supreme Court of the Netherlands in respect of legal cases in Aruba, Curaçao and Sint Maarten, and also in Bonaire, Sint Eustatius and Saba, shall be regulated by Kingdom Act.
2. If the government of Aruba, Curaçao or Sint Maarten so requests, the said Kingdom Act shall provide for the addition of a member, an extraordinary member or an advisory member to the Court.

Article 24

1. Agreements with other powers and with international organizations which affect Aruba, Curaçao or Sint Maarten shall be submitted to the representative assembly of Aruba, Curaçao or Sint respectively at the same time as they are submitted to the States-General.
2. If an agreement has been submitted for the tacit approval of the States-General, the Ministers Plenipotentiary may, within the time-limit set for this purpose for the Upper and Lower Houses, communicate their wish that the agreement shall be subject to the express approval of the States-General.
3. The preceding paragraphs shall apply by analogy in respect of the denunciation of international agreements, with the proviso in the case of paragraph 1 that the representative assembly of Aruba, Curaçao or Sint Maarten respectively shall be notified of the intended denunciation.

Article 25

1. The King shall not bind Aruba, Curaçao or Sint Maarten to international economic or financial agreements if the government of the Country, indicating the reasons for considering that this would be detrimental to the Country, has declared that the Country should not be bound by them.
2. The King shall not denounce international economic or financial agreements in respect of Aruba, Curaçao or Sint Maarten if the Government of the Country, indicating the reasons for considering that a denunciation would be detrimental to the Country, has declared that denunciation should not take place with respect to that Country. An agreement may nevertheless be denounced if exclusion of the Country concerned from the denunciation is incompatible with the provisions of the agreement.

Article 26

If the Government of Aruba, Curaçao or Sint Maarten communicates its wish for the conclusion of an international economic or financial agreement that applies solely to the Country concerned, the government of the Kingdom shall assist in the conclusion of such an agreement, unless this would be inconsistent with the Country's ties with the Kingdom.

Article 27

1. Aruba, Curaçao and Sint Maarten shall be involved as early as possible in the preparation of agreements with other nations that affect any of them, in accordance with Article 11. They shall also be involved in the implementation of agreements that affect them accordingly and are binding on them.
2. The Netherlands, Aruba, Curaçao and Sint Maarten shall conclude a mutual arrangement on the cooperation between the Countries for the purpose of establishing regulations or other measures necessary for the implementation of agreements with other Powers.
3. If the interests of the Kingdom are affected by the absence of regulations or other measures necessary for the implementation of an agreement with other nations in one of the Countries, while the agreement can be ratified for that Country only once the regulations or other measures have been established, an order in council for the Kingdom, or if necessary a Kingdom Act, may determine how the agreement shall be implemented.
4. If the regulations or other measures necessary for the implementation of the agreement concerned have been established by the Country, the order in council for the Kingdom or the Kingdom Act shall be rescinded.

Article 28

In accordance with international agreements entered into by the Kingdom, Aruba, Curaçao and Sint Maarten may, if they so desire, accede to membership of international organizations.

Article 29

1. Loans outside the Kingdom in the name of or for the account of one of the Countries shall be contracted or guaranteed in agreement with the government of the Kingdom.
2. The Council of Ministers shall agree to the contracting or guaranteeing of such loans, unless this would be contrary to the interests of the Kingdom.

Article 30

1. Aruba, Curaçao and Sint Maarten shall lend such assistance and support to the armed forces within their territory as the latter require for the discharge of their task.
2. Provisions shall be laid down by national ordinance to ensure that the armed forces of the Kingdom stationed in Aruba, Curaçao and Sint Maarten can discharge their task.

Article 31

1. Persons resident in Aruba, Curaçao and Sint Maarten, may be compelled to serve in the armed forces or to perform alternative civilian service only by national ordinance.

2. The constitution of Aruba, Curaçao, or Sint Maarten may determine that persons subject to compulsory service in the army shall be sent elsewhere without their consent only pursuant to a national ordinance.

Article 32

The armed forces for the defence of Aruba, Curaçao and Sint Maarten shall consist as far as possible of persons resident within the Country concerned.

Article 33
1. Requisitioning and use of property, restrictions on title and rights of use, the requisitioning of services and billeting for defence purposes shall be effected only with due regard to general rules to be laid down by Kingdom Act, which shall also contain provisions concerning compensation.
2. Whenever possible the said Kingdom Act shall instruct the authorities of the countries to issue further provisions.

Article 34
1. In the event of war or a threat of war or if a threat to or the disturbance of internal peace and order might seriously damage the Kingdom's interests, the King may, to maintain internal or external security, declare any part of the territory to be in a state of war or a state of emergency.
2. How such a declaration shall be made and the ensuing consequences provided for shall be determined by or pursuant to Kingdom Act.
3. Such legislation may determine that, and in what manner, powers of the civil authorities in respect of public order and the police shall be transferred, wholly or in part, to other civil authorities or to the military authorities and that, in the latter case, the civil authorities shall be subordinate to the military authorities. Whenever possible the Government of the Country concerned shall be consulted with regard to the transfer of powers. Such legislation may depart from provisions relating to the freedom of the press and freedom of association and assembly, and from those relating to the inviolability of dwellings and correspondence.
4. In an area where in the event of war a state of emergency has been declared, military criminal law and military criminal jurisdiction may be declared wholly or partially applicable to any person, in a manner determined by Kingdom Act.

Article 35
1. Aruba, Curaçao and Sint Maarten shall contribute, to an extent consonant with their resources, to the cost of maintaining the independence and the defence of the Kingdom, and to the cost of the conduct of other Kingdom affairs, to the extent that they benefit Aruba, Curaçao or Sint Maarten respectively
2. The contributions of Aruba, Curaçao or Sint Maarten referred to in paragraph 1 shall be determined by the Council of Ministers for one fiscal year or for a

number of consecutive fiscal years. Article 12 shall apply by analogy with the proviso that decisions shall be taken unanimously.

3. If the contributions referred to in paragraph 2 are not determined in due time, the contributions determined for the previous fiscal year in accordance with that paragraph shall apply for a period not to exceed one fiscal year.

4. The preceding paragraphs shall not apply to the costs of measures for which special provision has been made.

§ 3. MUTUAL ASSISTANCE, CONSULTATION AND CO-OPERATION

Article 36

The Netherlands, Aruba, Curaçao and Sint Maarten shall accord one another aid and assistance.

Article 36a

(Lapsed)

Article 37

1. The Netherlands, Aruba, Curaçao and Sint Maarten shall consult wherever possible on all matters involving the interests of at least two of the Countries. To this end special representatives may be designated and joint bodies created.

2. The matters referred to in this Article shall include:
    a. the promotion of cultural and social relations between the Countries;
    b. the promotion of effective economic, financial and monetary relations between the Countries;
    c. problems in respect of coinage and currency, banking and foreign exchange policy;
    d. the promotion of economic resilience by means of mutual aid and assistance;
    e. the conduct of professions and business in the Countries by Dutch nationals;
    f. matters relating to aviation, including policy on unscheduled air transport;
    g. matters relating to shipping;
    h. cooperation in the field of telegraphic, telephone and radio communications.

Article 38

1. The Netherlands, Aruba, Curaçao and Sint Maarten may enter into mutual arrangements.

2. They may decide by mutual consultation that such arrangements and the modification thereof shall be laid down by Kingdom Act or order in council of the Kingdom.

3. Private law and criminal law matters of an interregional or international nature may be regulated by Kingdom Act, provided that the governments of the Countries concerned agree to the provisions thereof.
4. Provision for the transfer of the registered offices of legal persons shall be made by Kingdom Act. Such provision must be approved by the governments of the Countries.

Article 38a

By mutual arrangement, the Countries may make provisions for settling disputes between them. Article 38, paragraph 2, shall apply by analogy.

Article 39

1. Civil and commercial law, the law of civil procedure, criminal law, the law of criminal procedure, copyright, industrial property, the office of notary, and provisions concerning weights and measures shall be regulated as far as possible in a similar manner in the Netherlands, Aruba, Curaçao and Sint Maarten.
2. Any proposal for drastic amendment of the existing legislation in regard to these matters shall not be submitted to or considered by a representative assembly until the Governments in the other countries have had the opportunity to express their views on the matter.

Article 40

Judgments given and warrants issued by courts in the Netherlands, Aruba, Curaçao or Sint Maarten, and engrossments of authentic acts issued by them, may be enforced throughout the Kingdom, with due observance of statutory provisions in the Country of enforcement.

§ 4. THE CONSTITUTIONAL ORGANIZATION OF THE COUNTRIES

Article 41

1. The Netherlands, Aruba, Curaçao and Sint Maarten shall conduct their internal affairs autonomously.
2. The interests of the Kingdom shall be a matter of common concern to the Countries.

Article 42

1. Within the Kingdom, the constitutional organization of the Netherlands is set forth in the Constitution, and that of Aruba, of Curaçao and of Sint Maarten in their respective constitutions.
2. The constitutions of Aruba, of Curaçao and of Sint Maarten are established by national ordinance. Any proposal for the amendment of the constitutions shall explicitly describe the proposed amendment. The representative assemblies shall adopt a bill for a national ordinance of this kind only by a two-thirds majority of the votes cast.

Article 43

1. Each of the Countries shall promote the realization of fundamental human rights and freedoms, legal certainty and good governance.
2. The safeguarding of such rights and freedoms, legal certainty and good governance shall be a Kingdom affair.

Article 44

1. Any national ordinance amending a constitution with regard to:
   a. articles relating to fundamental human rights and freedoms;
   b. provisions relating to the powers of the Governor;
   c. articles relating to the powers of the representative assemblies of the Countries;
   d. articles relating to the administration of justice,
   shall be submitted to the government of the Kingdom. Such national ordinances shall not enter into effect until the government of the Kingdom has signified its agreement.
2. Bills for national ordinances as referred to in the preceding paragraphs shall not be submitted to the representative assembly or be examined by the assembly if it has initiated such a bill, until the opinion of the government of the Kingdom has been obtained.

Article 45

Amendments to the Constitution with regard to:

a. articles relating to fundamental human rights and freedoms;
b. provisions relating to the powers of the Government;
c. articles relating to the powers of the representative assemblies;
d. articles relating to the administration of justice,
shall be deemed - without prejudice to the provisions of Article 5 - to affect Aruba, Curaçao and Sint Maarten within the meaning of Article 10.

Article 46

1. The representative assemblies shall be elected by Netherlands nationals who are residents of the Country concerned and have attained an age to be determined by the Countries, which should not exceed 25 years. Each voter shall cast only one vote. Elections shall be free and by secret ballot. In case of necessity the Countries may impose restrictions. Any Netherlands national shall have the right to stand for election, subject to such requirements of residence and age as the Countries may define.
2. The Countries may award to Netherlands nationals who are not residents of the Country concerned the right to vote in elections for the representative assemblies, and to residents of the Country concerned who are not Netherlands nationals the right to vote and stand in elections for the representative assemblies, provided in the case of all the foregoing that the requirements for residents who are Netherlands nationals are observed.

Article 47

1. Before taking office the Ministers and the members of the representative assemblies in the Countries shall swear or promise allegiance to the King and the Charter.
2. The Ministers and the members of the representative assemblies in Aruba, Curaçao and Sint Maarten shall take the oath, or make the promise, in the presence of the King's representative.

Article 48

The Countries shall take account of the provisions of this Charter in their legislation and administration.

Article 49

Rules may be established by Kingdom Act with regard to the binding force of legislative measures which are inconsistent with the Charter, an international instrument, a Kingdom Act or an order in council for the Kingdom.

Article 50

1. Legislative and administrative measures in Aruba, Curaçao and Sint Maarten which are inconsistent with the Charter, an international instrument, a Kingdom Act or an order in council for the Kingdom, or with interests whose promotion or protection is a Kingdom affair, may be suspended and annulled by the King as Head of the Kingdom by virtue of a decree stating reasons. The recommendation for annulment shall be made by the Council of Ministers.
2. This matter shall be regulated for the Netherlands, if necessary, in the Constitution.

Article 51

1. If any organ in Aruba, Curaçao or Sint Maarten does not or does not adequately perform its duties as required by this present Charter, an international instrument, a Kingdom Act or an order in council for the Kingdom, the measures to be taken may be determined by Kingdom Act, setting forth the legal grounds and the reasons on which it is based.
2. This matter shall be regulated for the Netherlands, if necessary, in the Constitution.

Article 52

With the assent of the King, a country ordinance may confer upon the King as head of the Kingdom and upon the Governor as an organ of the Kingdom, powers with respect to Country affairs.

Article 53

If Aruba, Curaçao or Sint Maarten so wishes, the independent supervision of the expenditure of funds under the budgets of Aruba, Curaçao or Sint Maarten respectively may be exercised by the Netherlands Court of Audit. In that event, after consultation with the Court of Audit, rules shall be established by Kingdom Act governing cooperation between the Court of Audit and the Country concerned. The Government of that Country shall be empowered to appoint, on the nomination of its representative assembly, a person who shall have the opportunity to attend deliberations on all affairs of the relevant territory.

§ 5. TRANSITIONAL AND FINAL PROVISIONS

Article 54

1. Article 1, paragraph 2, shall be lapsed by amending the Constitution once the position of Bonaire, Sint Eustatius and Saba within the polity of the Netherlands is provided for by the Constitution
2. This Article shall expire if Article 1, paragraph 2, is rescinded pursuant to the preceding paragraph.

Article 55

1. Amendments to this Charter shall be effected by Kingdom Act.
2. A Bill for an amendment passed by the States-General shall not be approved by the King until it has been accepted by Aruba, Curaçao and Sint Maarten. This acceptance shall be enacted by national ordinance. Such a national ordinance shall not be adopted until it has been approved by the representative assemblies of the Countries in two readings. If the bill is passed at the first reading by two-thirds of the votes cast, it shall be deemed approved forthwith. The second reading shall take place within one month after the bill has passed the first reading.
3. If and in so far as a bill for the amendment of this Charter differs from the Constitution, the bill shall be dealt with in the manner provided for in the Constitution in respect of proposed amendments to the Constitution, with the proviso that in second reading the two Chambers may adopt the proposed amendment by an absolute majority of the votes cast.

Article 56

Authorities, binding legislation, ordinances and decrees existing on the date of entry into force of the Charter shall remain in effect until they have been replaced by others pursuant to this Charter. In so far as the Charter provides otherwise with respect to any matter, the terms of the Charter shall prevail.

Article 57

Acts and ordinances previously applicable to the Netherlands Antilles have the status of Kingdom Act or order in council for the Kingdom respectively with the proviso that, if they can be amended by national ordinance pursuant to the Charter, they have the status of country ordinance.

Article 57a

Existing Kingdom Acts, Acts of Parliament, national ordinances, orders in council for the Kingdom, orders in council and other regulations and decrees that are contrary to an amendment of the Charter, shall remain in force until a provision for this is made in accordance with the Charter.

Article 58
1. Aruba may declare by national ordinance that it wishes to terminate the constitutional order enshrined in the Charter in respect of Aruba.
2. A bill for such a national ordinance shall be accompanied on its submission by an outline of a future constitution, containing in any event provisions on fundamental rights, government, the representative assembly, legislation and administration, the administration of justice and amendments to the constitution.
3. The assemblies of the Countries may only approve such a bill with a majority of two thirds of the sitting members.

Article 59
1. Within six months of the approval by the representative assembly of Aruba of the bill referred to in Article 58, a referendum to be regulated by national ordinance shall be held, at which those entitled to vote in elections to the representative assembly may express their opinion on the Bill.
2. The bill shall not be enacted as a national ordinance until it has received the approval of a majority of the voters in a referendum.

Article 60
1. Once the national ordinance has been enacted in accordance with Articles 58 and 59 and once the future constitution has been approved by the representative assembly of Aruba with a majority of at least two thirds of the sitting members, the date on which the government of Aruba feels that the constitutional order should be terminated in respect of Aruba shall be determined by Royal Decree.
2. This date shall be no more than a month after the constitution has been adopted, which in turn shall be no more than a year after the date of the referendum referred to in Article 59.

Article 60a

1. The drafts for a constitution of Curaçao, respectively of Sint Maarten, established by the island councils of Curacao and Sint Maarten by island ordinance, shall, on the date of entry into force of Articles I and II of the Kingdom Act amending the Charter pertaining to the dissolution of the Netherlands Antilles, obtain the status of constitution of Curaçao, respectively of Sint Maarten, if:
   a. the view of the government of the Kingdom was gathered before the draft was presented to the island council concerned, respectively before a bill initiated by a member of parliament was examined by the concerned island council;
   b. the draft has been approved by at least two-thirds of the votes cast and;
   c. the government of the Kingdom has agreed with the draft established by the island council concerned.
2. If a draft has been approved by an island council by a smaller majority than two thirds of the votes cast, the condition mentioned in paragraph 1, section b, is satisfied if the island council has been dissolved after the vote on the draft and the draft has been approved by the, pertaining to that dissolution, newly elected island council with an absolute majority of the votes cast.
3. If a draft has been approved by an island council with a smaller majority than two-third of the votes cast and the island council concerned has not been dissolved, this island council shall be dissolved by the lieutenant-governor. The decision to dissolve comprises the call for elections for a new island council within two months and the first gathering of the new island council within three months after the date of the decision to dissolve. If the newly elected island council approves the draft with an absolute majority of the votes cast, the condition mentioned in paragraph 1, section b, is satisfied.

Article 60b

1. The draft national ordinances of Curaçao, respectively Sint Maarten, established by the island councils of Curaçao and Sint Maarten by island ordinance, shall, on the date of entry into force of Articles I and II of the Kingdom Act amending the Charter pertaining to the dissolution of the Netherlands Antilles, obtain the status of national ordinance of the Country of Curaçao, respectively Sint Maarten.
2. The draft national decrees, respectively draft national decrees containing general measures of Curaçao, respectively Sint Maarten, established by the Governing council of Curaçao or Sint Maarten by island decree or island decree containing general measures, shall, on the date of entry into force of Article I and II of the Kingdom Act amending the Charter pertaining to the dissolution of the Netherlands Antilles, obtain the status of national decree, respectively national decree containing general measures of Curaçao, respectively Sint Maarten.

Article 60c

The governing councils of Curaçao and Sint Maarten may together and with one or more governments of the Countries of the Kingdom make draft mutual arrangements that shall obtain the status of mutual arrangement within the meaning of Article 38, paragraph 1, on the date of entry into force of Articles I and II of the Kingdom Act amending the Charter pertaining to the dissolution of the Netherlands Antilles.

Article 61

The Charter shall enter into force on the date of its ceremonial promulgation, after approval by the King. Prior to its approval the Charter must be accepted in respect of the Netherlands in the manner provided for in the Constitution; in respect of Suriname and the Netherlands Antilles by decision of the representative assemblies. Such a decision shall require two-thirds of the votes cast. If such a majority is not obtained the States shall be dissolved and the decision shall be effected by the new States by an absolute majority of the votes cast.

Article 62

(Lapsed)

Index for the Constitution

The numbers refer to Articles.

Index for the Constitution

Index Charter for the Kingdom

Index Charter for the Kingdom

www.ingramcontent.com/pod-product-compliance
Lightning Source LLC
Chambersburg PA
CBHW061154220326
41599CB00025B/4479